What if everything
you know about the
world is wrong?

Master of My Universe

How to Get What You Want
And Live Your Dream

A simple instruction manual

Alice Elliott Brown

Self-Help/Inspirational

Master of My Universe: How to get what you want and live your dream

Pergados Press, 7371 Atlas Walk Way #203, Gainesville, Virginia 20155.

www.AliceElliottBrown.com

email: Publisher@AliceElliottBrown.com

Print Edition: DriveZero, an imprint of Pergados Press

ISBN-10: 0-9725368-9-2

ISBN-13: 978-0-9725368-9-9

Library of Congress Control Number: 2010943168

Printed in the United States of America

This book is dedicated to my fearless readers
Who may not have been ready,
But forged bravely ahead.

*And with many thanks to the mythological studies
of Joseph Campbell*

It matters not how strait the gate, how charged with punishment the scroll, I am the Master of My Fate; I am the Captain of My soul.

--William Ernest Henley, Invictus, 1875

The Point

Everything you've ever heard, read, or experienced is an illusion. Up is down. Left is right. Truth is imaginary. Wrong is a viewpoint. You cannot be certain that you are not plugged into the Matrix. You do not know *for sure* if you are awake or dreaming. You cannot *guarantee* that there is an After-Life, or *prove* there was no Before-Life. You *do not know*if life exists in other star systems, or whether there is a Wal-Mart *under construction right now*on some far-flung planet. What you know about reality is what you choose to believe. You take your reality on faith. Regardless of all that, you still have to go to work, pay the bills, manage your health, cook dinner, and care for the children. How can you keep *doing*such things, in the face of overwhelming cosmic uncertainty?

What can you do to claim good health, paid bills, a happy family, and inner peace as your birthright?(After all, didn't the good fairies promise this to your parents on the day you were born? Was that promise just some fairytale?)

This book is not Tony Robbins. It's not <u>Simple Abundance</u>. It's not the <u>Four-Hour Workweek</u>. This book is the version of success without shortcuts. It's the method without plastic and insincere "feel-goods."It's the unvarnished and unpolished nitty-gritty of how to get what you want.This is the book you read when you are not afraid to let the toothpaste of understanding out of the tube of popular delusion. This is the information you cannot deny, once you truly know it. This book tells you how to live your dream **for real**. If you can bear the knowledge, read on.

But consider yourself warned.

Contents

Introduction:
Who is The Real You? How you can choose your destiny when the roof is leaking, the bank is foreclosing, and your world is crashing around you.

Chapter 1: Be careful what you wish for.
Knowing what you want is more than half the battle.

Chapter 2: Defining the problem.
Why aren't you happy right now?Is there something keeping you from happiness? Why aren't you happy just staying where you are? Why follow a path at all?

Chapter 3: Considering the options.
What do you need that you don't already have? Have you seen all the hidden paths available? Is that grinning Cheshire cat deceiving you?

Chapter 4: Finding the Time.
Setting goals and Achieving Balance. Finding time for what pleases you. Weaving a web of happiness into the fabric of our time. Integrating and entwining family, friends, fun, and finances.

Chapter 5: Paying the Bills.
Measuring Outcomes and Establishing Structure. You will never be happy with bill collectors snapping at your heels. How to get rid of them.

Chapter 6: Expanding your Family.

Picturing Alternatives and Adjusting to Your Environment."What if" this and "what if" that. Everybody needs somebody to love them. Learning to discern who really cares about you.

Chapter 7: Reclaiming your Health.

Paying Attention and Rewarding What Matters.Without our health, nothing else will be important. Learning why we do what we do. Recognizing the payoff. Making sure we get paid for the things we really want. Putting an end to paying the piper.Calling your own tune.

Chapter 8: Following Your Bliss. Revealing your true self, and recognizing why you are meaningful, unconditionally, in a universe that needs you. Unleashing the subconscious.

Chapter 9: Wrapping It Up.

Laying out the program for becoming The Real You.

Supporting material
    A. Bibliography:

The works that influenced this book, from Basic Circuit Theory to the Zohar.
    B. The Completely True Story of FantasyLand
    C. The Roots of Cognition: The EDNA Database

About the Author: More Books by Alice Elliott Brown

Preview: The Homestyle Gourmet: Cooking for Balance and Beauty

Then Alice came to a fork in the road. A grinning Cheshire cat sat in the tree. "Which path shall I take?" Alice asked the cat. "Well, where are you going?" the cat answered.

"I don't know," said Alice.

"If you don't know where you're going, any path will take you there," said the cat.

---- From Lewis Carroll, "Alice in Wonderland"

Introduction:

Who is The Real You? How you can choose your destiny when the roof is leaking, the bank is foreclosing, and your world is crashing around you.

We all have wants. Desires, dreams, and ambitions call to us from early childhood. An adult asks, "What do you want to be when you grow up?" At age five, we might answer, "a mommy" or "a daddy". As time goes on, the question nags us. One day, we realize the realities of our life make the question irrelevant. Without warning, we suddenly know it is not possible to realize our childhood dreams. By the time we grow up, the only vestige of a dream remaining could be a wish for relief from the constant stress of bills, health problems, and family tensions. In the end, good health, paid bills, and a happy family, may be all we desire. Yet, sometimes, we have a vague sense inside that these basics of life are not enough. We wonder if the emptiness inside can be filled with a shopping trip for new shoes, a faster car, an expensive watch, an island vacation, or another serving of fast food fries. Even when we have everything, we search for an inner peace. We feel driven to look for our purpose and meaning in life. We wonder if we have a destiny to fulfill.

In **Master of My Universe**, we explore the proven techniques of management that people who succeed use to achieve their goals and create wealth. You may not recognize yet how these project management techniques apply to your life. Perhaps you have always thought life just "happens." Maybe you have been the person who signs up for a college class, but calls the professor to say, "I apologize that I did not get a chance to complete the assignment." Life management is not about what you "got a chance" to do. It is about what we each purposefully and actively choose to do, and make our time priorities. For all of us, life can get unbearably burdensome sometimes. In this book, we will postulate that there is no "chance" involved. In place of "chance," there are only **pivotal moments, critical choices, break-through insight, gut-wrenching challenges, and invigorating milestones**. These are the everyday building blocks of a passionate life. To attain our goals: good health, paid bills, a happy family, and inner peace, we can apply the techniques of successful project management to our everyday routines. When we find our meaning and our purpose, we feel truly at peace. Until then, we may find that we have thoughts streaming through our heads like this:

I do everything right. Okay, maybe I do most things right. Or, pretty many things right. At least, the big, important things right. Anyway, I get up and go to work every day, or I work hard in the home.

I love my family. I try my best to take care of them. I try to feed them right. I try to watch my weight. I try to do the right thing. I try to give my kids a better life. I try to get along with my neighbors, and my Uncle Archie, even though I think he is mean and stupid. I try, in every way I know how, to be a good, loving person. However, no matter how hard I try, too often, bad things happen. Bad things like accidents, illnesses, unexpected bills, and crazy, random events that make no sense. I feel as if I am just running in place, a hamster in a cage, unable to make progress or get anywhere. I've felt this way for a long time. I want things to be better, but I've tried so hard, for so long, I no longer believe in the dream. After decades of hardship and countless moments of despair, my health is failing. Sometimes I feel lucky if I have a day without pain. I now **expect** tragedy.

When I was young, I had dreams. Now, though, I realize those dreams were unrealistic. They were pipe dreams. They were just the foolishness of youth. I'm grown now, and I know better. I've stopped chasing rainbows. I've become a responsible, practical adult. Life is random. Life is unfair. I know that, so I just grin and bear it. I push on, continuing to do my best, given the circumstances. Life is hard. It is not my fault. I did my best. I can only hang my hopes now on the promise of the hereafter. We **endure** life, until we obtain our heavenly reward.

You are thinking like this, and then you see it: the fork in the road, which means a decision lies ahead. Alice in Wonderland's Cheshire cat may not be waiting there, but all the same, you feel lost and uncertain. You don't know which way to turn, where you want to go, or how you ever got here. You don't know anything. You only feel. You feel scared. You waver between selecting a path forward at random, sitting down where you are, or turning back the way you came. Worried that others will see your fear, you paste that Cheshire cat's silly grin on your face and stand still, paralyzed with indecision.

Master of My Universe

If you've had dreams and lost them, if you still have dreams and don't know what to do with them, or if you wish you could pull yourself out of your crushingly burdensome life long enough to take time to dream, this book is your godsend. Stop whatever you're doing; get some paper and pens. Mark this date on your calendar, find a quiet place to be alone, and sit down to read. You are about to rediscover The Real You.

The Real You (**TRY**, for short), is the person you were when you were eleven years old. **TRY** had many dreams and wishes. Back then, TRY believed in fairy tales, magic, superheroes, happy endings, and the unfailing ability of the good guys to defeat the bad guys within a one-hour television show. We all knew that right triumphed over wrong. Good beat evil. Love conquered all. TRY had mind-pictures of happy endings. You believed in Happily-Ever-After. You envisioned days of unending bliss. Over the years, TRY's dreams ran out of town, chased by bullies who wanted to trample them and stomp on their glimmers of hope. Life's disappointments and outright cruelties chased TRY away. Once your innermost dreams and wishes collapsed, TRY felt great waves of shame, humiliation, and even guilt. TRY felt guilty for having dreams. You believed they were foolish, so you hid them.TRY fell into a deep sleep.

Now, TRY has lost the ability to make choices. You no longer trustyour inner instincts. You are not sure where you should be going, but you knowyour current path seems hopeless. You haveroamed around in an endless maze for years, making no progress toward getting what you want. By this time, you have convinced yourself that what you want is a new car, a Movado watch, a big screen TV, a better spouse, nicer kids, and a cruise vacation to Belize. You thinkyou want your credit card bills paid, your kids in college, and a snow blower for your driveway. You imagineyour life would be better, if only you had a landscape gardener, the air conditioning fixed, and a larger apartment. Occasionally, TRY peeks out from hibernation and expresses desires for exactly these things. The pain you feel causes you to keep feeding yourself the blue pills of denial. Anything, to keepTRY sedated. You cannot bear the insistent demands, so you keep TRY quiet and asleep.

This book will awaken the TRY within you, and call TRY's essence back from despair. You might feel afraid to let TRY come back, worried about being disappointed anew, scared to open your heart to more pain, or hesitant to make yourself vulnerable to humiliations long forgotten. You might feel a well of emotion rising inside you when you even think about letting TRY out of that deep hole, where you have locked up your dreams for eternity. It is okay if you feel that way. It is normal. Anybody would fear being hurt again. Everybody uses denial to avoid that pain. All of us skirt the issues, avert our eyes, and refuse to see ourselves upon inner reflection. Our survival instinct kicks in. It wants to protect us, so it encourages us to shut down and turn away from self-knowledge. Self-reflection hurts.

Self-reflection – the ability to see ourselves objectively in the mirror – is not only painful. It is sometimes nearly impossible. For more than twenty years, I struggled with a weight problem, which I never had! People do that. I worked at weight loss, feeling defeated and frustrated. After many years of yo-yo dieting, weight loss programs, and prescription drugs, I managed to starve myself into a metabolic dysfunction that produced an actual weight problem. It was years later that I saw some old photographs and realized that in my earlier days, I had never been fat! My "friends", in their size 2 clothes, had falsely convinced me that the size 10 it took to accommodate my ample breasts meant I was a blimp! Too many of us just do not recognize our differences as normal and acceptable. We "swallow" the norm of the group, and attempt to become what the group perceives us to be. This happens when our friends sanction us. Sadly, it happens even more intensely when a beloved parent delivers the information about our self-image.

In this book, we will take a journey to FantasyLand, a place where TRY, our inner child, lives. It is a journey through the mirror of self-reflection. There we will meet dream characters, who are constructs of the inner mind. Elves, faeries, mad hatters, and a number of cats, dudes, and gnarly toads will greet us. We will examine our beliefs about how the universe operates. In the end, we will understand how our belief system changes our perception and distorts our experience. We will practice the skills that push the buttons that make the world go around. When we complete our journey, we will each arrive

somewhere. It may be a different place for everyone, but in our own way, we will each go where we belong.

You might not be ready to endure the pain of looking inside for the answers. You might not be willing to examine your soul. That's okay. If you're not ready, put the book back down. Lock it in a safe; bury it in your underwear drawer; wrap it, and donate it to your sister-in-law. You don't have to be strong enough yet to take that journey into your soul. Maybe this is not your time.

However, if this is your time, if you do love yourself, if you miss The Real You, if you want your dreams to become reality, if you are ready to look your true self in the "I" and if you are strong enough to meet your soul, then sit down. Pour yourself your favorite beverage.   Settle down in the best seat in the house. Take off your socks. Get comfortable. Fluff the pillows. Relax. Breathe deeply. Look that Cheshire cat in the eye, and get ready to meet your soul.   Be prepared to take the journey of self-reflection, so you can say to yourself:

Welcome home.

Do what you can, with what you have, where you are.

---- Theodore Roosevelt

Chapter 1: Be careful what you wish for.

Knowing what you want is more than half the battle.

One day, a venture capitalist visited Peru. He happened upon a man who was making beautiful metal sculptures in his back yard. "These are a gold mine," said the venture capitalist. "Let me build a factory to copy these. We can sell facsimiles of them on the Internet. You can be in charge of supervising the factory. We'll work day and night for twenty years, and at the end, you'll be fantastically wealthy."

"What will I do when I am wealthy?" the Peruvian man asked.

"Why, then, you can do anything you want," said the venture capitalist. "Fish.Play with your grandchildren. Make metal sculptures in your back yard. Whatever pleases you."

The Peruvian stared, perplexed at the proposal. "I fish, play with my grandchildren, and make metal sculptures in my backyard everyday now," he said to the odd American visitor. "I am doing what pleases me. If you don't mind, I'll skip the twenty years of working day and night, and be happy beginning today."

Master of My Universe

Money, and the price to get it, may not be all it's cracked up to be. As the Peruvian pointed out, **time is what life is made of**[1].Enjoying life occurs when we enjoy each of our daily moments. The Peruvian saw through that ruse which the venture capitalist never fathomed. Yet, the Peruvian had success, by his own measure. In this chapter, we will introduce the five tenets of belief that allow a person to be successful. Having examined these principles, we will thenlearn the practical skills that make these tenets work to operate our universe.

Begin at the Beginning

Wait. This was supposed to be a book about getting money, a new car, a true love, a decent job, and kids that don't talk back! The reason I can't pay my bills is thatthey are too high, not because I haven't hitchhiked to Alaska to find myself. I don't need to look for my next job by meditating. Nobody's going to cure my thyroid problem by rubbing a moonstone on my head! I need real solutions, for real problems, in the real world. My problems are not imaginary, thank-you-very-much. I certainly did not cause them. I am seriously looking for answers, and I want answers that work. I do not want any yoga-Ashram-breathing business. I am a responsible taxpayer, not a worthless loser! This book better turn around fast, or I am accidentally losing it by leaving it on the table in the fast food restaurant.

Was that your self-talk mumbling in the background? Do not be alarmed; we all have self-talk. Psychologists know about it. Psychiatrists prescribe drugs to shut it up. It is annoying for each of us, but there is nothing to do about it. It is generated by the softwarethat runs our brains. Ignore it. It is like one of those sci-fi monsters that feed on appreciation. The more you listen to

---

[1]"Time is what life is made of." Quote attributed to Benjamin Franklin

it, the worse it gets, so just pay it no attention and distract yourself by . . .

Oh, what's that you say? There's a party? Great, I love a party. Did the phone just ring? Hey, how many times are those kids going to come in and out of that door? They're letting the flies in. Amanda! Those cookies are for after dinner! Jeez, Constance, I can't take you to soccer practice; I promised to get these costumes ready for Joshua's play. And I can't do the costumes because Aunt Martha's sick! I said I would take her these new pajamas. Is that really The Guiding Light coming on TV right now?

Distraction is a best seller. With enough distraction, we avoid hearing ourselves think, and that is the point. If we do not hear our self-talk, we will not feel bad about ourselves. If we don't hear our minds running the tapes from the time our first grade teacher called us an idiot, or our big brother Butchy labeled us a retard, or our dad said, "You stupid brat", then we will not know that subliminal messages are sabotaging our efforts to succeed. If we do not acknowledge these messages running in background, we will not be obligated to do something about them. If we do not know there is something important we choose not to hear, then we will not recognize that the ear infection, which handicaps our efforts to finish a project, is self-inflicted. As long as we are so distracted that we cannot hear the self-talk, we can safely stick with our view that the world is random. We can continue to assure ourselves that the problem, or the loss, or the accident, or the misfortune is not a consequence of any action.

Jane thinks it's all random. She said so. I heard her talkin' on the phone.

Hush, hush.Don't bleed into the book pages. Self-talk must be hidden and quiet.

The universal law

The whole issue, in learning how to get what we want, is, after all, an issue of randomness in the universe. We need to know to what extent one can make the universe operate by our own hands. Is there, or is there not, a rule of Universal Law? It is a simple question. Either the universe has laws by which it operates, or the universe is random and senseless. We want to know, because if there are predictable rules, we can learn them. If we can learn them, we may be able to manipulate them, play them, and control them. Then we can get what we want. That's the point. *So, we ask, is the universe random? If it is not random, is it predictable?* It is an eternal question with far-reaching implications. It touches deeply on our concepts of belief and faith. It impacts our image of self. It reaches so deeply into our soul that our survival instinct kicks in to distract us from hearing the answer. We use distracting self-talk to tell ourselves that accidents and misfortune are random; ergo, we say, the universe is random. Some people believe prayer can manipulate the universe, attributing a characteristic to God, which is disposed to favor those who pray over those who do not pray. Some take the attitude: Trust in God, but exert all human efforts to the best of your ability. Others see the universe as unresponsive and random. They see no relationship between intent and probability. Some do not believe that human thought patterns emit waveforms that interact with the cosmos. Yet, when an accident, a misfortune, or an illness occurs, we each tend to wonder what caused it.

But . . . whose fault is it?

We want to know whose fault it is, because if we can assess blame and analyze fault, maybe we can reverse the action or prevent it from happening again. When a loved one dies, we agonize over those last minutes we spent with the person, assessing blame, looking for some action for which we can be at fault. Deep inside, we hope that, if we can find guilt, we can atone for it. We can be forgiven, and change the result. If it is not our fault, whose fault is it? Obviously, we tell ourselves, it's nobody's fault. It is just random. The world is random. The Earth revolves around the sun, the stars are speeding toward infinity, paramecia are growing and dying meaninglessly, and antibiotic-resistant bacteria are overrunning the universe. Don't forget that the polar ice caps are melting, the ozone layer is disappearing, and social security is almost out of money. The liberals are spending our money on welfare, the hawks are spending our money on war, the progressives are spending our money making insurance companies richer, and the cigarette companies have purchased the food companies. This is all out of our control. We can't do anything about it, so we just do our best. We keep that phony smile pasted in its place. We cover up the internal agony, so no one will know we are in pain.

Did the chip on your shoulder cause the pain in your neck?
Then, because we kept ourselves from hearing that self-talk of sabotage, we will not notice the connection between the chip on our shoulder and the resultant neck pain. If we smother our self-talk, we will not be aware that the excessive workload we carry results in a herniated disk. We will deny that a betrayal of our trust resulted in an asthma attack. We will never connect the dots between our children's foibles and our heart arrhythmia. If we keep trying, keep pushing forward, keep doing what we are supposed to do, keep following all the rules, we will never notice the rheumatoid arthritis screaming that it will disable us if we make one more move.

Master of My Universe

Whose fault is it? It's nobody's fault. It's just the random universe. Whole big universe operates on a couple of mathematical forces, like four or maybe five of them. Runs by a pair of dice, operating everything off probability. Oops. You lose; wipe you out. Roll again and play another hand. No sense to it, just random patterns. Flip flop. Drib drab. Tag, you're it, drop dead. Who cares, just another road kill.

The universe did it.
Do you believe that? Do you really believe, in your deepest values, that the universe is random and unthinking? Do you honestly think that nothing you do matters,that you are vulnerable to being struck by lightning at any moment, and that germs from a doorknob cause a cold? Okay, maybe germs from a doorknob do cause a cold, but what about those other two?

Excuse me.

Whoops, there's my self-talk butting in. I will never get this chapter finished if I keep stopping to listen to it.

Excuse me, but I object to the idea that germs cause a cold. I think that is scientifically unfounded.

You should ignore that disruptive, italicized self-talk, like I do. It only goes away by starving it, and it feeds off attention. *Now that I think of it, though, I do agree there is some question about what causes a cold. After all, germs are everywhere, inside and outside. Upside and downside, germs literally come out your ears. So how come one person gets a cold and another person doesn't? It makes no sense, bad-mouthing germs just because they happen to be co-incident with colds. Flies are co-incident with garbage, but they do*

Chapter 1: Be Careful What You Wish For

not cause it, do they? I amfairly certain I don't believe in viruses, or is that virii?

Self-talk distracts. I did not intend to talk about or think about germs and doorknobs. This is a chapter about the beginning of dreaming, and being carefulwhat you wish for. If I'm going to succeed at writing this chapter, I have to have control over my thoughts, and my self-talk.I'm trying to write about dreams, but I can't get anywhere! My self-talk is sabotaging me! *I wonder.Does everybody have a little voice inside that creates havoc and interrupts progress? Or is it just me? Am I unique in having this running dialogue in the back of my mind? Or do you have it, too? If only my imaginary friend from childhood could stop by again and explain this. But, I stopped believing in her when I hit puberty, and she went away. What was her name? I haven't seen her for years.*

Some tools of childhood help us create, innovate, and dream. To dream, we need the power to focus.

The fairies did it
The power to focus is one of our magic abilities, which the fairies who attended your birth conferred upon you with their wands. Probably, your parents did not want to mention it to you, because right after the good fairies gave you your individual personality, the bad fairy cursed you with the power to snatch defeat from the jaws of victory. Fortunately, after hearing the bad fairy's curse, there was one fairy left, who popped up and gave you the power to focus. This power gives you the ability to overcome the curse of choosing defeat.

My goal right now is to describe the beginning of dreaming. I will use my power to focus to achieve it.

The beginning of dreaming.

How do we know when something begins? Did the chicken come first? Or was it the egg? Is morning the beginning of a day, or the end of a night? Is Sunday the first day of a new week, or the last day of a weekend? Is puberty the beginning of adolescence, or the end of childhood? When we move to a new house, are we starting a new life, or ending an old one? Every beginning of one thing is also an ending of something else.

The beginning of a life-where-dreams-are-smothered is the end of a life-where-anything-is-possible. Before you lost your dreams, you believed they would happen. At some time, maybe in one moment, maybe in a series of moments, you lost your belief that dreams could come true. You started seeing the Universe as random, its actions as arbitrary. You accepted the concept that life might not have meaning. You allowed for the possible indifference of the Earth. You felt betrayed by the conflict between your observations and the sayings your parents taught you. You realized you would have to choose between believing your parents'ideas about how the world works, and trusting your personal observations. You had to decide between listening to your mother, and listening to your gut.

The impossible dream

For example, you might have believed you could be a professional ball player. Your mother, wanting to be sure you could get a job, might have told you that was an impossible dream. She might have encouraged you to study accounting instead. Or perhaps you had a crush on a boy when you were in elementary school. Maybe his parents lived on the wrong side of the track, and your mother told you that boy's family was "no good." You listened to your mother, and you tried to accept what she said as true, because that is what we all do. Your disappointments built, until one day you woke up without the belief in dreams-that-come-true anymore. It was a sad day. You might remember it; you might not. Whether you remember it or not, that day was significant for you. It was the beginning of a life without hope. When we have no hope, we stop dreaming. When we have no dreams, we cannot make a dream come true. The first tenet for getting what we want out of life is then:

Tenet 1. You must have a dream.

A dream is not some willy-nilly, shoulda-woulda-coulda "wish list". Wishes are very different from dreams. A wish is something you want, if it is given to you, but it is not something you want so badly you would make a deal for it and pay its price. You do not want consequences attached to what you wish for; you just want some unseen force to hand it over. Getting something for nothing generally turns out to be a raw deal. You usually find out that wish-granting genie was a trickster. For example, you might wish to win the lottery, but you dream of being a big star on American Idol. In the first case, your only effort to make your dream come true is the purchase of a lottery ticket every week. You make a small effort, hoping for a big reward. In the second case, you might work for years to perfect your singing ability, and then plan to audition for the contest. You invest significant energy into your dreams. The reward is part journey, part result.

"Free money" is not what dreams are about. Dreams have substance. Dreams are long-term visions. Dreams bear a price worth paying. When what you want is your dream-come-true, you are willing to deal with the universe to make it happen. This book shows you how to make your dreams come true, and get what you really want, by dealing with the laws and the forces of the universe. So there you have it. Tenet #1 is "You have to have a dream, if you're going to make a dream come true." Now that you have your dream, what are you going to do about it?

What Matters for You

I am not much of a free handout person. I do not believe in it. Not that it makes any difference to you, what I believe in. What matters to you is what **you** believe in, because what you believe shapes the world you experience. There was a guy from the back roads of an underdeveloped country visiting Washington DC, and he saw a man enter a large silver box. A few minutes later, the box opened, and the man turned into two women. Magic!This is why he took the stairs, instead of the elevator, to his hotel room. In his perception, because he did not understand the concept of an elevator, he saw the silver door open to let one man in, and then open again to find the man missing, and two women in his place.

Everything we see, we see in the context of our set of beliefs. You hear a dog barking. The only reason you know the sound comes from a dog is that you haveseen dogs before. If you had never seen a dog, maybe you would think it was a werewolf, or perhaps a barking hippopotamus. Our perceptions are formed early in life. We make associations in our minds. Forever thereafter, we see only what we believe.However, in scientific reality, what is real? Steven Hawking, well-known physicist, tells us there are eleven dimensions, some curled inside others[2]. The only reality is the forces swirling in electrically charged, mysterious and undetectable, dark matter. Everything else is a construct of our associative and sensory mind. We see what we be-

---

[2] Hawking, S. The Grand Design

lieve, based on our sensory experience and perceptive associations.

Tenet 2: You will see it when you believe it.

Most people think they believe it when they see it, but this is a misconception. We can only see what we first believe to be possible. Maybe it would help to explain it if I tell you a completely mythical and untrue story. This is a story that lived in the back of my head for many years. Do not even think about this story as being possible. It is so mythical, that it lives only in fantasy. Of course, the back of my head, like the back of your head, is where the primitive amygdala records the history of humanity. Maybe this story was true in some other world, at some other time, in some other dimension. This story only moved to the front of my mind, which is where the consciousness of the frontal lobe lives, very recently. *It may be carrying some baggage from its travel.* We say that stories have a "ring of truth" to them, depending on how they "resonate." Wavelengths, and different frequencies, would have a lot to do with those curled up dimensions, wouldn't they? See if this story rings true for you. This is the story of Jane's inner mind.

The Story of FantasyLand
FantasyLand is a place far, far away and long, long ago. It is totally different from life here on Earth. In FantasyLand, the only way to succeed in life is to achieve an exactly zero balance in your bank account. Residents of FantasyLand, unlike residents of Earth, cringe when their bank account goes above zero. You see, each day in FantasyLand, actions that you take and events that occur automatically cause debits and credits to your bank account. When you were born, you were born with a balance in

your account. If you were born with a lot of talents or money, your balance would be below zero, because you would have a debt to society in return for all of your privilege. You would have to pay into the account, by doing good deeds, to bring your balance back to zero. A person born to privilege would be deeply indebted to society; this person would have to live a life of doing good deeds. On the other hand, if you were born with little ability and poor, your balance in the account might be high. You could take from the account, in order to achieve the goal of zero. Society would owe you something.

Doing good deeds
Let us call this account, just for the sake of drama, "Karma". To understand life in FantasyLand, you have to recognize that you can lower your Karmic debt by doing good deeds and performing kind services. If you are born with many Karmic assets, they become a crushing burden, and you must relieve yourself of them by investing in seeds. The only seeds that lower your Karmic balance are seeds of transformation. You have to spend your Karma on buying them, so you can create "change". Your life in FantasyLand consists of a daily dance with Karma, in which you must balance between lowering your debt by doing good deeds, and relieving your burden by investing in seeds of transformation. Only when your Karma is completely balanced, can you end your life as a winner, and die. In this way, even if a very young person died, it is perceivedby the society as a victory for that person. He could not have died if he had not achieved Karmic balance. Death becomes a celebration of achievement. It means the purpose in life has been fulfilled. Of course, in FantasyLand, no one believes Death is evaporation. Everyone knows the universal law that energy can be neither created nor destroyed, so it is assumed that all people who die have simply moved on to the next world.

Chapter 1: Be Careful What You Wish For

Following your Destiny

Throughout your life, you have the opportunity to exercise your free will and make decisions about your path. Among all the possible paths, there is only one path that will lead you to your Destiny. At the point of your Destiny, there is a Giant Magnet, which is pulling you toward it. You feel attracted to the magnet, so you are constantly adjusting your path, trying to find the one path that will lead to your end goal.

Each decision you make intends to bring you closer to the magnet. However, sometimes, the path doubles back on itself, or twists in an odd manner, and you get confused. When this happens, you may inadvertently make a wrong decision or go down a wrong path. As magnets do, this conflict snaps a twist in the force field between you and your destiny. The magnet gets worried that you may be going rogue, skipping off your path, or losing power. It sends out an alarm signal. When the alarm sounds, the path rises up to shake, push, nudge, shove, smack, or roll you back on track. These disruptions to your path are called "accidents", but they are not accidental. They are Destiny interacting with you. This continues to happen until you meet your destiny.

Synchronicity

We know this story is mythical.But, what if you believed this? What if, every time you experienced an accident, a coincidence, an odd circumstance, a chance encounter, or a strange synchronicity, you believed it to bean action of the magnet of Destiny? If you believed it, then accidents and problems would look like opportunities to adjust your direction. You would experience the bad things in life as if they were good and helpful things. When you lost something, you would think you did not need it. You would think when you broke your arm on the way to a meeting, you were not meant to do that deal. You would think when you broke a lamp, you must have had some use for an extra lamp-shade. If you believed in the laws of FantasyLand, every bad thing that happened would be perceived as guidance from the universe. You would come to expect all experience to be positive. You would feel gratitude for the course correction, rather than frustration and dismay for the obstacle. You would feel gratitude, rather than rage. This would be a totally different way to look at difficult situations than the way you probably look at them now. *If you felt gratitude to the magnet for guiding you to your destiny, instead of frustration and despair*, **do you think your health would improve?**

Emotional response is chemical reaction in the body, which results in hormonal imbalance and causes disease. Do you believe that feeling positive gratitude about frustrating things would change your emotional response to any situation? Do you see that your innermost core belief system impacts your emotional response, which changes your chemical reactions, which impacts your hormones, which results in your state of disease? Do you see that believing in the laws of FantasyLand would change your health, whether the laws of FantasyLand were true or not? Do you see that it is your belief in FantasyLand, rather than the truth or falsehood of its existence, which would change your emotional response, and impactyourchemical balance? If you see it, can you believe it?

It's not all fiction
The Earth is a magnet, you know. That is not fiction. So there you have tenet #2. You must believe it to see it. First, you have to have a dream. Then you have to put that dream into the context of a belief system that tells you at your inner core that it is possible for you to make it come true. Until you believe it, you

will never see it. You must envision your dream as true, before it can ever happen. When you believe that your dream is your destiny, the path will rise up to meet you.

But, enough of this foolishness. You wanted to know how to get what you want. What was that you wanted? A new car? Your debts paid?A job?An all-beef patty?Or, did you want to meet your destiny? I don't know about you, but for me, the fun of a new car wears off. **I want what I want when I want it.**However, when all is said and done, more is said than done. What I truly want, at the core of my being, is inner peace. I get that when I know I am on my path to Destiny.

Enough about me.

Have you noticed that sometimes my self-talk (the words in the italics), is reasonable and intelligent? It adds information or gives guidance. Other times, my self-talk is emotional and negative. It whines, complains, and denigrates. Self-talk comes from varying perspectives inside us. Some of it is helpful, and elevates our abilities. Some of it is useless. It deserves to be banished to a corner and ignored. The problem comes when we have no control over the tapes playing in our minds. Without a functioning controller, we cannotchoose which messages we want to accept, so we protect ourselves by shutting them all down. We purposely choose to keep from hearing ourselves think, by distracting our minds. With half our mind shut down to keep from hearing the babbling, we do not have everything we need to be our personal best. When we are purposely not listening to our inner selves, who knows what kind of mischief and trouble our "darker half" might be getting into?*The dark side does not like being ignored. Like a spoiled child, it schemes about what it can do to get attention.*

Master of My Universe

Oh, thank you, Mother. I heard that! I heard it in my mind, of course. I did not hear a voice in my head. When I heard it in my mind, it sounded like the voice of my mother. The voice I heard in my head said something that I thought sounded useful and worthwhile, so I listened to it, and I wrote it on this paper, so you could hear it, too. If you heard that voice in your mind, you might call that "thinking." You are much too sane and sober to hear voices in your head!

Is channeling the same as thinking?

In FantasyLand, totally unlike Earth, people do not "think". They just "channel". That is, people are like antennae with receivers. Inside their brains, they have different channels to receive information, and they can tune in or tune out to whatever they want to hear. The Big Server in the Sky sends information to them at varying frequencies, and they can pick and choose what they want to hear. It feels just like thinking, but of course, it is not. Thinking is not the same as receiving information from the black hole at the center of the Milky Way! There are actually two giant servers that live at the core of the Milky Way. In FantasyL-and, they are inside the black hole. The Milky Way circles this black hole, and interacts with FantasyLand's magnetism, to call people to their Destiny. The black hole inside the Milky Way has been named Sagittarius A Star, by the scientists who believe they have found it.

What is "thinking," anyway?
I have a lot of different thoughts, and sometimes I debate topics in my own mind, looking at the pros and cons of things, trying to decide. Sometimes I disagree with myself. If I pay careful attention, I can tell that my thoughts are not always speaking in the same voice. I can hear my mother's voice, and I can always trust

that one, but there are other voices speaking in my head, too. They try to use my own voice most of the time, so I think I am thinking. That's good, because if I told anybody my thinking was using other voices, other than my own, they would get out the Prozac. You've heard of the fine line between genius and insanity. Well, I choose to walk that line, because the "voices" sometimes have worthwhile and insightful things to say.

If I were fearful of those voices, I might choose to keep my channel to that part of my mind closed. Then, I would not have "thought" of this useful and relevant information. My intelligence would have been limited, because I was not using my whole mind. I would have appeared to be a person who had somewhat of a "closed mind." Of course, if my mind is closed, that is because I am trying to shut up the dark side, which is the home of both genius and insanity. What a dilemma! You shut the door to keep the demon out, and it ends up locking the brainy and creative part of yourself right there in the closet with the nasties! Which brings us to:

Tenet 3: Creativity and ambition come from the dark side.

You can't live your life happily with the dark part of you locked up.**That dark part is your creativity!***It is also your backbone.*A smile can't be your umbrella. You cannot paste a smile on your face in an attempt to hide and deny the nasty feelings inside. Nasty feelings, kept hidden in the closet, try to chew their way out. They nag at you from the inside, eating away at all that is good. They gnaw at you.

This causes stomach problems. You say, "I can't stomach that." You say, "That makes me want to vomit." You say, "You expect me to swallow that B.S?" Meanwhile, you go to a doctor and get pills for your acid reflux.

There is a nerve, called the vagus nerve[3]connecting right from the stomach to the brain. When you take painkiller drugs, they divert the calming hormones from your stomach to your brain, so you feel soothed. This is why painkiller drugs cause constipation. Digestive problems lead to malnutrition. Malnutrition leads to all sort and symptoms of imbalances which doctors will label as disease, and give you more unbalancing drugs to suppress the symptoms. Locking the nasties inside makes you sick. Drugging the nasties does not cure them.

You are not a nice and good person if that nice and good part is only "for show." The only way you can be truly nice and good is if you are nice and good all the way through, inside and out. You have to throw open that door to the dark side, and air out its foggy recesses. The nasties and the negative self-talk cannot be just locked up. First, they show, even though you think they are hidden. That insincere smile looks phony. Scientists have categorized all the muscles of the face. The emotion we feel shows in our expressions.[4]Emotion is not only chemical; it is also muscular. It shows in your facial expression and body language. People know from the set of the muscles in your face. They can see the nasties locked up in your head, based on the mini-muscles in your face. Nasties cannot be hidden. They have to be removed. Eradicated, dissolved, banished, exorcised, released, eliminated.

---

[3] The pneumogastric nerve, the tenth of twelve paired cranial nerves. It conveys sensory information about the state of the body's organs to the central nervous system.

[4] Gladwell, M. Blink: The Power of Thinking without Thinking

Chapter 1: Be Careful What You Wish For

Eliminated.There's a good word. I like that word.

Pooped out.Flushed.Ex-Laxed.   In this book, we will have some exercises to help you create the environment that gets rid of those nasty thoughts. No matter how dramatic and torturous your childhood, there are still simple ways to rid yourself of its impact. Once you leave your parents' house, it is your responsibility as an adult to counteract whatever psychological harm occurred while you could not defend yourself.   I have heard old retired guys still walking around saying, "I can't help it;that is how my parents raised me."   That is no excuse. From age eighteen on, your actions are your own responsibility. There is an expiration date on blaming your parents for your closed mind and bull-headed stubbornness[5].

Well, that explains it then. It is your parents fault. I thought you said it was nobody's fault, and the universe was just random and unfeeling. How can you expect me to follow this disjointed rambling when you won't tell me whose fault it is?

Okay, that's enough! I've had it with this stupid self-talk! I'm putting an end to this. I'm going to talk to myself.

Self-talk, what is wrong with you? Why do you care whose fault it is?

If I knew whose fault it was, I could put them in jail so they wouldn't do it again. ThenI'd be safe.

How do I know **you** didn't do it? What's your name?

---

[5] Paraphrased from a speech by J K Rowling at Harvard University

What do you mean? I'm**you**. You're talking to yourself. Like a crazy person. Anyhow, I didn't do it. Don't blame me. It's not my fault.

Right. You didn't do it. I didn't do it. So who did it? The candidates are: my parents, society, the random universe, God, the liberal left, Al Qaeda, Dick Cheney, Glenn Beck, or Hugo Chavez. Which is it?

Uhhh. I pick Hugo Chavez.

As you see, talking with the Nameless Demon in my head is a futile effort. The conversation points out, however, that Nameless is looking for someone to blame, because Nameless is worried that Nameless is to blame. Looking for someone else to blameis an attempt at reducing the feelings of guilt. We see from this conversation that guilt is one of those residual feelings that creates negative self-talk. We're not actually guilty, but we feel guilty. That guilty feeling, locked inside, reduces our capacity for creativity and ambition. It uses up our creative space and drains our energy. Guilt, shame, fear, humiliation, embarrassment, and anxiety all create an energy drain. That direct line from the stomach to the brain sends the transmission: Help! I'm sick! Send medicine! Then the hormones rage, the immune system is activated, the blood pressure rises, the pulse increases. If we happen to go to a doctor while this is occurring . . . zap! We come home with a prescription drug. Of course, the problem hasn't been solved, but we've stopped noticing the symptoms.

Stop the torture

To eliminate the negative self-talk, we have to find a way to stop feeling guilt needlessly. Now, if we were actually guilty of something, that would be easy. If you're guilty, you can confess, make amends, accept the consequences, and move on. It's like when the TV-bad-guy tortures someone who is innocent. They have nothing to confess, so they end up being tortured to death. Your negative self-talk is the guilty feeling that has no basis. It can't confess, so it never stops feeling tortured. As long as this tortured soul is locked inside your closet, you will be far too busy guarding the door. This guarding effort will prevent you from getting any creative, ambitious work done. How do you get rid of this guilt? The same way that all negative self-talk gets eliminated. You stop feeding it. It eats self-pity.

Which side will win?

There is an old Native American proverb[6]. An elder of the tribe tells the children they have competing forces inside themselves. One force is a mean wolf, fighting desperately for life against a good and kind, friendly dog. "Which one will win?" the children ask. "The one you feed," the elder answers. When we stoke the fire of negative thoughts, and give them oxygen with our words, we are feeding the mean wolf.

If you have nothing to confess, then why not deal?

If you can't stop the torture by confessing, what can you do to make yourself free and creative? How can you reclaim all that wasted space in your mind, which you are currently using to torture yourself over baseless guilt? If you can't find someone to blame, how can you fix it?

---

[6] Source unknown. It's a story circulating on the Internet.

Master of My Universe

Fix what?

Fix the universe. Fix it so it stops randomly assigning accidents. Fix it so it stops raising taxes. Fix it so we don't run out of oil. Fix it so the polar bears don't fall into the ocean when their ice floes melt. Fix it so my car stops breaking down. Fix it so my little niece doesn't need another operation. Fix it so my mother doesn't die from a heart attack brought on by the flu. Fix it so my young nephew doesn't die from a blood clot brought on by prescription medicine. Fix it so the illegal aliens learn to speak English. Fix it so the autoworkersdon't lose their pensions and the Wall Street vultures do.

You already did that. You elected Barack Obama.

Well, that's true. That did make me feel empowered as a person. But only for a moment. I had a little elation there for a short time, thinking I had actually done something. But, I quickly learned that nothing meaningful changed in my world so the moment of euphoria passed. Now I'm back to normal. I want change. I want something done. I want my electric bill to go down. I want a new job. I absolutely need, need, need more money.

And your back hurts?

From carrying the crushing burden, yes.Only when it rains.But look what's happened. I'm conversing with my self-talk again! This time, though, my self-talk sounds like my mother instead of Nameless, so it's okay. I like talking with my mother. It's helpful and positive. Not like that demon, Nameless!

He-who-shall-not-be-named?

Chapter 1: Be Careful What You Wish For

Right.Like in the Harry Potter books[7]. The major demon is this guy whose name you can't say aloud. Naming something empowers it. This is a well-known, universal truth. That brings up a major point, which is about to lead us to Tenet 4. We human beings like to think we're so unique and special. Yet, we all have many thoughts in common. The psychologist Jung called these thoughts "archetypes." Archetypes are universally accepted sets of truths. They float in the ether and invade other people[8]. We all get these thoughts in our heads, no matter what background or experiences we've had. They are forces that we receive with our mind antennae, even if we never told each other about them. That explains why we tend to have common themes in our dreams.

Or in our sexual fantasies.

Yes, Mother. Oddly, people have common themes in their sexual fantasies. The universe is very interested in sexuality, you know. The universe has a desire to keep its people reproducing[9], so it sends out signals to . . .

The universe sends out signals? You're starting in on that gibberish again? We're not getting all New Age Metaphysical here, are we? Because I don't go for that.

Okay, that wasn't Mother. I'm not interested in hearing any voices except those of my mother, so just scurry on back to your hole, please. I'm working. I will not feed you. In fact, from here on

---

[7] J K Rowling, Harry Potter series
[8] Jung, C. Man and His Symbols
[9] Ridley, M. The Red Queen Hypothesis

out, whenever you run your mouth in my chapter, I'm just going to say, "No Soup For You", and that will make you shrivel up and go away. Get it?Got it? Good.

"No Soup For You."
Reader, if you're having trouble with your own self-talk, feel free to use my "no soup for you" phrase to make your own demons run away. I borrowed the phrase from Jerry Seinfeld[10] anyway. As I was saying, of course the universe sends out signals. What do you think electricity is? Or magnetism? Or gravity? Or the strong nuclear and the weak nuclear forces? We accept that these forces exist, although we can't see them. We accept them because we can measure them, reproduce them in an experimental environment, and harness them for our own use. We can control them, or we at least think we can.

But what about the force that handles our thoughts? What about the force that generates the dreams that we dream when we are sleeping? What explains the common themes in psychological problems, dreams, sexual fantasies, and motivations? How can an author write a book if the behavior of characters is not predictable?   We all know that the behavior of human beings has common threads.   Where do these threads come from? How do stem cells know whether to become kidneys or toenails? What universal force carries the information that allows us to think? Why do we all feel sad, happy, joyful, or grieving, about similar things?   What triggers our emotion?   What stimulates our thought?

What causes thinking?
We don't know, and our best scientists don't know, what causes thinking. From a practical perspective, we don't need to care. To

---

[10] The television series *Seinfeld*

learn how-to-get-what-we-want-when-we-want-it, we don't need to be concerned about whose fault it is. We also don't need to know what force causes thinking. We just need to know: it isn't our fault, and we don't control the universe.

But to be clear . . . there really is a black hole in the center of the Milky Way, there really are floating frequencies, and the Earth really is a magnet. Look it up!*11*

So now,we've learned:
(Tenet 1) we have to have a **dream**.
(Tenet 2) we have to **believe** that dream can happen and envision it done, and
(Tenet 3) we have to unleash our deepest, darkest **creative** energies, and not bottle up our dark side and negativity. We have to release our negativity into the Earth, through our feet, where it will cause no harm[12]. Then we will be free to access our genius, our ambition, and our backbone, which come from the dark side.

If we don't control the universe, what controls it?
Some say nothing controls it. Some say it is just a product of a perfect storm of forces, which randomly stuck themselves together with no sense or blueprint, and accidentally put a world in place of exactly the right temperature, with exactly the right environment, to create and sustain life. Others say God created the universe, which of course leads tothe question of what created God[13]. This causes us to wonder what was the beginning of the beginning, which opens up the whole area of what is the

---

[11] See the Bibliography of this book.

[12] Negativity released into the Earth can be cleansed by the eco-system. Else, it will pop out of our mouths, where it causes great harm.

[13] For in-depth analysis of this question, see Meyer, *Signature in the Cell*

nature of time?   Fortunately, we do not have to answer any of those questions in order to figure out how to get what we want. It's a good thing we don't, because if we waste all our time trying to find that answer, we'll miss the key politics required to . . .

The politics?You're bringing politics into this?

(No soup for you)

Politics, meaning "of the people". We get what we want by doing things that people are able to do. We get what we want by doing the best we can, with the tools we have, in the place we are. It's not magical or mystical. It's just uncommon sense. Practical, useful, proven, intuitively obvious, but uncommon, sense.
That is our fourth tenet:

Tenet 4. You make a deal with the universe.

The universe is ruled by forces unseen and unknown. We're just the tiniest speck of the teeniest dust on a rolling ball in a vast-ness we can't imagine or describe. We only see three of the eleven dimensions. We can't figure out who runs this vast universe, why He, She, or It did it, what was the point, or who is to blame. We don't know that, and we are unlikely to know it, at least while we're alive. We can believe something about it, and that belief is our faith, which we choose; butit's called faith, because there's no evidence. We can't prove it. What we can prove, how-ever, is that the universe interacts with us. It responds to our actions.

If we poison its water, it will kill us when we drink it. If we pol-lute its air, it will smother us when we breathe it. If we desecrate its land, it will wither our food supply. If we play with its matches, it will detonate us with its inner bombs. The universe, and most particularly the Earth, operates on a give and take designed for survival. You live on Earth. Earth is in the universe. The universe runs through forces that are measurable and detectable. The universe knows you are here. **The coincidence and the unusual circumstance are its interactive tools.**

In the following chapters of this book, we will show you how to contract with the universe to get what you want. Contracting with the universe sounds odd, I know. Here's a way to think of it:

Our contract with the universe
In FantasyLand, whenever someone plants a seed, the seed will probably grow into exactly what its parent was. If its mother was corn, the seed will also be corn. The farmer can pretty much count on this contract with the universe, to reward his effort of planting a seed, and nurturing its growth. Then, when the corn grows into a full plant, the farmer has the right to eat the corn, or sell it. He also has the right to take the seeds and make another planting of more corn. This is the contract the farmer has made with the universe. The farmer can count on the universe to continue to provide him more food, as long as he provides the skilled labor, which cares knowledgeably for the plants.

I know what you're thinking now. You're thinking that's the same as on Earth. You're thinking FantasyLand is really like Earth! But you would be wrong about that. You see, on Earth, companies like Monsanto have genetically modified corn. The contract with the universe is void. On Earth, if a farmer saves his seeds, he can be sued by the Monsanto company. The genetically modified corn made by Monsanto infiltrated the air around the farmer's natural corn. By the processes of nature, the farmer impinged on Monsanto's patent. So, you see, Earth is nothing like FantasyLand. But, what if it were? If Earth were like FantasyLand, then when you planted a seed, and you watered it, nurtured it, fed it, and made sure it got enough sunlight, you would reap what you sowed. *Too bad, too bad. That's not how it is on Earth any more.*

When you deal with the universe, you live by its laws. Its laws are not right or wrong. They are true or false. The laws of the universe are the laws of predator and prey. The zebra's viewpoint is that the lion is wrong. The lion's viewpoint is that the zebra doesn't get a vote. The universe's laws are consistent, but they are amoral. When you decide to make your deal with the universe to get what you want, keep that firmly in mind. *Be very, very careful what you wish for.* The genie you let out of the bottle will not differentiate between getting rich by your efforts, and harming others to take undeserved wealth. **This is where you make your personal decisions about your own integrity.** It is where you prove to the Author that you deserve to be the Hero in your own story. It is where you live up to your destiny and step forth to claim it.

So, yes, the fourth tenet is that you must make a deal with the universe. First, you **dream**. Second, you **believe** your dream will happen. Third, you release all your **creative** energy into it; and fourth, you nurture your seeds. **Deal** with the universe. That brings us to Tenet #5, the last tenet.

Tenet 5: What Gets Rewarded, Gets Repeated

If you are doing something repeatedly, it's because you want the reward that comes with it. If your children are throwing tantrums, it's because in the past, you rewarded their tantrums with attention. (Even negative attention is attention.) If you are consistently overwhelmed and running late, it's because you enjoy feeling the importance of being in demand. If you are regularly irresponsible, it's because you want someone to step in and help you. If you are constantly misplacing your keys, it's because you desire to get yourself stranded, so someone can "save" you. If you are chronically depressed, it's because you choose unhappiness. If you are repeatedly too ill to go to work, it's because you hate your job. If you are constantly busy, busy, busy, it's because you fear knowing what you truly want.

Ready, Fire, Aim

I know every person reading this is now hopping mad. How dare you suggest that I gave myself cancer? You are all screaming indignantly. How dare you blame the victim? How dare you imply that little children who get ill are at fault? How dare you suggest that I wanted to be hit by a car? How dare you suggest that I wanted an airplane to fall on my house and set my living room on fire?

Do you remember Nameless, who's hiding in the closet ready to pounce on anybody who suggests the bad things that happen to you are your own fault? Nameless is a filter in your mind. He wants you to have trouble hearing correctly, and he encourages you to interpret every little suggestion as a supposition of guilt. I didn't say the bad things that happen to you are your fault. I said the behaviors you do repeatedly are the ones that give you reward. The circumstances that befall you are not your fault, but the behavior you choose in response to those circumstances is fully your rational decision. You choose to respond based on your understanding of the consequences.

You must choose to pay the price

Master of My Universe

Circumstances occur for many reasons and many rhymes. The universe is in charge of circumstances, and you are not in charge. *Because you are not in charge, you must make a deal, sign a contract, and negotiate an outcome with the universe, to get what you want.*

I said this was a book about how to get what you want. This is the answer. **You deal.** This deal will involve serious work. It will come with a price. You must choose whether the reward involved will meet your expectations. You must decide whether you will pay what the universe demands, upfront. You can't just wish upon a star.

Example: You lose your job. What are you going to do? Reach for the anti-depressant pills? Go on a drinking binge? Waste the last of your savings on a lawyer to sue the company? Treat your spouse and children badly? Or re-think your career and re-invent yourself in a new and better way?

Example: Your fiancé is in a car accident. What are you going to do? Flunk out of college because you're so depressed? Worry until your eczema starts flaring? Postpone the wedding because he won't look good walking down the aisle on crutches? Cancel the wedding because you don't want your health insurance rates to go up? Or cheer him up and keep a positive outlook?

Example: A hurricane blows your house down and the insurance company refuses to pay. What are you going to do? Keep paying the mortgage company because it's "right?" Or declare bankruptcy, send the mortgage company a copy of your insurance policy, and say, "Let's you and him fight." Sometimes you need to stand up for yourself.

Chapter 1: Be Careful What You Wish For

Circumstances are not your fault, but playing the victim is not the role you choose for your life. This life is your story. Select the role of the hero, not the villain or the victim. *Wouldn't the Author expect that?*

In FantasyLand, the Author of the World worries about His characters. He tries to nudge them gently back onto their paths when they stray, but too often, their activities interfere with the operation of the default forces, and cause volcanoes to erupt. So He decided to post some signs in the sky. It would be like a point system. Five points for noticing that your stomach hurts after eating MSG[14]. Fifteen points for recognizing that you're mad at your boss at work, not your kids at home. Three hundred points for acknowledging that a heart **ache** and a heart **attack** are kissing cousins. The Author thought maybe the little signs in the sky would be rewarding, and people would strive to attain them. He knew, from those experiments with Pavlov's dogs[15], that people repeat behaviors that bring rewards.

Recognition is a major reward

But, alas, just as He had implemented His Sign-in-the-Sky program, Facebook put out its next release, and no one looked up to the sky any more. They all had their heads down, staring at their computer screens, getting their feedback from each other. Nobody even noticed His signs in the sky. Nobody paid attention to His world view. The Author didn't know what to do. Rewards that came from the sky couldn't compete with the lure of peer-to-peer Facebook feedback. Feedback was recognition, and recognition was a major reward! The Author felt despondent. His program was doomed! What to do? All the People Units He had

---

[14] Monosodium glutamate, sometimes called "natural flavors"

[15] Pavlov fed dogs only when he rang a bell. Soon, the dogs would salivate when the bell rang, even when there was no food offered.

created were set to respond with a hormone rush when they felt acknowledged and rewarded. He meant that to be a hook, which He could use for control. It was an important measure to allow free will without destroying the universe. But the people used it to acknowledge each other, instead of to interact with Him. Something was going terribly wrong.

Choose your rewards carefully.
We must be extremely careful about what rewards us. We will do what gives us positive feedback. Drinking beer gives positive feedback, in the short term. Many addictive behaviors: shopping, over-eating, taking drugs, gossiping, chatting online, gambling, and playing World of Warcraft, for example, give short-term rewards without contributing to long-term happiness. If we want to get what we actually want, we must choose which rewards to accept, for getting rewards consumes our time, and **Time is what Life is made of.**

Dream. Believe. Create. Deal. Reward.
Those are the five tenets of getting what you want. When you understand them, you will learn to behave in a way that attracts success. You will be able to follow the eight practices that derive from the tenets. We will learn how to follow these practices in subsequent chapters. You will get what you want when you want it, every time. When you learn the skill that comes from these practices, you will know the power that tells you: **Be careful, very careful, about knowing what you really want, deep inside.** The universe will deliver exactly what you wish for. In fact, right now, right this minute, the universe is already delivering exactly what you wished for. You just may not know what you asked. It is very important to understand what we are asking *because the Universe is One with us All.*

Memorization is a key ability you will need to learn to get what you want. This is the easy way to memorize; make a simple label and turn it into a mnemonic. Like this:

Tenet #1: Dream

Tenet #2: Believe

Tenet #3: Create

Tenet #4: Deal

Tenet #5: Reward

DBCDR or Don't Be Caught Dead Right.

Just remember: "Don't Be Caught Dead Right". Then memorize Dream, Believe, Create, Deal, Reward.

Let's Review

Five tenets (or principles) determine the interaction between you and the universe, and act upon the delivery of what you want. The five tenets are:

#1. <u>You have to have a dream.</u> If you've stopped dreaming, how can you make a dream come true? Your vision of success has to be clear and well defined. It has to be firmly planted in your mind, including its details. You need to picture it completed, and view that picture regularly.

#2. <u>You'll see it when you believe it.</u> Our belief system filters our perception. If you don't believe something will happen, you will fail to notice the coincidence and circumstance lining up to cause it.[16] You will pass on the opportunities presented to you by the universe. Your failure to believe will keep your dream from happening. Your inability to respond to guidance with gratitude will damage your health. *As we learned from Peter Pan, if you don't believe, Tinker Bell will die!*

#3. Creativity and ambition come from our dark side. You can't live a full, creative, productive life with your dark side locked in a closet. Phony smiles that cover dark thoughts are unacceptable. Your nasty thoughts have to be exorcised, banished, released, remanded, and extinguished. They cannot be allowed to share a body with you. Clean them up or chase them out. You need full capacity to be all you can be, and that includes calling your deepest inner recesses into service. Those dark corners cannot afford to be hiding secrets. They are reserved for our personal, quiet genius.

#4. You make a deal with the universe. Coincidence does not just happen![17] There are no accidents. You make your luck. You contract for your performance in life, and life pays what you negotiate. You, however, must hold up your end of the bargain. It takes a lot of work on your part to get the contract signed, but your option is to work without one, and that is often an exhausting and unsatisfying experience.

#5. What gets rewarded gets repeated. Everything you do repeatedly and consistently, you do because you choose its reward. Be careful what you wish for, for the universe grants your wishes indiscriminately and literally, especially those you make sub-

---

[16] These are the hundred million miracles that happen every day. From Rogers and Hammerstein: *The Flower Drum Song.*

[17] To learn more, research the Mandelbrot set. Chaos is chaotic, not random.

consciously. When you like what something produces, you may find it very difficult to stop the behavior that causes itsreward.

These five principles are complex and difficult to grasp. They are not common knowledge or conventional wisdom. In fact, they are often counter to common knowledge and conventional wisdom. In this chapter, we've briefly introduced the five tenets. As yet, we have not discussed how to act on them.

Exercises for Chapter 1

Now that we've learned how important it is to select carefully in choosing what we want, we will have to examine who we are in detail. Until you know who you are, you cannot really know what you want. This exercise is called "Self-Assessment." It is used in many classes in advanced management. You will need that paper and pens now. You need one pen that writes in black and one that writes in red.

Set aside an afternoon for this exercise. Using the paper and the black pen (not a computer), sit down quietly and start writing your life story. Start at birth and move on through up to now. Write quickly. Don't be concerned about proper sentence structure, grammar, spelling, or even a good read. Just start writing as fast as possible, and let everything flow and spill onto the paper. Do not censor what you are writing. Do not go back to read it before you have finished. Write the whole thing in 2 to 3 hours. The key to a useful document will be that you did it very quickly, without taking time to think it out.

If you have trouble starting, your first paragraph should say: "I was born on <u>date</u>, in <u>place.</u> My parents were named <u>Mom</u> and <u>Dad</u>." Then pick up from there.

Your document is not intended to be read by anyone except yourself. **The most important thing to understand is that you must not lie to yourself.** You must write the truth, as the truth exists inside your head, without covering it up, wafting perfume over it, avoiding the juicy parts, or censoring the humiliations. As soon as you finish this exercise, you will burn that paper to make sure nobody ever, ever gets his or her hands on it. But for now, just set aside your reservations, make time in your day, sit down and write it out, quickly, in one sitting. When you have finished writing it, go to:
http://AliceElliottBrown.com/secrets.html

This link will tell you the next step for analyzing your document.

Continue to Chapter 2 to learn more secrets of How to Get What You Want and Live Your Dream.

The morning dew brings jewels, CaveBear. And the rising sun shines just as intensely on those who have no money, as on the richest king.

– Toepia, from "Toepia and CaveBear", yet to be written.

Chapter 2. Defining the problem

Why aren't you happy right now? Is there something keeping you from happiness? Why aren't you happy just staying where you are? Why follow a path at all?

Facebook Posting:

"I've had it! I'm done! When do you call it quits in this life? I can't get a job. I can't find a partner. I'm living with my son. His wife hates me. I have carpel tunnel syndrome. The insurance won't pay."

Response 1: Hey, bud! Don't despair. Come hang with us.

Response 2: Life sucks, don't it?

Response 3: Been there. Call me.

Response 4: This too shall pass. Lean on your friends. We're here for you.

Etc, etc, etc

Poor me! I can't catch a break! Let me post my sadness on Face-book, so others can console me and pay attention to me. That'll solve it.

Before we can get what we want, we need to check to see if we already have it. Why can't you be happy now? What's the problem? What don't you have, that you need?   Is something getting in your way, so that happiness is beyond your reach? Let's consider what might be standing between you and happiness. Here are some possibilities:

1. Are you ill? If you are, that is a real reason to be unhappy. It has to be the most important focus of your work in this book. As you work through the exercises, your primary goal will center on recovery and restoration of your health. Without health, nothing else can be accomplished, so all your goals will be subordinate to regaining health. Illness, in this context, includes problems such as drug or alcohol abuse, obesity, depression, and addictions. Through the life management techniques you learn in this book, you will help your body be the best that it can be. Health is achieved through the action of our immune system. Your primary goals focus on strengthening your immunity so that the body can perform its work.

2. Are you living in an abusive relationship? Many times, people believe there is no way out of these bad situations. Usually, they think that is true for financial reasons. In this book, you will learn there is no such thing as a financial "reason." There are only financial excuses. Money is not the problem.   If you are thinking that money is the problem, the exercises in this book will open your mind to possibilities you had not considered. Hopefully, you will change your perceptions and find the way out of your bad relationships. Your primary goals will be to change your behavior so that others will stop getting a reward from abusing you.

3. Are you in debt beyond your ability to pay? Having bill collectors threaten you is agonizing. Losing your home, losing your job, being unable to pay for basic necessities – these are all things that validly stand in the way of happiness. This book will give you practical techniques to get out of financial trouble, and stay out. If this is your problem, debt restructuring will be your primary, over-riding goal. Of course, being in debt causes stress. The stress could make you ill, and could trigger abuse in your relationships. If debt is your problem, you could have multiple goals to accomplish on all those fronts. We will work through this in these chapters and exercises. This is a problem that can be solved, but it requires unconventional approaches.

4. Are you Calamity Jane or Runamok Roy? Is your freedom constrained? Are you saddled with burdens and responsibilities, which you cannot handle? Do you feel trapped at home with the kids, stuck in a humiliating job, or stifled by demanding but un-satisfying relationships? Is somebody suing you? Do problems just pile up, one after the other? Do you have bad luck after bad luck? Changing your current life requires skill in life manage-ment techniques. You may need to change your attitude toward the ties that bind you. We will examine the concepts of commit-ment and obligation, and decide what they really mean to you. Managing a life also means managing the expectations of others toward you, and teaching them how to behave around you, based on how you choose to respond. Relationships take two people. When you change your responses to others, the payoff changes for them. If you are overwhelmed by burdens, others may be taking advantage of you.

5. Do you have "everything", but still feel a sense of emptiness and depression? When you look up at the stars at night, do you feel a bone-chilling loneliness? Is it a deep emptiness, whichcannot be solved by sharing your thoughts with a partner? Has your suburban dream turned into a smothering nightmare? Do you have a good life partner, wonderful kids, an abundant bank account, and an overwhelming need for alcohol, drugs, shopping, gambling, overeating, or online chat rooms? This, too, can be part of what keeps us from being happy. As you develop life management skills, you will see a path out of these forms of self-immolation.

The first four of these problems may be valid obstacles to happiness. We will discuss techniques and learn skills to fix each of these problems. Many people have found, however, that fixing these common problems only leads them to problem number five: a meaningless sense of emptiness and despair. The problems themselves may have been merely symptoms. The underlying cause of unhappiness remains.

Health, relationships, debt, unreasonable constraints, and a meaningless sense of emptiness, are all valid reasons why you may not feel happy today. But the good news is: today is the first day of the rest of your life. No matter what happened in the past, no matter what mistakes were made, no matter what circumstances evolved, you can change the situation beginning today. You have the power to change yourself, and changes in yourself change the world surrounding you. Your responses, your reactions, your choices, and your behaviors are what change your world. It is not necessary for you to wait for anybody else to do anything.

First Demon: I knew she would do that. I knew she'd blame me again.

Second Demon: Yeah. Like it's our fault she married the wrong guy, got sick, was born into the wrong family, had kids too young, got into debt, lost the house, lost her job, and can't get discovered on American Idol. I told her to buy more lottery tickets. It's not my fault.

First Demon: Let's throw this book behind the couch. Nobody will ever clean back there to find it.

No soup for you.

When preparing to solve a problem, we must first release from our minds any desire to assign blame. Blame has no useful purpose; it clouds the vision necessary to solve the problem. Whatever got you into this predicament, the only need now is to get out of it. When there is a hole in the dam, don't waste any moments looking for the culprit who made the hole. Just stick your thumb in it, and get on with plugging the leak. Your problems now, whatever they are, have an essential conflictat their core. Let's put aside a discussion of the problem of the day, and think about the concept of "conflict."

In FantasyLand, where I lived when I was nine, I saw a globe on display in a clothing store. The globe whirled; a white picket fence surrounded it. I asked my grandfather to buy it for me. For the rest of my childhood, he joked that I wanted "the whole wide world with a little white fence around it." I never saw anything wrong with that. I was fully an adult, expelled from FantasyLand and living on Earth, before I realized he was joking. In those days, when asked if I thought "I was right and the world was wrong," I believed that question deserved deep consideration and a thoughtful answer. I did not realize that people were speaking sarcastically. If you have ever considered yourself unique and special, you know how hard society works to "knock you down a peg." Friends and family compete for that assignment. They love you and want to see you conform.

Human beings, as a tribe, are co-dependent. We enforce sanctions on our members, to teach them our society's definitions of "right and wrong." Wearing white shoes before Memorial Day or after Labor Day was wrong, my grandmother taught me. Over time, society has varied these definitions of right and wrong. In some times and places it was "right" to show a woman's cleavage, but "wrong" to show her ankles. It is "right" to use your left hand to hold your fork while cutting meat with a knife, but it is "wrong" to eat the meat from the fork while the fork is still in the left hand. Unless you're European. If you are European, then it is "right" to keep the fork in the left hand. Parents teach all of these rights and wrongs to children in their homes. The children come to believe them to be moral judgments, rather than recognizing them as a society's sanctions of its members. When the children grow up, and meet people whose parents taught them different values, the children assume the people they are meeting have moral failings.

A child from a poor household, for example, may grow up and go away to a fancy Ivy League college. This happensbecause fancy, Ivy League colleges have blind admissions and liberal financial aid policies. When the young person arrives at college, her ignorance of the cultural rules of rich families will make her stand out from the crowd, and label her as "morally deficient". Social standards and moral judgments tie together in our society. Ever since that day in the cradle when you received your birthday gifts of powers and curses from the good and bad fairies, your parents, siblings, cousins, assorted other relatives, and friends have worked at socializing you to fit into the community mold.

Pulling ourselves outside the situation, we see that human beings divide into various related groups of people. (We could call them "tribes.")Each tribe teaches specific behavioral rules to the children from birth. These rules help the child fit into the group. They also serve to encourage the child to marry within his or her own subculture. As a law of nature, this is part of survival. Nature wants each species to reproduce itself. Building and enforcing social structures is part of that natural survival of the tribe. People born with money, for example, want to make sure they marry other people who were born with money. They set up social systems to erect barriers around their tribal members, to preserve their "bloodlines."

Now, what does this concept of "tribe" have to do with determining why you are not happy with what you already have?

Patiently bear with me. I'm unfolding the answer. In Chapter 1, we talked about the basic principles, the five tenets, which guide the universe. These are the principles you must use to get what you want. The principles we discussed were conceptual, not tactical. Discussing them didn't give us solid and objective tools to take action. In this chapter, and all the following chapters, we will work in detail to figure out the specifics of what to do. Talk is cheap. To get what you want, you have to go past talk, and get into action.

Why My Facebook Friends Love Me Best

In Chapter 1, we said: "what gets rewarded gets repeated." Facebook posts are repeated by the millions, every minute. Many people you know are hovering on Facebook all day long, playing application games and posting comments about their bowling scores. Why is this happening?

It's happening because you are posting back, and your post back is a Reward. Feedback is attention; it is approval; it is acknowledgement. People feel better when someone "likes" their comments, and sympathizes with their viewpoint. Everybody wants to be noticed and included. Facebook is about finding someone to agree with you, to like you, and to see your merit. Everybody likes that! *It's how we are built.*

One of the tenets we discussed in Chapter 1 was: Make a Deal with the Universe. We described how the Earth knows you are here. We said you are born with a destiny, and although your path to that destiny may be winding, the Universal Force will nudge, push, and shove you back onto it. ***Now we have described a potential conflict.****The magnetic pull of the Universal Forceis not the only force that is pulling and pushing on you. There is a competing force also exerting its influence. Society, through your parents, neighbors, friends, and teachers, also want to push you around. They have exerted a lot of pressure and demands for your attention. They want you to use your free will to make choices that conform to their expectations.*

On the one hand, you have a destiny calling you. On the other hand, you have a desire to please and associate with your friends and family. This creates a conflict that literally may be "tearing you apart." Your emotional conflict could trigger the imbalances, which result in disease. You want to fulfill your destiny, but you have social expectations pushing you in another direction. **This conflict, interpreted through the primitive lizard brain of your associative mind, can cause disease.**

In FantasyLand, the entire world was created by a Magical Being whom we will call, for the purposes of Political Correctness, "The Author". Now the Author has in mind how the story ends. He or She has envisioned the final scene, and has pictured a happy ending. Good stories all have happy endings, in FantasyLand. All the people who live in FantasyLand are characters, who were created by this Author. The people don't know they are characters, so they have no knowledge that there ever was an Author. (Characters are never required to believe in the Author.) Now the Author has been writing this story and playing this game for a long time, so the Author has the system figured out. To prevent boredom and ensure that He, She, or It can continue the game indefinitely, the Author has decided to let all the characters make their own decisions. Each character has full capacity to pick a path, make a change, and introduce a conflict. The Author knows that all conflicts will be resolved in the end, but the Author chooses not to interfere in the resolution process. The characters, as far as day-to-day living in FantasyLand, have complete free will.

If each character were to choose to progress in a straightforward manner toward destiny, the FantasyLand story would be short and sweet. Everybody would have a wonderful life, all characters would enjoy inner peace, and the happy ending would idle peacefully to all eternity. There was a movie made about that place of happiness once. It was called "Pleasantville." In the movie, Pleasantville, nobody did anything outside his or her comfort level. Every basketball made it through the hoop, but the lack of excitement and drama in their story made people feel dead instead of vigorous, alive, and colorful. Let's concede that the Author understands this issue, and believes that all the drama in our stories is a necessary evil. Maybe we can't know joy unless we've known sorrow. Maybe we can't feel pleasure unless we can feel pain. Maybe there is no light if we cannot compare it to darkness. Maybe the low lows in our life are just there to balance out the high highs. Maybe you'll never be "up" if you have no possibility of somehow being "down."

The characters don't progress in a straight and unwavering line to their destiny, however, because in addition to the draw to their destiny, they also have to deal with regular living. Living includes jobs, families, and monkey wrenches such as hurricanes, floods, and natural disasters. The Author throws those monkey wrenches in to heighten the drama and keep the story complex and unfathomable. They aren't gratuitous, of course. The natural disasters and problems thrown into the mix by the Author all provide guidance toward the destiny of each. Contrast is required before one can see the picture. We cannot see the design of the carpet because we are too closely following the individual thread. The goal is to get to the destiny, and nothing else matters.

Of course, as we discussed in Chapter 1, FantasyLand is not real. We all know we are not free-willed characters in an authored play, right? We all know we don't each have a potential happy ending, correct? We all know it isn't possible that there might be some Fantasy Author, whom we do not know about because characters are not required to believe in the author. We all know it isn't a simple matter. Finding our true path and connecting with our destiny could not be what makes us happy. But what if it were?

Chapter 2: Defining the Problem

In FantasyLand, for every minute of every day of every decade of your life, Destiny will pull, ping, and torture you if you turn and run from it. This is a very big problem. New cars, elaborate swimming pools, plasma TVs, Gucci handbags, Prada shoes, trips to Mali, and even prescription anti-depressants will fail to satisfy the longing created by the need to meet your destiny. The magnetic draw of destinycreates a deep desire. You crave doing what you were "put on FantasyLand to do." No material possession or transient entertainment will calm that craving. You cannot buy happiness.

If it were true on Earth, like it is in FantasyLand, that connecting to our true path and moving toward our destiny is the way to be happy, then a book about how to get what you want would say:

Everything you want is contained in the path to your destiny. If you find that path and stick to it, the Author will arrange the story so that coincidence and circumstance rise up to ensure you have food, water, shelter, and all those things that sustain life while you're traveling the path.

Of course, that's pure fantasy from FantasyLand. For that to be true, you would have to believe a lot of stuff that just can't be real! First, you would have to believe that there is an Author. Second, you would have to believe the Author is paying attention to the individual details of every person's daily life, and wants each person to be happy. Third, you would have to believe each person had a destiny. Fourth, you would have to believe Destiny was calling. It is crazy to believe we each have a song. Isn't it?

Master of My Universe

First nameless demon: What's crazy is to think the Author will pay your bills, fix your car, replace your water heater, and save your marriage, when the Author can't even save the baby seals and repair the ozone layer.

Second nameless demon: Right, yeah, I agree. The Author is letting teenagers in Somalia operate pirate ships. The Author is standing by while terrorists knock planes out of the sky, and imperial powers bomb weddings. The Author is letting the fish in America's rivers die from chemical poisoning. It seems to me the Author has a little bit more on His plate than He can handle. I'd be waiting for pigs to fly before my number would come up on His agenda.

Hmmm. It sounds like my self-talk is expanding to be a whole crowd of selves talking. I wonder how many different people I have in here. But that is a really good point. How crazy is it to believe that if you are on your path to your destiny, God will provide? Or the Author, or the Great Energy Force, or the magnetic field of Earth, or whatever it is that is a force outside yourself that is bigger than you and you don't control? Maybe we should take some time to consider how crazy this idea really is.

It's got to be the money

If you are not happy now, you probably believe it's because you need more money. If you had more money, you would a) solve all your problems, and b) make new problems with bigger price tags. Within two years, you would need more money again. This is a scientifically observed, undocumented fact. There are plenty of rich people in this world. Overall, are they happier than poor people are? They still get themselves chased out of the house in the middle of the night by an irate wife with a golf club in her hand. Having known many rich people, I can testify with certainty that money cannot buy happiness. However, money can temporarily get you out of a jam you have created for yourself. Maybe right now, that's what you think you want. Remember in Chapter 1, when we talked about the laws of the universe being the laws of predator and prey? If money is actually your problem, you get more money by behaving as the predator instead of the prey.

Credit card companies (predators) loan you (prey) money at 0% interest, knowing you will spend it and be unable to pay it back before it pops up to 29% interest. Health insurance companies (predators), charge you (prey), an exorbitant monthly fee when you are not sick. When you do get sick, they deny your claim. After you exhaust yourself fighting with them, they make a few nominal payments and stick you with the rest of the bill. Processed food companies, many of whom are owned by cigarette companies (predators), package up sub-standard, chemical-laden pseudo-food, fill it with addictive substances, advertise it to an unsuspecting mass audience (prey), and profit from causing the very illness that the health insurance companies also profit from. That's how predators get money.

Within the laws of the universe, predators win over prey. Lions eat zebras. Cats eat mice. This is how money is made.

In FantasyLand, the Author stands back and lets the characters find their own way. The Author has made it possible for each character to play their pre-defined role in the story. If each character dreams, and follows their dreams, that deep feeling in their heart will guide their way. The Author placed this guiding feeling in each heart, for every character. All the characters need to do is follow their hearts, and they will each find their path. Every religion of the world teaches this. But, with all the competing advice of societal pressures, too many characters misunderstand. Time after time, the characters use their free will to stray from their path. Dangers and misfortunes follow them, pushing and shoving them to find their way, urging them to return to the journey. But fear and habit become their new masters, and they give up their dreams, choosing to become enslaved. If they only knew that the feeling in their heart is guidance from the universe, they could find happiness and live their dream. But they do not know, so they wallow in pain.

Now, the Author in FantasyLand: that's just an analogy. FantasyLand isn't real, so that isn't like God or anything. On Earth, we all know it is completely unrealistic to chase dreams and follow rainbows. On Earth, some people believe in leprechauns and some people don't. Whether or not leprechauns exist is not dependent on whether or not you believe in them. Leprechauns aren't Tinker Bell, or Santa Claus, or some crazy imaginary Author, right? Even if you don't believe in gravity, gravity will still keep you from falling off this spinning ball that's hurtling through space, won't it?Now, before you learned that the Earth was round and hurtling through space, you thought you were standing on solid ground that didn't move. You believed the Earth was stationery. You know now that what you believe doesn't change what is. You can't walk on the ceiling just because you don't believe in gravity. The only thing your belief system controls is your emotional response to things that happen to you. Truth is truth, right? So whatever is true about forces that operate the universe, your belief or non-belief doesn't change them.

What we believe may not be true, but as far as our health is concerned, it might as well be.

Our emotional responses are chemical reactions that trigger hormonal response. As we grow up, we develop associations in our mind. Some of these associations are based on things we believe that are simply not true. Our mind convinces us we know things which are not true. We remember things that did not happen. We have stored associations from childhood experience, which are not valid. Because of the way the software of our mind works, our intelligence builds programmed patterns. Once these patterns are set in place, we will use them to make our decisions, repeatedly. The patterns might be lousy patterns. They might produce disastrous results. If you do not recognize that you are following the same destructive pattern repeatedly, you will grind yourself into mush, all by the action of your own mind. There will be no relief from the steady stream of problem after problem, until you look for your decision-making patterns, and recognize what you must change. You will dig the same holes each time you pull yourself out of them. These patterns *become* your belief system. You stop challenging their validity and accept them as Truth. Your senses respond by turning off, like a nurse who stops smelling the ammonia. You can no longer discern true from false, because you have ceded to a pattern that defined right from wrong. You accepted your lot in life. TRY scurried back to the basement.

When life gives you lemons
No matter how many times you are rescued, or you rescue yourself, from the problems in your life, a destructive decision-making patternwill re-create new problems. Yes, it is true that life throws curve balls, that disaster could befall anybody, that tragedy can strike any of us at any time. But it is our response to

the lemons life gives us, which determines whether we will live with a sour taste in our mouths, or own a lemonade stand. The circumstance does not define our situation. We define it by how we respond.

Quantum physicists of today tell us that the numbers and form of the laws of nature do not demand one solution. The universe may take on many values, in any form that leads to a self-consistent mathematical solution. Within the eleven dimensions, there are many possible universes.[18]

Maybe it's true that I have a universe. You have a universe. She, he, it, they, and we have a universe. Where our universes touch, we have a common experience, but possibly divergent perceptions. Our choice is contained in the role we play on our world's stage. Our question is whether to be mastered, or to be enslaved. You have to *choose* to be Master of Your Universe. Else, you will be merely a pawn in someone else's.

What type of decision-maker are you?

Common Decision Making Patterns by Type

A. Safety first. *Cautious.* If you are a Type A decision-maker, you followed the advice to save for a rainy day. You follow conventional wisdom. You get an annual checkup at the doctor. You buy good insurance. You check the weather report before leaving the house, in case you need an umbrella. You stock up when there is a sale. Your lifelong decision patterns reflect caution and consideration before making any changes. You would not quit your old job before you had an offer for a new one.

---

[18] Hawking, S. The Grand Design

B. Go with the crowd. *Tribal.* Type B decision-makers are trend followers, not trendsetters. When invited to a party, you ask who else is coming. You buy shirts with those little logos on them. You dress in the fashions that are "in." You buy what everyone else is buying. You do what is expected of you, and believe there is a reward for doing the expected. You had little turmoil or confusion over what college to choose, or what major to select, as you did what everyone else believed to be right.

C. Analysis paralysis. *Fearful.* Type C decision-makers could be called indecision-makers. When you do take an action, you second-guess yourself and try to go back and change it later. Rather than accepting that no decision is ever perfect, you strive to be "right," and feel bad when you believe you were "wrong." You postpone action, waiting for better information. You don't want to make the wrong choice about your career, so you do not choose. You stick with whatever you have now, because choosing is painful.

D. Throw caution to the wind *.Impulsive.* Type D decision-makers are nearly the opposite of Type C. You choose even when no choice is required. You burn bridges, block off options, and get yourself blackballed in places where a little discretion could have kept you in good stead. You reach for the brass ring, even when there is no possibility of success. You react on impulse, rather than calculation. You respond to even the smallest stimulus, and make moves when no movement is necessary. You may have experienced several jobs in a short timeframe. You don't have a savings account.

E. What's in it for me?*Greedy.* You have no constriction against manipulating others, if the outcome favors your cause. You believe this is the correct and appropriate means of decision-making, and it is the one taught to you by your social tribe. Everyone you know makes decisions by calculating the value of the personal outcome. You can't imagine why anyone would do anything else. You may think you are following the principles of self-interest described by Ayn Rand, although Ayn Rand may disagree with your assessment. You have ambitions to go farther in your career, and you would like to advance in whatever position you have now. You put great store in buying the right things, and displaying them for others to see.

F. Cost justify. *Rational.* When you bought your last car, you analyzed the gas mileage, balanced it against the annual maintenance cost, and agreed to fewer features to get a better deal. You think buying at a discount is equivalent to saving money. You recognize that a state college is more cost effective than a private one, regardless of the reputation of the academic programs. You made a spreadsheet to analyze the cost of living between two cities where you had competing job offers. You car pool. You turn off the light over the stove when you're finished cooking. You live on a bus route, just in case. You don't change jobs because you don't want to lose the un-vested employer-contribution in your 401K plan. You probably work and live within driving distance of the place where you grew up.

G. Follow your heart. *Instinctive.* You've worked hard at knowing yourself, and recognizing your own desires. When you have a strong draw to a path, you are likely to take it, whether its end-point is certain or not. You don't consult others about your decisions, although you may ask their opinion as a matter of intelligence gathering. Regardless of their answers, you act based on your inner voice. Those who oppose your decisions go to the bottom of your guest list. You spend less time with them. You are likely to be working in a career you love. You seldom second-guess yourself, but you are not afraid to change your mind when your inner feelings change. You do not see decisions as "right or wrong." They are simply the choices you made at the time, but they are subject to change without regret.

Let's Review

If you are unhappy now, buying something won't fix it. If you bought a book about how to get what you want, thinking you wanted a muscle car or a diamond necklace, you were wrong. That is not what you want. After you get that, you'll still want something else. Things you can purchase do not plug the holes in a heart.

The conflict you feel inside is the pull between society's expectations of you, and your own desires to sing your own song, write your own ticket, and blaze your own trail. It is normal to have that conflict. The conflict itself is written into the system. The challenge is getting yourself balanced between the clashing demands. Dropping out of society is not the answer, but foregoing your own destiny will simply not work.

A want is different from a need. You need food, shelter, and a loving family. You want inner peace. Inner peace comes from following your true path. Food, shelter, and a loving family are-written into the program by coincidence and circumstance, which the Author of your story provides. Inner peace is the journey of the soul, which you must decide to travel.

Master of My Universe

You could be the Author of your own story, but then you'd be stuck keeping the planets aligned, checking the salt level in the oceans, replacing the 6 inches of topsoil for the plant life, and co-coordinating the hurricane schedule to keep the temperature of the Earth balanced. You're much too busy for that, so you're stuck with just being a character on a world stage.

As long as you're a character, you might as well choose to be the Hero, rather than the Victim. If you think about it clearly, it is most likely that the Author will have selected your true path to be the one in which you act with integrity, respond heroically, and select virtuously. Just playing the numbers, you have a much better chance of reaching your destiny if you take the high road.

All you have to do is get on your path to destiny, and food, shelter, heat, and love will find you.

This is both less simple and simpler than it sounds. It's a paradox.

This set of theories does not need to be true in order for it to work. It is enough for us to believe it is true. Our belief system colors and biases our basic emotional response. This response triggers hormonal changes and cause us to behave and experience the world differently. **It also keeps us healthy or makes us sick.** *You know that. If you're fighting the concept right this moment, TRY is using both hands to hold onto that lid before the toothpaste gets out of the tube. You can't unring that bell, so you're developing hearing loss.*

In the next chapter, we will get more specific about how to determine what you want, and what exactly you have to do to get it. We will take numbers and name names. We will assess situations, assign responsibility, and allocate tasks. We will gather the resources. We will mobilize the troops. We will get the ball rolling. We will blow the whistle on the plays.

We will walk confidently in the direction of our dreams, and experience a success unknown in common hours. -- Thoreau

Exercises for Chapter 2:

In chapter 1, you quickly wrote your life story. Then you went to a website to learn what to do with it. After you did what you had to do, you got rid of that handwritten paper before somebody else read your secrets. As a result, you now have a typewritten sheet of paper that gives you a list of decisions you have made throughout your life.

Consider that list now. As you look over it, think about other decisions you've made that may not have made it onto your paper. Your paper reflects what you wrote very quickly. That means what came out records only those experiences that were highly meaningful to you. Make a note of other important decisions that didn't make it onto the list. In the next chapter, you will think about why those other decisions didn't make it to the list. If you did not do the exercise in Chapter 1, go back to do it now. If you are not ready to face yourself yet, continue through the book and come back to the exercises later.

Take your list of decisions. Find a quiet place where you can sit down and be comfortable for an hour or two. Make arrangements so that you will not be disturbed during this time. You need to be able to focus, without distractions.During your quiet time, make a chart. Take each decision, think back to the time in your life when you made that decision, and carefully write on your chart:

Column 1: The decision you made.

Column 2: How old you were when you made it.

Column 3: The other choices you had at the time, which you rejected.

Column 4: The reason you rejected the other options and chose the decision you made. Be sure to give the reason you had at the time you made it. Don't use your hindsight to sugarcoat it.

After you have filled out your chart for all the decisions, look carefully at your reasons for choosing what you chose. Do you see a pattern in your choices? Did your reasoning for choosing one option over another remain consistent? Sometimes, actually . . . most times . . . people make decisions for the same reasons, over and over. Years go by, decisions are very different, but the reasons for choosing one option over the other are the same. These reasons could be faulty, and yet, they cause us to continue to bumble through life, continuing to make the same mistakes.

For example, maybe you continually choose to "uphold your responsibilities" even when others around you do not care or appreciate what you do. Maybe you hold onto actions because you believe them to be "right," even when no other person cares or even knows what you've done. Maybe you see things as black or white, ignoring the many shades of gray.

Do you regularly choose to fly in the face of convention? Do you routinely pick the most difficult option? Or do you always pick what others think you should pick? Are you bold and daring in your decision-making? Or do you stick with the safety nets? Do you select options that require big, dramatic changes? Do you run away from situations when they get complicated? Do you stay the course, even when circumstances change? Whatever your decision-making pattern has been in the past, it is most likely to continue to follow that same pattern in the future.

If you like that pattern, great. But if that pattern is what got you into trouble, continuing to follow it will ensure that you stay in trouble, no matter how many times you pull yourself out. You must find the pattern, so you can decide if you need to change it. It is difficult to evaluate yourselfobjectively. You will need to put effort into finding your pattern. Human beings make decisions based on criteria that they use over and over again. You have a pattern in the choices you make. If you plan to get what you want, you will have to find that pattern. When you feel comfortable that you have identified the pattern in your decision-making, write the pattern on the back of your charts. Save the charts for the next exercise. Review the examples of common decision-making patterns. Yours may be a hybrid of some of these.

Continue on to Chapter 3: Considering the options

No one can be your boss without your permission.

--- Anonymous

Chapter 3: Considering the Options

What do you need that you don't already have? Have you seen all the hidden paths available? Is that grinning Cheshire cat deceiving you?

For those whose inner being rebels against thoughts of an intelligent universe, interacting with its carbon-unit occupants, rest easy. It isn't necessary to know, or important to resolve. You don't have to believe, in order to operate the controls that guide a life. You can believe any story, any faith, or any fantasy.It won't change the laws of physics. You can swear that your faith is the one true faith, and all others are delusions. Regardless of what you believe about the "why," however, there are specific things you have to do to get what you want. As long as you do what must be done, it doesn't matter what you believe about what happened. Gravity, electricity, magnetism, and nuclear energy still behave the same. TRY is still waiting in your psychological basement. The only thing that changes based on your belief system is your own response to the circumstance that comes your way.

Happiness is a decision.
The problem is: you are not happy now because you are not on the path to your destiny. Now we need to know the solution. In

Chapter 1, we described the five basic tenets, or principles, of how the universe works with you to get what you want. We said you must Dream, Believe, Create, Deal, and Reward yourself in ways that keep you aligned with your dream. In Chapter 2, we defined what you want. We said: you want to meet your destiny. That's the problem. As long as you are not on the path to your destiny, calamity will befall you, and nothing will satisfy the yearning inside. We envisioned that the magnetism of the universe itself would rise up to send earthquakes your way, to nudge you back on your track.

This, of course, is patently ridiculous. It does not explain why children are harmed. It does not explain random acts of violence and their devastated victims. It does not feed the children of Ethiopia. It does not give the baby born to a crack addict a fighting chance. It does not stop a pandemic flu. It does not keep America's hospitals from infecting a large percentage of their patients with a disease they didn't have when they checked themselves in. It is, in short, just a mythology of belief.

There are no accidents
In our described mythology, the universe is quite simple, and enormously complicated at the same time. If the principles described in Chapters 1 and 2 are true, then there are no accidents. **If these principles are <u>not</u> true, then behaving as if they were true will change your response to them. This alters your reality.**This book, and its concepts, may be completely off base, totally irrelevant, and abjectly meaningless. Its vision could be 100% false. There could be entirely different explanations for what is happening in the world. But, if your problem of needing to find inner peace, get a better job, improve your marriage, pay off your debt, and heal your eczema, are solved by following its directions . . . then what difference does it make if the

concept was ludicrous?   Why do you care whether there is an Author of your story, as long as your story is happy and satisfying?   Why do you ask questions for which you have no action to take, upon hearing the answer?   If you know how many questions are on the exam, does that change your method of studying for it? If it doesn't, then why do you ask?

If you know "how," who cares "why?"
You don't need to know the conceptual reason, the "why," of what fixes your problems. You need to know the "how" of what fixes it. Those first two chapters were just setting the stage, throwing in a few bones to the stockpot, stirring up the inner belief system, and encouraging you to open your mind to possibility. We don't need to know who or what created the universe, what its motivations are, what happens after death, or what will happen the day after tomorrow. I do not know which is the "true" religion, or if any religions are true. I am wholly uninformed regarding the date of the end of the world. I don't even know if germs on a doorknob cause colds!   The important message is: **it doesn't matter why. It only matters how.** These concepts are proven project management techniques. They are not feel-good, placebos, get-rick-quick schemes, or empty Ponzi promises. If you try them, they will work whether you believed in them or not.

"Why" is not known. It is not known by anybody, anywhere, in any field. Religions are built to answer the questions of "why", and people choose to believe various versions of them.   Religions aren't based on knowing; they are based on faith without evidence. There is no evidence of "why" the universe operates. "How", nevertheless, is well-documented science.

It's not about "trying"

Master of My Universe

Eight practices cause success. The rest of this book is about teaching you to do them. It's not about believing in them, talking about them, discussing them, analyzing them, cooking them, eating them, or publicizing them. It's about doing them. Remember TRY, from the first chapter? You called on TRY and wanted TRY to come home. TRY is that person who ran away, the person who was you, before puberty. It's not about *trying* to do them. It's not about *trying* to be a good person, *trying* to do right, *trying* to succeed. It's about succeeding. We do not succeed by *trying*. We succeed by doing. Succeeding is a "no excuses" thing. *"Trying"* builds your excuse right into the action.

"I *tried*, but I failed."
You haven't failed until you *stop* trying. If at first you don't succeed, try, try again. When you sent TRY away, and relegated her to the basement of your memory, you stopped TRYing. You can't stop TRYing! If you stop TRYing, you might as well stop living! You've blown the whistle and called the game! "Oh, well, at least I *tried*." And now, you've failed and you're giving up and hanging your tail between your legs and accepting defeat? Every play on a football field expects to be a touchdown, but almost all of them fail. So what? You just reconsider, re-evaluate, re-assess, and re-attempt, based on the new information. Then you huddle, re-group, and go after it all over again. You don't pronounce yourself a failure, take your ball, and go home!

Don't try the same way twice
On the other hand, you don't play the same play again next time. Thomas Edison said, "I have not failed. I have successfully found ten thousand ways that won't work." You can't stumble across innovation if you keep doing the same thing over again when it isn't working. You TRY and TRY and TRY, but you don't TRY the same way twice! Something may not turn out the way you

planned, but it isn't necessarily a failure. Maybe it's guidance to go in a different direction.

You've called TRY back from the depths of despair, and now you have to teach TRY to keep at it, keep TRYing, and never give up. At the same time, you have to teach TRY to stop doing the same thing over and over again when it isn't working. The only way to know whether or not an approach is working is to know what you expected it to do, what the conditions were at the time and place that you did it, what options and variations you have available for making changes to your approach, and what outcomes will fit into your range of acceptable results. You have to know whether the reward is worth the effort, whether the pot of gold is actually at the end of the rainbow, how many bodies you have to step over to get to the prize, and whether the prize is valuable enough to pay the price to get it. Above all, you have to know the price extracted and the value expected for your actions. Personal responsibility is the name of the game when you master your own universe.

The Eight Practices
When you get all of that figured out, you will know how to get what you want. Once you know how to get what you want, you will have the option to decide if you want it badly enough to make the deal. The deal with the universe, that is. The *amoral* universe. The one that operates on the principle of predator and prey. The one where the lion eats the zebra.

And this is where the conflict arises. Back in FantasyLand, let the games begin!

In this corner, we have Rocky Balboa, downtrodden victim turned inspirational hero. Rocky is ready to prove his mettle against the evil forces who rule the Dark Side. Rocky is every-man, who tries and tries and tries against all odds. Rocky needs to go the distance, so he can get rich and win the hand of the lovely but unexceptional female, Whats-her-name. Rocky must fight, fight, fight the evil and malevolent forces, until Rocky wins, so he can claim victory and become the dark side himself.

In the far reaches of the Fantasy Kingdom, at a deserted outpost, we find Luke Skywalker! Fair-haired and blue-eyed, Jedi Sky-walker must find and defeat the evil Darth Vader, paragon of Evil, in an oedipal fight to the finish!

Smack dab in the Middle Earth of FantasyLand, we find the brave and earnest Harry Potter, who must fight to the death against He-Who-Shall-Not-Be-Named, proponent of Evil and Darkness.

These are all FantasyLand problems. On Earth, there is no issue of Light vs. Dark. On Earth, we know Light can't defeat Dark! Both must exist nearly equally, or it knocks our biorhythms to-tally out of whack!

You see, on Earth, our humanity evolved to depend on cycles and balance. We can't afford to see life as a battle between good and evil, light and dark, white and black. If we did that on Earth, we would end up with desperate problems of domestic violence, drugs, crime, and illegal aliens in the workforce! An attitude of splitting the world into "us vs. them," "dark vs. light," or "good vs. bad," is the attitude of a street gang, not a world of evolved hu-manity. Our universe, unlike FantasyLand, requires time for sleep and time for waking. Time for work and time for play. Time for friendship and time for meditation. Time for fun and time for duty. Balance in all things is our watch word. We *must* live in harmony with the Earth's cycles. Unlike that crazy, Hollywood-created FantasyLand. On Earth, we know *there is a season for everything, a time for every activity. A time to be born and a time to die. A time to plant and a time to harvest. A time to kill and a time to heal. A time to tear down and a time to build up. A time to cry and a time to laugh. A time to grieve and a time to dance. A time to scatter stones and a time to gather stones. A time to embrace and a time to turn away. A time to search and a time to quit searching.*[19]

Deal with the universe. You can't defeat it.
You aren't in a fight with life. You are, however, in a contract. We deal with the universe, in accordance with its laws and behaviors. We harmonize, not demonize. To succeed, we learn how the world *is,* and we mesh with it. Here are the eight practices you master in order to succeed:

1. You have to **set goals**. You can't get what you don't define.
2. You have to **achieve balance**. Life is a delicate dance with a mixture of work and play.
3. You have to **establish structure**. Time is of the essence. It is the only value that cannot be increased. A structure keeps your balance aligned, while you're sprinting toward the goal.
4. You have to **measure outcomes.**What gets monitored, gets done.
5. You have to **expand your options**. You can't limit the possibilities, if your goal is to win.
6. You have to **adapt to your environment.**You don't run the world. However the world exists, you have to change yourself to meet it.
7. You have to **pay attention**. Observe your surroundings. Note the subtleties. Collect data points. You cannot draw conclusions

---

[19] Ecclesiastes 3: 1-6: The Holy Bible

before the data is in. You must watch for the signals from the universe.

8. You have to **reward good behavior**. What gets rewarded, gets repeated. Watch your rewards like a hawk searching for canaries.

You are probably not fully aware of what is rewarding to you. Yet, you reward yourself constantly. It's necessary, by your nature, by the nature of all human beings. Know what you are doing to reward yourself. You may be surprised to learn that the rewards you've selected are sabotaging your true desires. Every day in every way, you are choosing small rewards for your actions. A cigarette may be your reward to yourself. A glass of wine. A plate of cheese and crackers. These little rewards may inadvertently be encouraging actions that will lead you away from your goals. Rewarding yourself with cigarettes, alcohol, and processed foods may sabotage you. You must set yourself up for success, by ensuring that your daily actions are rewarded in a way that leads you to act in your own self-interest for your longer term goals. Your rewards must be frequent and small, but directed positively.

Hold onto your Dumbo feathers

To learn these practices and perform these eight actions daily, you don't have to believe any special things about why the universe exists. You don't have to buy into the "universe as a drama with an Author" theory. You don't have to believe they will work in order for them to work. Their proven action is not a placebo. They are not a "Dumbo feather", which a mythological elephant holds in his trunk in order to believe he can fly. They are just solid project management, applied to the project of your life. Mastery without is a function of mastery within. Light vs. Dark and Goodvs. Evil, is a Hollywood plot, not a plan for meeting our Destiny.The world as it exists is shaded gray. Your job as captain of your own ship is to navigate successfully through murky waters. Only then can your ship come in.

TRY has a role to play
A long time ago, as we discussed in Chapter 1, you cast TRY into the lower cellar of your history. You've kept the basement door locked all that time. Now, maybe you're sitting here thinking this:

I need to improve my family life. My kids are disrespectful. My husband and I have nothing in common. Our home has no warmth to it. I'm developing a cough. I think I'm allergic. I feel unloved. Our budget isn't working. We can't make ends meet. The creditors are calling. I'm stressed. I'm not fulfilled in my job. I've gotten into some legal trouble with my neighbors. I'm having nightmares. I'm getting frightened. I'm having panic attacks. I think I'm getting arthritis. I feel anxiety. I lash out at the people I love. I'm worried. I feel out of control. Sometimes I wonder if the world is crazy. I feel violated when I realize I can't walk down a city street without worrying about a drive-by shooting. I have to go back twice to check the front door to make sure it is locked. I'm insecure. I don't know why God would let the world be like this. I have doubts.

You're unloved. You're unworthy. You're stressed. You're unfulfilled. You're scared. You're worried. You're insecure. You're disconnected. Is that eight problems? Would a more fulfilling job, possibly at a lesser salary, be separable from a problem with creditors? Would you feel healthier if you felt more loved? If you felt more loved, would you feel less threatened and insecure in the universe? Are there eight problems here, or is it one problem, manifesting in many ways? Is anything on this list more than a massive imbalance in the energy surrounding you? To test this theory, try answering this set of questions:

If I could learn to control how I respond, in my personal energies, efforts, attitudes, actions, words, and emotions:
Would my children behave differently?
Would my allergies go away?
Would my boss straighten up his act?
Would my body change shape?
Would my neighbor change his hostility toward me?
Would my finances work themselves out?
Would I sleep better and dream peacefully?
And most importantly, if I change my behavior, will the world I experience change?

Deep in your subconscious, that little voice we've named as TRY, just piped up. It said, Yes.

Yes, if I change my Self, I will change my world.
Yes, if I give love, I will receive love.
Yes, if I think good thoughts, I will perceive good responses.
Yes, if I forgive, my body will express forgiveness.
Yes, if I display honesty, I will be treated with sincerity.
Yes, if I embrace humility, my needs will be provided for.
Yes, if I release my ego, I will achieve an inner peace.
And that horrid, unspeakable demon, Nameless, shriveling in a fetal position within the temporal lobe of your inner mind, just breathed a sigh of tortured relief. You're finally guilty. He can confess, and end the torment.

Yes, your problems are your own fault. Yes, you are the culprit. Yes, if you change your Self, you can change your world. Celebrate. You're back in control. Now let's get started on learning to act with integrity, inside and outside, so the world can run like clockwork again. You'll need to implement those eight practices, and develop some skill with them. Once you've got them mastered, however, you'll be at the top of your game.

You need to be mastered, however, not slaved.

I understand, Mother.

Which Master shall you choose?

Please don't bring religion into my book, Nameless Demon. I'm trying to write Science here.

Then in the interest of Science, tell us a story.

In FantasyLand, the Author had a problem. His Characters were out of control. They didn't understand that they had to follow their Destiny to be happy! They were giving up their free will, and becoming slaves to a host of irrelevant masters. Debt, jobs, possessions, social acceptance, jealousy, envy, status, and vengeance were taking over as their gods. They were forgetting that they had their own dreams to guide them! At this rate, none of them would remember their reason for living, and their stories would never get to the happy ending which the Author had proscribed.

The Author agonized over what to do. At first, He tried scaring them. He appeared in the sky and boomed at them, saying, "I am the Lord Thy God. Thou shalt have no other gods before Me." He was talking, of course, about gods like money, status, television reality shows, and iPhones. But nobody noticed. So the Author thought and thought about how to fix the problem. Then He decided to try making a software upgrade to the cognitive mind of each character. In His brilliant software scheme, He thought He would divide the mind of each character into separate components. He would name these components "Aspects" of the mind software. They would be an architecture that was common across all minds, so that He could deliver some clear guidelines. Inter-species communication was hard, the Creator-Author thought. His great brilliance was too much for the mere carbon-based units He had created. When He tried to talk to them, it made them crazy! Every time He directly spoke to someone, they ended up locked in the psycho-ward! So He decided to enhance the mind software to make it easier to connect with them. He started by partitioning their mental hard drives into segments.

The first aspect He made, He called "Shadow", be- it was the survival instinct. It ensured that each character would put its own survival first. When we make cautious, Type A decisions, we are acting primarily in our aspect as Shadow! The survival instinct is important and useful. It has many appropriate times to be called into action.

The second aspect, He called Bee. **Bee was the sense of connectedness among all beings**. She was like the network router. Bee believes in consensus and the group experience. She is the tribal, Type B decision-maker.

The third Aspect was Toepia. **Toepia was the repository of the history of each person.** History and experience can bring on the worries, so Toepia is in charge when the Type C, fearful, decision-maker is in place.

Next came Gem. **Gem was the inner child**. She was the TRY of everyone. She remembered all the dreams and kept them alive. Because she remains hopeful, she can be impulsive at times. She represents the Type D decision-maker.

Katrina was the conscience. She thought about the integrity of each act. Her function as the arbiter of self-interest can cause greed in Type E decision-making.

Next, He made Ariana. **Ariana was Rational Thinking.** She reflected on the meaning and reason of things. She is the calculator of the soul. She is the Type F, rational decision-maker in each of us.

Finally, the Author made Q. **Q was the intelligence.** The instinctive decision-maker of Type G represents an integration of the interests of all aspects of the self. Although the conscious mind may not fully grasp the instinctive decisions of the heart, Q is smarter than consciousness alone. Q incorporates both the subconscious and the conscious desire to guide the way to destiny. Q is the controller of all the aspects working together. Each person's mind contains all seven aspects, who must function as a team to realize that person's full human potential.

The intelligence became the leader

The Author put the intelligence in charge of all aspects, so they would have a leader. He was pleased with His software scheme. He saw these as common architecture, or "archetypes" which could span all Characters. With these Aspects in place, He could exert more control, without eliminating free will. After all, the Author had to live within the constraints of physics. If the Author did not voluntarily comply with these laws of physics, there would be no consistency in the universe. The Author was committed to providing a consistent universe for His carbon-based characters. He knew they needed consistency to feel safe, and to realize their own potential. These seven aspects would operate the characters, and help them each find their way. Sadly, however, inserting the aspects into the mind software came with a price. That price was the opportunity for distracting self-talk, and it opened doors for Nameless Demons to enter. The Author sighed. It couldn't be helped. He sadly accepted the price for the law of the Karmic bill.

All along the way, bad things happen to each of us. In our childhoods, we are vulnerable to being deeply psychologically harmed. The TRY within us, Gem, is our inner child. We each have a Gem, and a Shadow, and a Q, and all the aspects, inside our minds. Your inner child will speak to you, just as all your other aspects will speak in your mind. You will call this "thinking." When your aspects speak, they are not insanity. They are the software of the mind, and its many firewalls to process memory.

Theories propose models that work
Science doesn't know how we think, or how our minds control memory processing. This theory of Shadow, the survival instinct, Gem, the inner child, Nameless Demon, the willies, and all the other aspects: this is as good a theory as any other. Crazy people let it get the best of them, and can't pull their main character out of the fray to keep it in charge. You, however, are not crazy, so there is no need to be afraid of asking yourself what all your different aspects think. If you're going to know yourself, and you're going to learn to put into practice all those eight practical skills that will get you what you want, you need to know what your deepest inner aspects are saying. You must know yourself in all your complexity, if you are to Captain your soul.

In FantasyLand, the Aspects sat around the conference table. They were discussing what to do about Calamity Jane, the human being whose mind they inhabited. They were each elements of the cognitive software architecture, which operated Jane's mind, and they felt bad that she seemed to have problem after problem haunting her.

Q, the Intelligence, started the meeting. "I'm worried about Jane," Q said. "She's got problems on top of her troubles! Every time she turns around, another disaster befalls her. We've got to do something!"

"I've noticed that," said Toepia, the memory. "I've recorded every incident, but Jane doesn't access her memory to learn from her mistakes."

Bee, the sense of connectedness, chimed in. "Jane has a lot of noise in her receptivity. She is not interpreting the signals correctly. When the universe tells her to Zig, Jane always Zags instead. She seems to have her wires crossed."

Shadow, the survival instinct, added, "That is a serious problem, Bee. Why is Jane failing to receive the signals from the universe? We must correct her reception capability."

Ariana, the rational mind, answered, "I believe the problem lies with Katrina, the conscience. I've noticed Katrina hasn't attended any of our meetings for a long time. I believe, Gem, the inner child, said Katrina is lying sick in bed."

Bee, the sense of connectedness responded, "That would explain it. If Jane's conscience is bothering her, she will be so distracted and confused that she will never get her signals straight."

Q, the intelligence, said, "I don't understand why Jane's conscience is bothering her. She hasn't done anything wrong."

Toepia, the history, looked up from her knitting. She peered over her bifocals and said, "Now I remember. Jane's mother labeled her when she was a child. Her mother told her she couldn't do anything right. Jane has been trying to live up to her mother's expectations ever since. What she's doing now is attempting to prove that her mother's assessment was correct."

Shadow grimaced. He always reacted strongly to stories about childhood injuries. "Labeling is a serious handicap," Shadow said. "Children are completely vulnerable to living up to their parent's expectations, but I had hoped Jane would be capable of overcoming her parent's mistakes as she aged. What can we do to help Katrina, Jane's conscience, recover from this unjustified attack on Jane's personality?"

Just then, Gem, the inner child, entered the conference room where the aspects were meeting. "I could TRY," said Gem.

"Yes," Q agreed, "you, and only you, could TRY."

Only our inner child has the power to pull together the aspects of our personality to overcome and correct the wrongs, slights, and damages done to our self-image when we were helpless children. This is why it is so important that we not allow our inner TRY to go into hibernation after puberty. The solution to our problem of finding our path to destiny resides in releasing those dreams of our youth, and allowing The Real You to remain in the forefront of our personality.

Let's Review

The practical skills involved in getting what you want are not dependent on any faith concept. You do not have to know "why" in order to learn "how" to operate the universe.

The skills that countless corporations use to train their people in management are useful tools to manage your own life.

The eight practices that will get you in a position to have and keep what makes you happy are:

> You have to **Establish structure**. Time is of the essence. It is the only value that cannot be increased.

You have to **Measure outcomes**. What gets monitored, gets done.

You have to **Achieve balance**. Life is a mix of work and play.

You have to **Set goals**. You can't get what you don't define.

You have to **Pay attention**. Observe your surroundings. Note the subtleties. Collect data points. You cannot draw conclusions before the data is in.

You have to **Adapt to your environment.** You don't run the world. However the world exists, you have to change yourself to meet it.

You have to **Expand your options**. You can't limit the possibilities, if your goal is to win.

You have to **Reward good behavior**. What gets rewarded, gets repeated.

You can remember those eight practices by making them into a mnemonic. **REAP SAME**. You will reap what you sow. When you behave with integrity, the world responds to your behavior,and gives back what you gave to it, three times over.

Bad things happen to good people. Children are vulnerable and dependent. They are not responsible for what happens to them in their childhood. When that childhood is over, however, they have to put it away, and take responsibility for their actions. This means you. Keep your inner child active in your adult life, so that you can TRY, TRY, TRY again.

Exercises for Chapter 3:

Your Legacy Statement

Many of the exercises in this book center around a meditative state, in which you write your thoughts on paper. Sometimes people resist getting themselves so alone that they can hear themselves think. Some worry about spiraling into depression if they are left alone with their own memories. If you are not yet ready to explore too deeply, try focusing instead on a Legacy Statement. A Legacy Statement is an essay about the impact your life will have on Earth. Start like this:"At my funeral, this is what I want people to say about me:"

You may not care today what people say about you while you are alive. When you are dead, however, people try not to speak ill of the dead. They are likely to say only what is good about you. In this exercise, write the impression you will leave behind that is good. You are describing what difference it made that you were alive. See only the best in yourself.

Here are a few example Legacy Statements:

Legacy #1: The leader. I was a leader in my community. I set the stage for others to see a life of generosity, good will, and community nurturing. I started the 4H Club in my town.

Legacy #2. The backbone. I was the backbone of my family. I provided the glue that held us together, established our traditions, and drew our guidelines. I raised children who are happy.

Legacy #3. The innovator. I was a contributor to the world of art. I created new insights and set them out for the world to see.

Legacy #4. The individualist. I was unique. I lived my life my way, followed the beat of my own drum, and blazed a trail. I gave the world a model of one who could not be patterned. I showed the strength of individuality.

Legacy #5. The friend. I was a friend to the friendless. I provided the focal point for those who needed love around me. I helped many people when they felt sad.

Legacy #6. The stabilizer. I endured through trials and tests. I remained steadfast and solid for others to lean on. I was a rock in a turbulent sea.

Legacy #7. The producer. I was an example of success through productivity. The use of my talent built a corporation that provided jobs for many people. I used all my talents to create wealth, and left behind a trust that will contribute to a worthy cause.

Your Legacy Statement must be one that truly pleases you, and gives you a feeling of happiness and inner peace. Spend as much time as it takes you to form a Legacy Statement that will drive your living and guide your days. You may want to take some time out of your routine, away from familiar places, where you can refresh your mental state. It is very important to craft a statement which pleases your soul.

To help in your thinking about your legacy, here is an example of a eulogy for a woman who died at age 59, after raising five children. Your legacy statement need not be this long. It is an example to stimulate your thinking about what your legacy may be.

On Death and Dying: A Eulogy for One Who Died Too Young

Last Sunday, our mother flew a kite with her grandson. The little boy lost interest and left the field, but Grammy had her kite flying high, so she stayed and flew it alone. She laughed and she yelled, "Look how high it is." Then a hard wind came and pulled the string fast through her fingers. The kite slipped from her hands and took the wind. Four days later, without warning, Grammy died of a massive heart attack. Her first. No one was with her when she died. No one said good-bye. She had not yet reached her sixtieth birthday. But last Sunday, our mother laughed when she flew her kite. When the wind pulled the string from her hands, we built her a new kite, and she went out and did it again. The grandchildren weren't there. She flew the kite alone. When she was all finished, she sat on the park bench by the stream. With unembarrassed delight, she laughed, "In all my fifty-nine years, I never flew a kite before."

Best, we all noted, to ensure we spend some time flying kites in our lives.

Our mother took great pleasure in simple things. She liked just a touch of luxury, a taste of the things that might be. Her last summer on Earth, she fulfilled a lifelong dream to leave her little spot in middle America and visit the glorious, glamorous "California." From her hotel room, she took a map and a rental car, and set off on her own. By dinnertime, she returned stimulated and exhilarated. Breathlessly she whispered, "I found Beverly Hills."

She liked nice restaurants, visiting her friends in her little Hyundai, sharing a cup of coffee with just a splash of Kahlua inside. She liked her independence, bounded within a safe world where she could love and be loved. Our mother was a truly loving person. She gave without a thought of receiving, and though she had nothing, she wanted nothing. Whenever she got something, her first thought was to whom she could give it away. She had so little, and all she wanted was the joy of giving. She loved unconditionally. The recipients of her love were never required to meet standards to gain her approval. Our mother granted her approval automatically, by reason of existence. She was never critical, never judging. She loved the way Love is meant to be – unconditional, irreversible, undemanding. Her children could have been axe murderers, and they would know she loved them.

---- Yet, her children were not axe murderers. They grew up in poverty, but they never turned to crime. Funny, how a mother's love can influence that.

She didn't get her full measure of the good things in life. Her husband was always out of work. There was never money for milk for the babies, let alone clothes for their mother. She was widowed at age forty-five. He had no insurance. She, of course, as the mother of five children in a home always two dollars richer than the welfare cutoff, had no education and no skills. When her husband died, her children rotated taking care of her. She lived with one, then the other. Her adult children assumed she was their responsibility. No one saw her as the prototype of society's welfare case. Certainly, she never became the government's problem. Her family loved her, and they took care of her, as families should.

But although our mother lived a short life, and never had a vacation, she believed her life was good. She loved her husband; she bore and raised five children; she had friends; she talked and laughed and dreamed. She was a close friend to her adult children; she played with her grandchildren. She built herself a world and defined it her own way. She was not like her mother, or her father, or her friends, or her daughters. She was herself, and she lived life to the best of her ability. And then, on Thursday, four days after her first ever time to fly a kite . . . without sickness, without loss of her ability to function, without deterioration of her body or her mind; she embarked on a magical journey. Quickly, like that kite string that flashed through her fingers and took the wind.

Those of us back on Earth were left reeling. We wished we could stop her from going. We wanted to run after her, and tie that kite string securely to a stump. We wanted to fix it, build a new kite. We wished we could do something, change something. We re-lived every moment, searching for a time when we thought she might have expressed some grief, or reached out for help. We examined the guilt inside ourselves, hoping desperately that if we did something wrong, we could do something right to reverse the outcome. We wished to be empowered to help her, to bring her back, to change things. We wished we had control.

But Control said, "No dice." And we knew it was not **chance** that took our mother, but the living God. And with that know-ledge, we were comforted. We wondered if we might build her a pyramid, and fill it with fruit baskets and treasures for her jour-ney. We wanted to carve stories on the wall describing her life and dreams. We wanted to bid her bon voyage to the life beyond. We reached out to do something, and we found the best thing to do was to comfort each other, and stand in the gap. And then we saw that when she was gone, she left a hole. And we realized that was the goal to work for in our own lives. We knew what we wanted our own obituary to say. We hoped we could learn to be worthy to attain what this one impoverished, unskilled and un-

educated woman's life had defined. And we made it our dream, when we are gone, we wish only
. . . to leave a hole.

And that, Arjuna, may be the ultimate accomplishment.

Write your own legacy statement now, working until you feel comfortable that you have prepared a statement that reflects your true feelings. Remember: we each must do what we can, with what we have, where we are.

To begin, you may want to say: "I wish it to matter that I lived. I want my life to have meaning to someone, somewhere, in the context of the world. I want to live my passion. My Legacy Statement is:"

When you have completed your Legacy Statement, you will know your dream.

Alternative exercise for Chapter 3:
If you wrote a legacy statement from the preceding exercise, you may not need to do this exercise. If you were unable to write a legacy statement yet, this meditative exercise may help you. You must relax and calm your mind in order for this to work.

In Chapter 2, you looked for the pattern in the decisions you have made throughout your life. Get out the chart where you analyzed your pattern. You may not feel that you have a pattern, and for now, forgive yourself for not having found it yet. It is there. You may need some time to understand that you know this pattern. You may not be ready yet to see it.

Chapter 3: Considering the Options

Sit down with that chart, and a blank paper, and your two pens, one red and one black. Be sure to make yourself comfortable, pour a cup of tea, light a candle, and unplug the phone. Be quietly relaxed, and free of distractions. Tell the family to give you some "alone time." Work in a quiet room. Calm your mind and speak to your inner child. Call her TRY, or Gem, or ask her what her own name is.

Wait quietly and patiently for the feeling that your red pen would like to speak. Just wait for it. Calmly and patiently, slowly and without emotion, calm your mind. Let it release the flood of chatter inside it. Fix your mind on the candle, if it helps. Sip the tea. Let the chatter in your head stop. Release it, release it, release it into the ground, through the bottom of your feet. Mentally envision a calm blue mist coming up from the ground and filling the room. When you feel calm and quiet, when the urge to pick up that red pen is strong, pick up the pen and ask TRY to speak. Write what she says, without reservation. Do not censor her. Let her say her peace. When you feel you have contacted TRY, ask her to answer this question: Who am I, and what am I meant to do in life?

Let TRY write for as long as she will. Do not be worried or scared about what comes out onto the paper. TRY may have been locked up for a long time, and she may be full of resentful and angry feelings. Let the rage come out. You might find that you are writing strange and frightening things, but do not worry about that. TRY has been asleep, and she is pulling herself out of it now. She may have feelings of despair. Let her vent. Better that this rage is coming out onto the paper, than that it reside deep inside you, where it can poison your lungs, your kidneys, and your digestive system. Let her spit heat onto the paper, rather than boil your blood (which is what raises your blood pressure.) When TRY has finished writing, thank her for expressing herself, and burn the paper. This was a cathartic exercise for you. It will allow you to begin to heal.

When you have completed this exercise, you are ready to begin the first steps of your transformative success plan: **setting goals** and **achieving balance**.

Please go on to Chapter 4: Finding your Time.

_____

Can one truly waste time without damaging eternity?

---- Henry David Thoreau

Chapter 4. Finding your Time.

Setting goals and Achieving Balance. Finding time for what pleases you. Weaving a web of happiness into the fabric of our time. Integrating and entwining family, friends, fun, and finances.

Back in the subconscious universe of FantasyLand, Q, the Intelligence, felt worried. It had been days since Gem, the Inner Child, volunteered to TRY to get the conscious mind of Jane to focus on her destiny. The inner mind aspects of Jane felt upset. Jane was attracting disasters and accidents, through her refusal to pay attention to her prime directive. As long as Jane bumbled around, with no focus on her goal, she would be bombarded with signals from the magnetic universe. The universe wanted Jane to wake up and get with the program! Jane's problems were escalating, so Q believed Gem had not succeeded in communicating with her.

"She won't listen," Gem complained. "I pinged her once, and she bumped into the coffee table, cutting her knee. I pinged her again, and she grabbed the headphones and turned the music up loud. I pinged her a third time, and she called an ambulance to take her to the emergency room."

"Oh," interrupted Shadow, the survival instinct. "I'm sorry. I guess that was my fault. When you pinged Jane, she felt queasy in her stomach. Her brain went on alert when it heard your call.

It doesn't want the memories resurfacing, from her childhood. Her immune system is mounting defenses, raising her blood pressure and upsetting her stomach. I forgot what happens to Jane when you re-awaken from a long sleep, Gem. I told her she needed medicine, and she interpreted my call as a need for the doctor."

Toepia, the stored history of Jane's mind, interjected, "Jane can't allow Gem to speak to her without recalling some painful associations. While Gem awakens, Jane will feel discomfort. We'll need to help her set up some stabilizing defenses. She needs tools to lean on or she may not succeed."

Katrina, the conscience said, "She will feel sad until she gets some positive feedback. She needs praise and rewards to assure her she is on the right track."

Bee, the connectedness said, "We'll make some forms for her to fill out. When she gets all the blanks filled in, she can put little stars next to her name, like in elementary school. That always calms the inner soul. She can collect points and win prizes."

Q said, "You're right, Bee. Without direction and guidance, Jane will flounder. She won't know which way to go. Jane thinks she's already doing everything she can do. She blames the random universe for her spate of accidents and bad luck."

Gem piped in: "Poor Jane. I'll get her to feel drawn to write some things down on paper. If she writes it herself, she'll think she's thinking it. Then she won't be so scared to hear me."

Ariana, the rational mind, said: "Good thinking, Gem. Let Jane ease into knowing you by writing her thoughts. She'll feel better believing everything is her own idea."

Back on the conscious Earth, poor Jane knew she was in trouble, but she didn't know why. She just felt pain.

So here you are, with obligations and responsibilities, and all is not well. You need to set it right but you don't know how. You want to recall the dreams of your youth, but you no longer dream them. Your youth is gone, and you can no longer plan to marry a billionaire. Or you did marry a billionaire, and having married for money, you now realize you are earning every penny of it. You don't have time to breathe, time to take a bath, or time to have a relaxing lunch. You are busy, but you are not doing anything. Left to its own devices, work expands to fill the time available. Time is the only currency of real value. It cannot be expanded; we have only so much of it. Whether we are rich or poor, our days still consist of 24 hours. Now that you've gotten in touch with your inner child, banished your Nameless Demon, and acknowledged your will to survive, it is time to learn how to practice the skills that will get you what you want. Time is the key.

In this chapter, we will carefully explain the first two time-related skills: **setting goals** and **achieving balance**. We will show how to find time in your life, by choosing what is important to you.

In FantasyLand, the characters are keenly aware of the value of Time. It almost seems like they play a game of musical chairs. In musical chairs, all the players walk around a ring, circling a set of chairs. When the music stops, they must get into a chair, or they are kicked out of the game. You never know when the music is going to stop, so all you can do is keep your eyes on the chairs, and listen carefully. There is always one less chair than there are players; somebody loses in each round. That's what it's like with the things you like to do. There is always one less bit of time than there are things you would like to do with your time, so some activity is always getting kicked out of the game.

If, for example, one of your goals is improving your skills at playing the piano, but you do not practice because you have PTA meetings, soccer practices, book club, and quilting club, then you clearly are choosing a different goal: social networking. You have to decide whether playing the piano is actually your goal. You must know if you would give up social networking for it. You will have to prioritize your goals, and decide which is more important.

Gem: That's what Jane's problem is! She is always busy, busy, busy. Like a hamster running in a cage!

How you spend your time is how you spend your life. Additionally, when you set goals, you have to consider all areas of your life: family, friends, career, finance, health, spirit, and personal fulfillment. Your goals must include balance, or your life will feel incomplete. That's why we consider setting goals and achieving balance together, as we contemplate the use of time.

Remember that dream you had, back in Chapter 1? Your goals are the implementation plan to make your dreams come true. How can you know what the goals should be? How can you envision the end result and determine the steps required to get there? What if you don't even know what it takes to get to your dream? What if the dream is just impossible? More importantly, what if you still haven't figured out what it is?

What if your goal is to get out of debt, lose weight, give your daughter a nice wedding, and take the grandchildren to the beach? What if your goal is to solve a health issue, settle a legal problem, or help a friend? These are critical issues, which need resolution. They are not, however, goals worthy of a dream. You will not solve them following this program, but they will solve themselves. As you align your time more closely with the high-level dreams of TRY, back from when you were eleven years old, balance returns to your universe. The giant magnet of destiny no longer feels compelled to throw obstacles in your path. Your problems dissolve.

The Chaos Game[20]

In FantasyLand, we play a game which allows us to feel comforted about the lack of randomness in the universe. To start, we need one die. This will be our random number generator. We only need three numbers for this game. Since the die hassix faces, we will let 1 and 4 represent 1, 2 and 5 represent 2, and 3 and 6 represent 3. The game board is a large piece of paper with an equilateral triangle drawn in the center. The points of the triangle are labeled 1, 2, and 3.

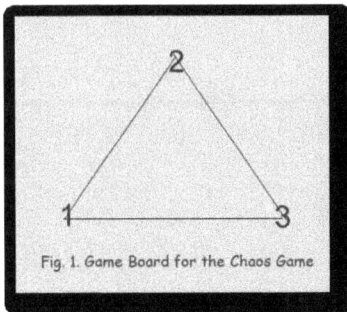

Fig. 1. Game Board for the Chaos Game

Figure 1: Game Board

The rules of the game are:

---

[20]Pietgen, H., Jurgens, H. &Saupe, D. *Chaos and Fractals*, page 298.

Master of My Universe

1. Pick any arbitrary spot, anywhere on the game board. It does not have to be inside the triangle. This is your starting point. Put a dot at your starting point.

2. Roll the die. Using a ruler, find the point that is exactly half-way between your starting point and the point labeled with the number that shows on the die. Place your second point there.

3. Roll the die again. Find the point that is exactly halfway between your second point and the point labeled with the number that shows on the die. Place your third point. Continue doing this until you have one hundred points.

When you have a hundred points, you will appear to have a random set of dots in a triangle. It will look like this:

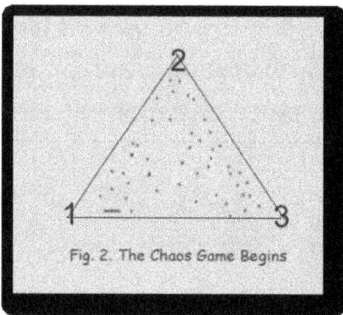

Fig. 2. The Chaos Game Begins

Figure 2: The Chaos Game Begins

Totally random, right? There is no way to determine where any point might fall, or the path taken by any point.

Now keep doing it, until you have ten thousand points. With certainty, the triangle will now look like this (figure 3). In mathematics, this is called the Sierpinski gasket.

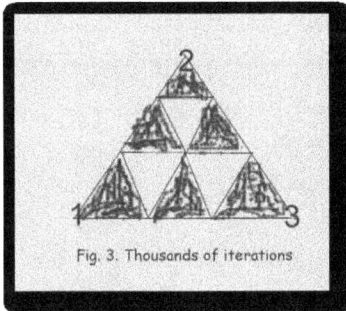

Fig. 3. Thousands of iterations

Figure 3: After thousands of iterations

A predictable pattern emerges from the randomly generated chaos. There are a number of these chaos patterns. In nature, they generate forms such as broccoli, coastlines, and ferns. Different arithmetic rules form different patterns. However, each iterative formula creates a pattern. We cannot predict where any one individual dot will fall, or what path it will take to get there. During the process, we may see only random dots. Given enough iterations, we can predict the final result with certainty.

Q says, "You see, Gem, this is the philosopher's free will versus destiny argument. Yes, we have free will. No one can predict where any one individual dot will fall, nor the arduousness of the path taken to get to the final pattern. But we know with certainty that a final pattern will emerge, given enough iterations over enough time."

Ariana, the rational mind, continued. "It's important to understand that the final chaos pattern will manifest regardless of our actions. This knowledge keeps us from chasing our tails, or running like a hamster on a wheel. There is so much time freed up, when we acknowledge that we are not in charge of operating the world."

Katrina, the conscience, agreed. She added, "Of course, this does not excuse us from doing our own jobs, meeting our own commitments, and fulfilling our own responsibilities. It allows us to give up on trying to control what is outside our own span. It prevents us from imposing our judgment on others."

Bee, the sense of connectedness, offered, "This attitude allows us to recognize that we are team members. We are not the whole team by ourselves. We do not have personal responsibility to keep six inches of topsoil on the Earth. We only run our own actions, within our own realm of responsibility. If we are assigned to first base, it is not up to us to play shortstop. Team members play their own position."

Just then Nameless demonrealized what Q had said. The demon interjected, "Oh, yeah? Well, what if you die before you get to your final pattern."

Gem was chewing on a peppermint stick at the moment, but she managed to chime in with, "In FantasyLand, we get a Do-over."

Toepia, the keeper of the history, looked up from her knitting."That's right," she added in her raspy grandmother voice. "In FantasyLand, we get new bodies and try again when we die. It's only after many lifetimes that we begin to get the concept, and learn our lessons on Earth."

"Oh, well, then," squeaked the demon, relieved to find a way out of the dilemma of multiple lifetimes. "That isn't anything like Earth. On Earth, we only live once."

Gem finished her peppermint stick and wiped her hands on a paper towel. She was sorry to hear the demon felt that way about multiple lives. "Too bad. Too bad," she commiserated. "It's a shame the laws of nature had to be suspended for human beings."

"Do nothing. The world will order itself.[21]"
Now, maybe you are reading this at age 45, or age 60. Maybe it is no longer an option for you to realize your childhood dream of becoming a ballerina, a Senator, or a Marine. Perhaps your family obligations will prevent you from realizing your dreams of traveling, becoming a ski bum, joining the circus, or dedicating your life to the church. However you came to be where you are now, the question is what to do next, not where did you go wrong. To have a happy and fulfilling life, free of worry, you must focus on the present and the future, not bemoan mistakes of the past.

Setting goals is the critical step to help you find your time. As the Cheshire cat said to Alice in Wonderland, if you don't know where you want to go, it doesn't matter which path you take to get there. By this time, though, you know it **does** matter which path you take. You must take the path that leads to your destiny. You may not reach your destiny, but TRY tells you to at least head in its direction. The journey is every bit as important as the destination. So how do you set goals when you can't even dream a dream anymore?

Well, I'm about to tell you something that may be a very unpopular notion:the reason you can't reach your goals is unrelated to the facts about your goals and your time. *Instead, it is related to*

---

[21] The Tao TeChing

your belief system about goals and time. This belief system colors your relationship to time, and distorts your responses and perceptions to what is happening to you.

The Meme Piece[22]

What you are about to read may trigger you to feel angry, or to suddenly feel tired. You may find that you instantly lose interest in reading this book, or accidentally forget where you put it. You may have this reaction because your mind may not want to hear this information. You have a defense mechanism inside which protects your consciousness from knowing certain things about yourself. These mechanisms are stored in your subconscious mind as programming.

Shadow, the survival instinct, whispers: Ahem. Are you ιbout me?

In Chapter 2, we talked about the conflicts introduced when your parents and the society in which you live told you that certain things were objectively true. Your conflict came about when you observed, through your senses, that those things told to you by your parents may not be facts. They may instead be opinions or perspectives on truth. Your parents and authority figures told you these things for two reasons: first, they believed them, and thought telling you would be helpful for you. Secondly, your parents told you these things because they themselves were programmed with them. They felt compelled to pass the messages along to the next generation.

---

[22]Brodie, R. Virus of the Mind: the new science of the meme

Maintaining the societal class system

Memes include attitudes and behaviors that will keep you in your "place" in the social order. They maintain the distinction between social classes, castes, or tribes. If you are born to the servant class, they will teach you to be a good servant. If you are born to the master class, they will teach you to maintain and defend your position as master. The sets of behaviors and attitudes your parents teach you comprise the stereotypes of your "subculture", or tribe, and they cause you to behave in concert with the ethnic, or neighborhood, or religion, or region, or class, or family, or caste, or tribe, or gang, into which you were born and raised. Once programmed with this set of "truths", or beliefs, or premises, about how the world works, you, as an adult, will have no awareness that you are acting on a flawed premise, or an imperfect "truth." Like the fish who has no awareness that it is living in water, you will so totally believe these premises that you will be unable to challenge them. When someone points out these premises to you, and identifies them as false, you will so violently reject the information that you may shoot the messenger. That's why I'm reluctant to tell you about this in this book right now. I don't want you to blame me. I didn't make this system up. I'm just the messenger.

If 1+1=2, then Paris is the capital of France. If 1+1 does not =2, then Paris is still the capital of France. Sometimes the Truth Table is irrelevant.

Burrow, burrow, like a mole

These memeswere taught to you as a child, where they burrowed deeply into your subconscious mind. They live there, controlling your model of how the world works. You believe them so completely that you have no knowledge that there is anything to believe. You think they are absolute facts, about which there can be no debate or controversy. These memes are the reason it is so difficult for the people of a Western Christian culture to understand people from an Eastern Muslim culture. Both groups of people care deeply about God and family, yet they have stored such contradictory beliefs, or memes, about God and family, that one cannot fathom what the other is thinking.

For example: the sky is blue. Actually, the sky doesn't exist. Your associative mind translates the reflective wavelength emitted by the movement of electrons in air. This causes your mind to perceive the color blue. There is nothing to see. Many animals don't see it. Your belief system has caused the translation, and you don't think about it or challenge it.

Memes work somewhat like this:
In a family that has been living as blue collar workers for generations, a meme might exist that says:

Meme 1: "People who go to college are a higher class of people than we are. They are better than us."

The parents would pass that meme on to their children, through exhibiting that this is something they believe. If you asked the parents if they believed that, they would say no. However, their children see that they do believe it, by their behaviors. The meme is passed on to the children. Two of the four children in this family do well in school, and the question of attending college arises. The father, knowing he does not have the money for college, denigrates the children for doing well in school. He says things like, "Doesn't that teacher know how to write anything but A's?" And "What do you want to stick your nose in a book for?" He rewards his other two children, the ones who don't do well in school, with his attention and approval.

Secretly, in addition to feeling embarrassed that he cannot afford to send his children to college, he also fears that they will think less of him if they become a higher class of person by graduating. His response is to belittle their desire to go to college and to learn. His attitudes are faithfully copied and spread throughout the family. Others join in, saying, "He thinks he's better than we are", if any child mistakenly achieves anything. The family shuns a child who succeeds or excels in any activity. This is subtle behavior, never admitted or acknowledged. It is implemented passively, and taught using manipulation.

The cycle of poverty
As a result, many generations of this family pass before any member attends college. Sociologists refer to this as the cycle of poverty. The memes pass to the generations through sanctions of behavior. Female children are rewarded for behavior that attracts a mate and leads to having babies. Males are rewarded for behavior that joins in with the other males of the group: working on cars, watching football, or drinking beer. Both sexes are sanctioned negatively if they rise above the crowd. A child from this family who wins a prize for academic excellence would have no one to tell about it, and no one to drive her to the award ceremony. She would be shunned in the family. Because she is not a part of any other group, she would be isolated in life. The child who finally graduates from college is likely to move away and never return home.

Passive-aggressive sanctioning
The cognitive dissonance inherent in any contact with the family fulfills the prophecy that she "thinks she's better than they are." This reinforces the belief that a college graduate is a higher class of person, who cannot be associated with the family. When their

college-graduate daughter succeeds, they will visit her fancy house and passive-aggressively attempt to embarrass her.

Alternatively, a second family of first-generation immigrants to the United States may have a meme that says:

Meme 2: "The United States is a land of opportunity, and if we sacrifice for our children, they will succeed and take care of us in our old age."

In this family, the meme is also spread to the children. The children know it is the parents' expectation that they will become financially successful, and take on the burden of caring for aging parents. The children know the parents are spending their retirement money to pay for the children's college. Now, one of these children, an only child, graduates from college but cannot find a job. His parent's dry-cleaning business, hit by the economy, goes under. The son feels deep despair, because he believes he has disappointed his parents. Over and over, he plays the tape in his subconscious mind that says, "I am a failure and I am not good enough to meet my parents' expectations." His emotional despair releases hormonal changes in his body. He becomes depressed and eventually commits suicide.

Meme 3. "People who go to college get a better job."

This meme doesn't need generations of children to spread it. It can be spread over the Internet, by online colleges looking for paying students. Unlike the first two memes, this one doesn't carry a moral judgment about the character of college graduates versus non-college graduates. This is a functional meme, which causes its believers to sign up for college classes. While it may be backed by many years of historical data regarding pay rates and job classifications, that historical data did not include a large body of students who graduated from online colleges. Online colleges don't have many years of history.

The data also did not include an economy with few manufacturing jobs, weak unions, and a declining financial base. People who hear this meme, through advertising, may decide to go to college, as a working adult. They may spend years of effort and money working toward this goal, sacrificing personal time. Having attained the goal, they may learn that there were many other aspects that determine success in the job market, including contacts, experience, passion, aptitude, and even appearance. If the person then fails at getting a better job, they may internalize the failure as personal unworthiness. (IF people who go to college get a better job AND I went to college but could not get a better job, THEN there is something wrong with me.) This could lead to a spiral of depression and illness. Illness is often triggered by a deep disappointment and feeling of low self-worth.

Meme 4. A college degree is a finishing school to allow the young to age before making a living. It is not a critical factor of career success. The factors that lead to success are contacts, aptitude, persistence, and talent.

A child who grows up in a family where this is the prevailing meme is likely to go to college. In their mind, success in life is not tied to going to college. They will have no expectations that the act of attending college will contribute to their success. Instead, they will search for what the factors of success actually are. This meme may lead to self-empowerment.

Hidden premises impact emotions

These four examples of memes, or deeply concealed, pro-grammed beliefs, exhibit how our hidden premises affect our behavior and our emotions. They impact how we perceive a sit-uation, and then what we think happened and how we respond. They show how four different people, with four different pre-programmed memes, could experience the same thing – gradua-tion from college but a failure to succeed – and have very differ-ent life reactions to it. Each of those reactions will be chemical. Emotion is chemical. Chemical reactions in the body either promote health or nurture disease. Our innermost beliefs are the precursor to a healthy state or a lack of a healthy state. These same innermost beliefs are what influence your choices of goals, and your decisions about how to prioritize them to fit into your concept of time. *Yes, Nameless Demon. If you don't have Time, it is your own fault.*

You do have time to meet your destiny
I don't know what memes have been programmed into your be-lief system, through your childhood upbringing, your sets of ex-periences in life, or your institutional conditioning. But I do know this: *each of us has time to do what destiny wants done.* When we approach that path in the road, and the Cheshire cat asks where we want to get in life . . . way deep down in the far-thest reaches of our subconsciousness . . . we do know the an-swer.

Skill #1: Setting Goals
How do you know your dream and set your goals? In my younger life, I refreshed my dreams by taking fifteen trips to Disney World. Every time I had a major decision to make, I went to Disney World. Disney World became my symbol of fresh thinking and a bright outlook. You will need to find your own

method to hear your heart speak. Your personal answer, which leads to your destiny, is written there. Deep down inside, you know this.Discerning the dreams, visions, and goals that are right for you is the key to re-orienting your path to meet your destiny. Setting your sight to that goal is the cornerstone of re-balancing your life and adjusting the energies that surround you. It is only when you are walking firmly toward your dream that harmony will return to your life. The memes that programmed you may derail you from your destiny temporarily. You may have to overcome them. As you hear yourself think, listen for the dangerous word "should." When the word "should" is spoken in your subconscious mind, you may have found a meme.

Balancing your goals
It may seem that you have just a few goals right now. Maybe you just want to get through the next month at work without being on the layoff list. In balance, you have goals in all the areas of your life. We achieve balance by honoring all the parts of our-selves. How many times have we read in the paper about a fan-tastically rich and successful person who just committed sui-cide? Or one who is caught doing drugs? Or who is going through a painful divorce? Or who has children who are in se-rious trouble? Success is not all it appears to be from a distance. Sometimes the price of success is not worth paying. Defining what we mean by success is extremely personal; success is meet-ing your destiny.

Skill #2. Achieving Balance.
You have some top level goals, but you must consider goals for all the segments of your life. Your life is divided into sections. You have Family as a section. Finances are another section. Ca-reer is a third section, different from Finances. Maybe you are working in a job that is not really your career at this time. For

example, maybe you work as a security guard at night, while interviewing for parts as an actor during the day. You might be doing something just to make a living, while simultaneously building your skills to get a job that is more meaningful to you. Health is a fourth section. Finally, Spirit is the fifth section. Spirit includes your personal philosophy or ideology. It does not have to include a religion or a formal church. Spirit is the part of you that interacts with the universe as a whole. Each of these five sections of your life needs to have its own goals. When you set goals for each of them, you will find that you are farther along in reaching your goals in some than in others. You have already paid attention to some of these sections, but you may have neglected others.

Regardless of our religious beliefs, we all have a spiritual nature and a faith in something. Whether that faith is in the consistency of science, the great energy force of chaos, the good-naturedness of the alien abductors, Santa Claus, the kind plantation owner, the king, or any form of organized or disorganized religion, our subconscious minds are built to have faith. The architecture of the primitive amygdala and the primordial id assume a faith in something, regardless of what it is. If you do not have faith in something, your ability to hold onto a dream is compromised. After all, if the universe has no rules, how will you learn what to do in order to play the game of life? A random universe would give us no hope; luckily for us, chaos is not random.

Goals and Subgoals
You will not feel fully at peace until you have all five sections operating toward your destiny. In your Family section, you might have a goal to keep everyone peaceful and happy, and stop some inner turmoil that is happening. Or, you may not have a Family

yet. You may have a goal to start one. Possibly, you may have to define your friends as your family, and set up a network of people who are there for you. In your Finances section, you may have a goal to get out of debt, to buy a house, to move, or to build savings for the future. In your Career section, you may have a goal to prepare for a new job. In your Health section, you may have some problems to solve. In your Spirit section, you may need to set aside time to become more involved in your own spiritual life. All of these are sub-goals of your bigger goal. These are the strategic level, lower goals. "Making ends meet" can be a goal at this level. We will do some exercises to set these goals at the end of the chapter.

What gets measured gets done
Perhaps you are saying, "Why do I need balance? Everything in my life is fine except my family, or except my career, or except my finances. I just need to focus on the area that is out of whack." The key here is to have goals for each area, because you are going to set up a structure to measure whether you are making progress toward your goals. If it is true that some areas are well covered, then your measurements will show that, and you will not spend time on those areas. But unless you define the goal, set the structure to measure it, and monitor your progress, you will not actually know that. The mind is masterful at tricking you into thinking things that are not true. Managers know that what gets measured gets done. Our program is a project management scheme, with **you** as the project.

As you prepare your set of goals in each of your balance areas, challenge your assumptions, your premises, and your memes about what is important in life. You know these answers. Don't let pre-programmed belief systems, leftover from irrelevant tribal sanctions, mislead you to answer that you do not know your destiny. You do know. You may be afraid to acknowledge it because your memes tell you not to want it. You may be afraid of disapproval, of ridicule, and of misdirected shame. The memes cause you to hide your desires even from yourself. Your inner child, TRY, or Gem, may have been buried in the basement by the devastating action of a meme. Her banishment may have been delivered like a knife to the gut by an unthinking, beloved parent.

The biggest lie we tell our children: Sticks and stones may break my bones, but words will never hurt me.Wrong. Words hurt, scar, maim and terrorize, often for life. Your grandmother told you words can't hurt you, in a futile effort to inoculate you against the painful impact of the bully whohumiliates smaller children in elementary school. She hoped to give you some protection from a powerful and dangerous weapon: Words.Words are so dangerous, we give our most heinous murderers a life **"sentence."**

Back in FantasyLand, Gem has finally convinced Jane to settle down and write her goals. Jane feels a strong desire to do this. She doesn't hear Gem talking; rather, she experiences a draw for some quiet, thinking time. But Jane is still filled with rage, leftover from her childhood trauma. She sits down to write, but those hurtful memories come rushing back. Jane worries that the only way to stop the memories is to avoid being alone with herself. She panics, and prepares to run away. To soothe her, Gem whispers in her mind, reading from the **FantasyLand Handbook of Meditative Practice.**

Find a place to be alone, where you will not be interrupted. If it can be outdoors, that is ideal. Bring a notebook and your black and red pens. Give yourself time to relax, to decompress from your daily worries. Do not play music or listen to the radio. Do not set a time limit that is less than 4 hours. Do not turn on your cell phone. Do not tell yourself you don't have time for this. The truth is, you do not have time to not do this. Every day that you do not do it, you are spending time that cannot be retrieved. If you spend your time doing things that are not part of your destiny, you are spending your life in wrong pursuits. Wrong for you. Time is your life.

Using your black pen, write in your notebook: What do I want in my heart?

Using your red pen, write whatever the red pen writes. Even if the red pen writes "peanut butter", write whatever the pen wants to write. You may be thinking, "What do you mean, what the pen wants to write?" What I mean is, do not think it out first. Just calm your mind and let your hand move without connecting to your head. Do not censor, rationalize, plan, analyze, or think what you want to write before you write it.

What you are attempting to do is reach into your subconscious mind for the answer. The answer that comes out initially may sound irrational and unacceptable. As you allow your subconscious mind to bring its thoughts to the surface, it may express rage and frustration. When you ask what it wants, it may say, "I want a divorce". It may say, "I want to walk away and start over." It may say, "I want to be free of my burdens."

Allow yourself this momentary rage. Let the rage express. After it has vented, it will move on to more useful and productive answers. Until the rage vents, we are blocked from feeling our own desires. Psychologists say we are not "in touch with our feelings." Let the red pen express all the emotion it wants to express. Detach yourself from it by calling it "the red pen" that feels that way, although you know it is you who feel that way. When the emotion has all come out, keep writing. Ask your question again. Eventually, the red pen will tell you the answer. You will never be able to set goals as long as you carry that rage inside.

As the universe will respond to your steps on the path to your heart's desire, so also the universe is responding to that rage you carry. Your internal rage is causing your problems. Yes, Nameless Demon, it is your own fault. When you have fully vented, and the red pen is finished and ready to tell you your personal truth, note the answer that is truly your heart's desire. Tear the rest of the pages out of the book, and burn them.

Important note: it is not sufficient to "think" this. You must write it. After you write it, you may want to destroy the paper so no one else ever sees it, but something about the way your mind works will cause you to write something different from what you think you are thinking. If you just think it, you will not get the same answer. On another day, after you have recovered from this experience, take your personal truth and your real heart's desire and start to make a set of goals from them.

Let's Review

1. Time is what Life is made of. The way you spend your time is your life.

2. If you don't have time to do something, that is because you have chosen to make other things more important. You may be-

lieve the choice was made for you. If you believe that, you are conceding your free will.

3. The only way to ensure that you are spending your time, which is your life, on activities that lead to your destiny, is to set goals that are in concert with your heart's desire.

4. Every coincidence that comes your way is not meaningful. Some of the coincidences are just bees invading the house. You have to recognize when a coincidence pings your heartstrings, and shut all the other little distractions out.

5. You can know your own heart. It takes some "alone" time, but you can do it.

6. When you know what you want in your heart, and you make the decision to go after it, the world will align to help you get it.

7. You must define your dream and set goals to get it. Then, you will be spending your time wisely.

8. Your childhood programming, your life experiences, and your institutional conditioning, will set you up for failure if you cannot recognize and acknowledge that your perceptions may not be based on reality. You must hear your heart. It knows your destiny. You may have to overcome and overwrite the societal memes that programmed you to membership in your tribe.

Exercises for Chapter 4:

Using the following guidelines, write your subgoals for each of the five areas in your life. Consider how each of them contributes to your legacy statement and your ten-year goals.

Guidelines for writing subgoals for your five points of balance:

Project "You"

Step 1. State your goal. Your goals will change based on your age, so the best way to start is to think of how you would like to see your life ten years in the future. You must paint a picture in your mind, in great detail. Envision how your future will look, sound, taste, smell, and feel. The more detail you add to the picture, the more likely you will be able to cause it to occur. Your subconscious mind will incorporate the image, and lead you to make the correct small decisions at every fork in the road. Here are some examples:

Example 1. Ten years from today, I see myself attending my daughter's wedding. My health problems have been overcome, and I am prosperous enough to provide her with a glorious banquet for 200 people. Our home is paid off, and we are able to retire in comfort. I spend my days working for my favorite charity.

Example 2. Ten years from today, I see a greenhouse built on the property next to mine. I own that land now, and I run a successful herb farmproviding comfrey to retailers for distribution. My divorce is final, and I have lost 20 pounds. I'm looking good and feeling empowered.

Example 3. Ten years from today, I have received my certification to be a nurse. I work in a city hospital and have my own apartment. I drive a Camaro. My apartment is furnished in blues and deep purples. I am fully independent.

Example 4. Ten years from today, I am working for a large corporation. My job requires travel and I go to Paris and London regularly.

Example 5. Ten years from today, I own a vineyard. My family all live on the land and we work it together. My vineyard holds wine tastings and parties with local celebrities.

Step 2. Setting the specific goals for each point of balance.

Now that you have identified what you want in ten years, use that ten year vision as guidance to identify the specific goals for each of the points of balance in your life. We each need a mixture of activities and missions, in order to have a meaningful and enriching life. When we focus too much on career, on making money, on pleasure, or on relationships, at the expense of other areas of life, we develop an unhealthy imbalance. Think of the person you know who is too wrapped up in having fun, too focused on work, too involved in the intricacies of relationships, or too concerned about making money. Any of these areas, when they dominate our lives, create emotional imbalances. Emotion is chemical, and its impact accumulates in our bodies. Over time, that imbalance in our focus becomes an imbalance in our body chemistry.

Make your list and check it twice

Prepare a chart for each of your subgoals. At the top, write your ten year vision. As you select your goals for each of the balance points, think about how these subgoals contribute to your legacy statement. If you feel strongly about a goal for your balance point, but it doesn't seem to fit with your legacy statement, you may want to re-consider your legacy statement. Keep in mind two important laws of the universe, while you ponder your balance point goals:

1. Emotion is chemical. Even positive emotion upsets the hormonal balance of your body for some time. Calm living is critical for long-term health.

2. Time is what life is made of. When time is lost, wasted, spent, passed, or idled, it is gone forever. Jealously guard your time, and ensure that it is used only for activities that advance your life goals. Time is the only asset of enduring value.

Under each of your balance points, come up with at least two, and up to five, goals relating to that area of your life. If you feel strongly that you have more than five goals, consider whether some of your goals may be sub-goals of another. Here are some examples of typical goals for each balance point:

Balance Point 1: Finances. This area includes budgets, savings, education, and working for a paycheck. This is where you would form goals to get out of debt, to change careers, to get an education, and to plan for retirement. Your career is what you do to make money. Homemaking can be a career, if you treat it with respect and do it as if it were your job. If you have a job that you do not consider a career, make plans to either treat it as a career and succeed at it, or change to a job that can be your career. A hobby can be turned into a career, given proper attention and planning. Your success program requires that you spend all your time with the proper attitude toward life. Even a menial job can be treated with the respect of a career, and you must do this to remain in a state of chronic health. All the minutes of life are important; none of them can be wasted doing something that denigrates you.

Example: I choose to establish myself as a photographer within the next five years. To do so, first I have to develop a portfolio of my work. I can take this portfolio to companies when I interview.

Example: I choose to work from home as my career. I have to look for companies that offer this alternative and apply for jobs using my word processing skills. If I can't find any companies who offer this, I will have to advertise for people who want to have office work done for them from my home.

Example: I choose to get a job in the electronics field. First, I will have to complete my network engineering coursework at community college. Then I will write a resume and send it to 200 companies.

Example: I choose to be a fulltime homemaker. First, I will have to rearrange our family budget so that we can afford to live on my husband's income.

Example: I choose to put myself on a promotion track at work. To do this, I will look for ways to do my job better, and be perceived more positively in the office.

Example: I choose to go into business for myself, selling my artwork and handicrafts. To do this, I will begin to form a business plan and look for ways to implement it.

Notice that each example describes a specific action that will need to be accomplished in support of the goal. Your goals all need action plans, specific statements of what action you can take to cause them to happen.

Other Finance goals.

Under your finances balance point, you also need to think about your budget, your debt, and your goals to save for the necessities like cars, vacations, education, and retirement. The goal here is to stabilize my finances, and keep them running quietly, so they don't take too much time out of my life. Time is what life is made of. I don't want to spend my time, which spends my life, making money. On the other hand, there are bills to pay, so some type of job has to rear its ugly head here. The best case, of course, is to achieve a state where my fulfillment goals actually earn me a living.

Balance Point 2. Relationships goals.

Your relationship goals include your interaction with your co-workers, neighbors, community, family and friends. Most importantly, they also include your relationship with yourself. You are a complex person, and you need to pay attention to the relationship you have with all the aspects of yourself, too. Relationships with yourself and others are the healing element of your life, so this balance point includes nutrition, health, and personal appearance as well as interaction with others. Your goals in this area should include at least one goal that is about your own healthful living, and at least one goal about your family and community relationships.

Balance Point 3. Passions.

This areacovers those activities which really give you pleasure. Personal fulfillment, creativity, vacations, fun, hobbies, and spontaneous relaxation fall under this area. If your career is not personally fulfilling, you may want to put more focus on an area that does make you happy, and work toward causing that activity to replace your current career as a financial goal. Following your bliss often leads to a career that is both passionately rewarding and also pays the bills. You may have a goal to satisfy a long-held desire, such as a trip to an exotic place. You may have a goal to collect old railroad cars, or guns, or coins. You may have a goal to learn carpentry and build a shed. You may enjoy gardening, sewing, woodworking, or giving parties. Whatever you feel strongly engaged to do, these are your passions, and areas for which you need to set goals. They provide the happiness in your days, and sprinkle the smiles through your duties. You don't need a reason to want to do something that you feel passionately about. Passion is not a rational response. Instead, it's just a trigger for joy. Select at least one goal in the area of passion, but no more than three.

Balance point 4. Duties. These tasks are things such as: pick up the dry cleaning. This is where you make your To-do list for housecleaning, laundry, baking, soup making and cooking dinner. These are circular tasks: that is, once they're done, you still have to do them all over again periodically. The idea here is that you write into your schedule the time that you need to pick up the house, change the sheets, and wash the dishes. In the process of figuring out where all those duties fit in, you may discover that it's time to share the workload with the rest of your family members, and start delegating some cleanup tasks to the spouse and kids.

In every day, we still have to make the bed, wash the dishes, do the laundry, and pick up the mess. We have to shop for groceries, get the kids ready for school, pay the bills, and answer the mail. Thinking of these activities as duties that help us balance our day can change them from drudgery to relaxing times for quiet thinking. The key to transforming making dinner and stocking the pantry into a calming sadhana[23], instead of an annoying disruption, is the balance that comes from dividing our day into a mixture of activities. We intersperse pleasure with duty, so that there is enough joy to last through the drudgery. In fact, with the optimal mixture of activities, we welcome the calming influence of a mindless task here and there. Where things go wrong is when we neglect these duties to the point that our homes are not comfortably clean, and our environment is not conducive to calm thinking. Alternatively, some people spend so much time on the drudgery that there is no room for joy. The goals that fall under this balance point relate to organization of the tasks of life. While some people's need for these tasks consists of instructing the staff on what to do, most people have to find a way to reconcile how much cleaning and cooking and diaper changing they can stand to do, and still have a life. The goal in this balance area is pretty much the same for everyone:

Example: I choose to keep a well-maintained environment. To do this, I need to identify and schedule the maintenance tasks that keep my life free of clutter and neglect.

For some people, a failure to attend to this balance area goal has already caused problems. Unpaid bills, unanswered demands, neglected health, and an unattractive living environment take a toll on a person's goal achievement, and drain energy that is needed for things that are more meaningful. You may have neglected some maintenance areas in your life to such a point that fixing the problems will take all your time for weeks. Accumulated debt, relationships that have been left to deteriorate, health issues that were not addressed, repairs not done, documents not

---

[23] Sanskrit word meaning a repeated practice performed with observation and reflection. It is a meditative way to get work done.

organized, closets that hide years of junk you don't remember you own, and a house that isn't clean, can stop your progress toward any goals.

When a depressing environment surrounds you, you feel down and discouraged. If you wake up to a pile of dirty clothes on the floor, unwashed dishes in the sink, and gray, colorless walls in your house, you feel less capable of accomplishment. This feeling, which is an emotion, is chemical. It builds up in your body tissues untilyoubecome too depressed to clean the house. Your dirty house makes you feel depressed, and your depression keeps you from cleaning the house. Conversely, some people feel so compelled to have everything in its place, and every spot of dirt cleaned the second it appears, that they spend all their time picking up and cleaning up, and have no time left for living. There has to be a reconcilable balance, and achieving that balance is among the goals of this life area.

Balance Point 5: Spirit
Regardless of our religious beliefs, we all have a spirit and a faith. That faith drives and compels us, whether we see Creation as the great energy force of chaos or whether we see Creation as Allah, Jehovah, Hariti, Jesus, Cernunnos, Erzulie, or Zeus. It is necessary to acknowledge that faith, because our primordial id uses it as a zero point, from which it derives its balance. Some of us currently choose to be agnostic (ie "I-don't-know- whether- there's- a- God- but- right- now- I- choose- not- to- worry- about- it") Even the agnostic, however, is saddled with the architecture of the primitive amygdala: your conscious mind may wish away the issue, but your deep primordial id is childlike. All children believe to the marrow of their bones that there is some type of a God, even if that God is Santa Claus. Your God may be the science of chaos and the inspirational pull of the human spirit. It doesn't

matter what you see as the creative force of the universe. You must attend to this childlike belief system, or it will throw tantrums of discord in your bodily organs. They're called organs because they can be played. Emotion plays them. We must live in *harmony* or our *organs* feel the discord. You don't need to join a church, but you must acknowledge that you have a faith, even if it's a faith in Science or Humanity.

Your spiritual goals are those that inspire you to be fully yourself. Inspiration is the result of attending to the goals of your spirit. They have to do with your faith, but your faith is what you believe in, regardless of what that is. Spirit tasks, like Passion tasks, are widely variable, and again, extremely intense. You might just set aside Sunday morning for them, but if Sunday morning is taken up by church, you have to be sure that church is fulfilling your spiritual goals. Sometimes there is so much social activity going on at church that you can't fit your belief system into the structure. Your spiritual goals are personal, and they are about your relationship with the faith held deeply inside you. Examine that faith, and determine how best to spend your limited time so that it can be accommodated. Make your Spirit task list focus on knowing yourself and knowing your beliefs, and centering your life on them.

Example: I choose to uphold the rituals and ceremonies of my faith, in order to invigorate my spirit. To do this, I must set aside specific times to focus on matters of my faith.

Example: I choose to examine my faith in more detail, until I satisfy myself of what I believe. To do this, I will plan to investigate the premises of my religion.

Continue to Chapter 5: Paying your bills.

Annual income, twenty pounds. Annual expenditures, nineteen pounds ninety six. Result: happiness.

Annual income, twenty pounds. Annual expenditures, twenty pounds plus ought and six. Result: misery.

---- Charles Dickens

Chapter 5: Paying your Bills.

Measuring Outcomes and Establishing Structure. You will never be happy with bill collectors snapping at your heels. How to get rid of them.

In FantasyLand, the White Rabbit and the pipe-smoking caterpillar, Caterpix, debate the relative merits of paying the cable bill versus installing another solar panel. Resource constraints have plagued FantasyLand ever since the Karmic bank lost a file containing everyone's Radio-Frequency-Identification codes. Now all the FantasyLand citizens worry about identity thieves putting money into their accounts, and building up their Karmic debts.

"In my younger days," puffed Caterpix, "I was part of a neuroscience research team. We studied the impact of electrical stimulation on the muscular action potential. I contributed significant breakthroughs to understanding brain synapse functioning."

"I assume you were the specimen on that team," commented White Rabbit.

"Been addicted to nicotine ever since those days," agreed Caterpix.

Back on Earth, neuroscientists work in modest laboratories. They form teams, torture worms and slugs, and attempt to make heads or tails out of bizarre behaviors no more rational than a coin toss. Sometimes they appear to solve a small piece of the puzzle of the human brain. When they do, some hope fervently to sell their results to a drug company.

News Flash: November 16, 2010. An FDA panel voted to approve a new drug. Two of the fifteen panelists voted no. They said the studies, done by the company selling the drug, did not show a significant improvement over older drugs already on the market. The FDA panel expressed concerns about infection, neuropsychiatric side effects, and risk of suicide. Only thirty percent of patients treated responded to the drug at all. On the announcement, the company's stock rose 9.3%.

Caterpix: You do know that 30% of people respond to a placebo, too, don't you?

White Rabbit: Show off.

Our scientists have not discovered much about the functioning of the human brain, and its impact on immune response in the body. Without conducting any studies, however, we can say with assurance that life worth living is a mixture of work and play. In this chapter, we will cover the skill sets: **Establishing Structure and Measuring Outcomes.** In the Exercises in Chapter 1, you wrote your life story. In chapters 2 through 4, you identified the pattern of decision-making you have used throughout your life. You got in touch with your inner child, TRY, and you asked her to help you find your dream. You set your goals for the future. You feel some excitement about reaching those goals, but as yet, you may feel that they are not practical. Perhaps you believe you cannot achieve your goals. You could be thinking that nothing can be done to work toward your goals, because you have huge debts, big obligations, terrible financial troubles, and deep commitments toward others that require you to continue to work. You could be thinking that you are a slave to these financial commitments, and you are like an indentured servant, who must work for seven years to pay back the debt incurred for being brought to America on the ship.

Nameless Demon: I have just one word for you. Bankruptcy. That's what it's for. Do it. Don't be worried that you "won't be able to get credit again." You don't need credit again. Credit is what got you into this trouble. Time is what Life is made of. You cannot afford to be enslaved. "Free Credit Report Dot Com. Tell your friends, tell your dad, tell your mom."

This is an example of a meme that has gotten itself written into a television commercial. It rhymes, so it sticks in your head. It tells you to believe something, and to pass that belief on to your friends, your dad, and your mom. What does it tell you to believe? That your credit is your key to financial success, and you must safeguard that credit in order to live a happy life. Makes sense, doesn't it? You need a good credit score to buy a car, get a mortgage, and even to get a job.

Wait a minute. You need a good credit score to get a job? When did that happen?

You're right, Nameless Demon. Credit checks to get a job are a somewhat new development. Companies started doing them within the last twenty years, as more and more people got into so much debt that there was some worry that a new employee might go unstable. If you think about what happens in the U. S. today, a young person graduates from high school or college and needs a job. If they went to college, they may already have a huge debt to be paid off, and a monthly payment hanging over their heads for the next ten or twenty years.

They don't have a car, but they need one to get to work, so they get a car on credit. Then it becomes necessary to join the co-workers for happy hour after work, to fit in. They need a credit card, because they don't always have the cash from paycheck to paycheck to pay the bar bills. The next thing you know, there is a zero percent interest credit card offer in the mail. They run up a tab; the introductory offer expires on the credit card. Within a few years, they are paying 29% interest on a debt for a couple of beers and a few fill-ups at the gas tank. In no time at all, the monthly payments become so burdensome that there is nothing left to live on from day to day. Saving money becomes a foreign concept.

Owe your soul to the company store
In the 1950's, a Merle Travis song became popular, called Sixteen Tons. The song was about working people in coal mines in the Great Depression. The lyrics said: "You load sixteen tons, and what do you get? Another day older and deeper in debt. St. Peter, don't you call me, 'cause I can't go. I owe my soul to the company store." This referred to the practice, in many factory towns, of allowing workers to run a tab at the company store. The company would own the house you lived in. You paid rent,

which was automatically deducted from your paycheck. Rather than money, the company would issue "scrip", which was redeemable at the company store. The company would let you buy necessities above the amount you had on file in scrip. You ran up the tab, and they would take a monthly payment out of your paycheck. Eventually, you would owe the company so much money that you couldn't afford to quit your job, because you couldn't pay the bill at the company store.

Outgo exceeds intake

Through the memes programmed into your mind during your life, and the pressure to fit in and go along with the crowd, you may have ended up in a situation where your monthly expenses exceed your monthly income. Whatever it takes to change that, you have to change it. You must spend less than you make. That may mean you have to move out of your house and find a cheaper place to live. It may mean you have to trade in your car for a used car with no payments. It may mean you have to declare bankruptcy, and stop using credit in the future. Or, it may mean you have to stop spending on trivial and unimportant things, so that you can use all your extra cash to pay down debt. Who needs to spend four dollars on a cup of coffee at a restaurant, when you can buy a coffee pot and a thermos jug and make coffee at home?

Avoiding embarrassment is not a valid life goal

But, but, but . . . I made promises. I have obligations to family. I have status in my community.

Those are "ego" arguments. You don't want to be embarrassed. You feel you would be perceived by others to be a failure. Now, in the process of making your goals, it's possible you will be able to make goals that allow you to continue your financial status as it is. If that is possible, then by all means, make that a financial goal. If it is not possible to continue in your same job, meeting your same financial obligations, and also follow your destiny, then which shall you choose? Your destiny or your ego?

Shooting for the moon.

Sometimes, if you shoot for the stars, you fall short and only reach the moon. That's not a failure at reaching the stars; it's a success at reaching the moon. You may have to be satisfied with a lower target. All the same, you will be farther along your path. Most importantly, since the journey is more satisfying than the destination, the trip itself will cause you to feel inner peace. Sometimes we select a goal, but when we actually get the prize at the end of it, we realize the prize is not satisfying. We can change our goals as we go along. These aren't flip-flops in our thinking. They are just progressions toward our destiny. Sometimes we are heading toward one goal, but when we reach it, we set a new goal.

What happened to me

I'd been out of business school for two years. During that time, I'd been deliriously happy with my work assignments. I was doing mergers and acquisitions, traveling the world. I traveled a lot, and one day I came back to my hotel room early, while it was still light. It was a garden-style hotel, with rooms all on one floor. Each one had a small courtyard, so guests could sit outside, surrounded by flowers and plants, and see the lake. I had recently returned from Holland. Now I was in California. Next week, I would be back in Washington, DC. There would be a lot of late meetings because our Italian clients were in town. As I sat by the lake with a glass of wine and ordered room service, I said to myself (or perhaps one of my inner voices said):

What are you doing? Do you live in some kind of TV show? You're running around the world, spending your time, which is your life, as the servant of a corporation, who benefits from your effort and gives you just enough crumbs so that you think you're well-paid, but you don't have time to spend the money. Meanwhile, you have no time to spend with your family. You have no time to make new friends. You moved to a new city two years ago, and you haven't met anyone to form a social network. The only people you know are the men you work with. You don't even have a single friend. You can't fit in dates, and you haven't met anyone to date. Is this a life? Or is this some kind of charade?

Goals can change

Before that evening, I thought I wanted to travel. I wanted to do the big deals, work on the hot teams. After that, I changed my goal. Too much of a good thing can be devastating. I refused to continue traveling at work. (I know some of you are saying, "Easier said than done." You can't just tell your boss you won't travel any more. You could lose your job.) I stopped traveling, knowing there may be longer-term consequences for my career goals. For my new project, I decided to join some clubs of things that interested me. My thinking was that I would meet people who had common interests, and form a network of friends.A short time later, I was fired.

You see, when you are focusing on How-To-Get-What-You-Want, you don't think about details like How-To-Get-What-Somebody-Else-Wants, or How-To-Get-What- Society-Expects, or How-To-Get-What-Conventional-Wisdom-Says-You-Should-Want. I didn't want to get fired, because I wasn't financially ready yet. I had no income. All of this stress made me sick. Stress is what makes you sick. *You knew that, right?*

I could barely get out of bed, coughing. I now had no references for a new job. Sound familiar? Do you have problems and troubles like that? There are times when everybody has troubles. Rich or poor, our lives have troubles. I was too sick to figure out what to do. I was coughing so hard, I just stayed in bed. I had two weeks to do nothing but think. My thinking concluded that I would need to achieve balance in my life. I had to work less. From my sick bed, I wrote a new resume. I selected local companies and targeted a lower level job, at less pay. I couldn't have it all. I would need to work where I did not have to travel, where I could come home every evening, and where there could be time for family, friends, and a modest career. I was going to have to stop the corporate climb. This decision calmed my world. In time, my coughing stopped;I married, and had two children. Then I hired a nanny, returned to a serious career, and got back on those airplanes. Now I felt safe that my family and social network were in place. Given an opportunity, the world orders itself.

"Brains. Brains, brains, brains. How do brains work?'

"What are you doing, Gem?" asked Ariana, who is both the rational mind and mother of the inner child.

"I'm figuring out what's wrong with Jane's head. She's becoming a fruitcake. Rashes are popping up all over her legs, and her bones are clicking," said Gem.

"Have you asked Q what's wrong with her? Q is the Intelligence of our family," Ariana asked.

"Q's sitting in his pajamas in his bedroom. He won't talk," Gem told her.

"Well, that explains it," said Ariana. "If Q is not functioning properly, Jane will be very sick. You could try telling Jane some stories."

So Gem whispered this in Jane's ear:
In the distant past of Earth, when Earth and FantasyLand were the same place, Earth people lived in caves. In those times, people were a lot like cats. They were curious and they stayed up all night looking at the stars. They were trying to understand what the stars were and where they went in the daytime. The people didn't have any paper, so they scratched marks on their cave walls. This was so they could remember things. In one cave, there was this mark:

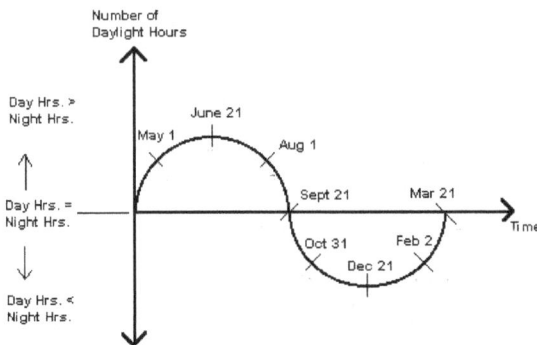

Fig. 4. How the Ancients saw time cycles.

Cavemen figured out that Earth had a cycle of day and night. They also knew there was a longer cycle of warm and cold weather. They noticed there was a time when flowers grew, and fish jumped in the rivers. There was a longest day, and a shortest day. They saw the days get longer and then shorter again. The cave men learned there were cycles in life, and there was also progress. They saw people grow and age. Some things were like circles, which came around and around again. Other things were like lines, with a beginning and an end.

Lines and circles, lines and circles, ones and zeroes, ones and zeroes. One Zero One Zero One OneOne
Hand, hand, fingers, thumbDum ditty dum ditty dumdumdum[24]

Jane likes it when I sing to her, Gem thought. It makes her brave.

And back on Earth, Jane thought:

For example, when I was a child, I wanted to have twelve children, so that I could build a dynasty and take over the world. When I grew up, in the 1950's, women did not have corporate management jobs.As a child, I could not envision a management career path. I had been taught it was an impossibility. Later, in my teens, I wanted to be an investigative journalist. When I finally chose a career, I chose technology management. When the Internet was invented, I became a citizen journalist in my community and started a Blog. The little pieces of us that are our various talents all want to come out and be used. This can happen in many ways at different times in our lives. Family can be dominant during some years. Career can be dominant in other years. You can change careers, change financial structures, and change direction, all without being untrue to your dreams. Your dreams are multi-pronged. You can follow one prong for a while,

---

[24] Dr. Seuss. Rhyme is soothing to the human psyche. Doctor Seuss rhymes with Mother Goose.

and then jump off to a different prong and develop it for a time. None of these "jumping arounds" implies that you are indecisive. They are just different ways of developing your full self.

Skill #3. Establishing structure. Now that you've established goals and sub-goals, you need to make the task list that will allow you to accomplish each one. The top goal, which you established in the exercises of Chapter 4, was your vision. Under that, you made sub-goals, which were the five sections of your life to achieve balance. These sub-goals are your strategies to implement the vision. Now you are going to structure your tasks, so that you can achieve the sub-goals. This is the tactical level of your implementation plan. It is very important that this tactical level plan be written. You can't just think of what you will do, because each of your tactics has to be measurable. You have to be able to observe whether or not you have done it.

Fine-tune as you age
Update your plan at least once every year. Your visions and goals may change. Your top-level goals change very littleover the years. They fine-tune, though, and what may have looked attractive at age twenty-two may no longer be interesting at age fifty-five. Your dream may transform from wanting to be a world-class ballerina, to wanting to give dance lessons. You may have multiple dreams and desires, and they may all take some part in your life at different times and ages.

A very young childwill say he or she wants to be a racecar driver, a veterinarian, and a paleontologist. Children want to be many things. The parts of us that have talent in various areas want to be used. Our talents don't like hiding under bushels. We want to use all our talents. Our talents don't necessarily fall under one category or one job.

Master of My Universe

In your Plan, you have defined your top-level goals and sub-goals. Finally, you will add your implementation tactics. These tactics may take years to complete. You were going to live those years anyway. You might as well live them while progressing toward your dreams. The structure you will establish to implement your plan will define how you spend your days.

Moments define our memories
Time is what life is made of. What you do with your minutes, defines your life. A life of quality is a life spent doing things that meet your own standards. The decision about how to spend each minute is your decision. The structure, to which you chain the activities of your minutes, is the very shackle that sets you free. We will set structures in the exercise at the end of this chapter.

You submit to these Time Masters voluntarily. When appropriate, you break your own bonds, and readjust your commitments. But most importantly, you recognize that the decisions of how to spend your time are the decisions of how to live your life. Given that you are mastered by these decisions, you enter the commitment with great care. These Time Masters are the rhythms of your life. They synchronize you with the harmony of the universe.

Gem: I think Jane just needs to re-program herself. If she used her powers of artificial intelligence, she could learn from her mistakes and try again. Each time she would get better and better. Like this artificial intelligence software. Jane should learn from her experiences, like this computer program does:

Press Release: 2010: Maximize Returns on Direct Mail with Neural Network Software

...BrainBuzz[25] Neural Network Software maximizes returns on direct mail. When a company uses the software, they only send mail to people who are likely to respond. This way, the mailing brings in more revenue at less cost. The software is trained to learn from its experience. It takes in data collected from previous mail campaigns. It compares that data on twenty-five variables. It iterates, testing various scenarios. It picks an option it considers best. It tries that way, gets feedback from the experience, and improves its guess for next time. The program keeps trying different options, and comparing results. It learns from its mistakes.

If Jane would set her goals, review the results, learn from her mistakes, and fine-tune her actions for next time, she could be just as smart as this robot software, Gem whispered.

But will Jane learn from her mistakes? Toepia commented. No, Jane does not want to accept that she has made a mistake, so she is unable to reconsider and change her approach.

Caterpix puffed by, in a cloud of smoke. That's why I like to keep it foggy in Jane's brain, Caterpix said. If she sees what she is doing clearly, she will be forced to take action to correct herself.

Just then Q appeared. Structure sets the boundaries for our behavior. It is how we know whether we are on the right track.

---

[25] This is a fake name. A fictional product. If there is a product named Brain-Buzz, it wasn't intended to be real. This is the real way neural network software works, though.

But we choose to follow a structure. If Jane does not choose her structure, she can safely blame her life catastrophes on randomness in the universe.

Chorus of nameless demons: **It's not her fault!**

Skill #4. Measuring Outcomes. Each of the tactics you defined in your skill of establishing structure must have a tangible and physical result. It is not a tactic to say, "Improve my health." You have to specifically identify what aspect of your health you plan to improve. You need to identify your task with a measurement of **how much** and **in what time period**. You might say:

1. Lower my systolic blood pressure by 20 points within two months without using drugs

2. Lose 5 pounds in one month

3. Make it through 30 days without an asthma attack

4. Exercise 3 times a week for 20 minutes a day

5. Cook dinner at home six nights a week, without using the microwave

6. Never open a bottle of wine before dinner

7. Always close the bottle of wine after dinner

You have to have simple tactics, things that you can point to as little things you've done. You have to be able to notice that you did them. For each of your other sub-goals, you must have measurable tactics on your list. Tasks that don't have observable results, within definite timeframes, might as well go on the To Do list right under "clean the Venetian blinds". You will not do what does not get monitored and reported. *That's how people are.*

Some other examples of measurable outcomes:

Under Finances, you might list:
1. Pay off one credit card by October of this year
2. Reduce the electric bill by 5% each month
3. Contribute the full amount to our IRA by April 15

Under Relationships, you might list:
Arrange to have dinner together as a family every Sunday
Establish a set of traditions for each of four holidays, that belong to our family alone
Give every child an individual "alone time" day each month with each parent, to do what interests them and really hear them
If you don't have a partner, you might plan to attend two group activities each month that interest you, in the hopes of finding someone of like mind
If you do have a partner, you might rekindle the romance by planning two formal "dates" every month

Under Spirit, you might list:
> Research the basis of my religion or ideology, by reading one book about it this month
> Set aside time to involve myself in my religious or ideological practices, every week
> Write down what I believe, on one page, before the month is up

You can set these tactical plans in any way you feel is appropriate. The important thing is that you make them specific enough so that you will know whether you have done them. Don't TRY on this. Do. This is where you progress beyond your inner child, and put your adult in charge. This is where you are **mastered.** When you have set up your Plan with these goals, sub-goals, and tactics, you will be ready to start living, and stop "marking time." Time is the only real value, and you must use it to head toward your destiny. Or else. *Or else, what?* Or else, you'll get sick. Have accidents. Meet misfortune. The path rises up to push you back on track. That's the point. If you rearrange your debt, so that you free up your time for the more important things in life, the forces of the universe will realign to make it work out. So the key to paying your bills is: restructure your commitments until your income is greater than your outgo. Do whatever it takes to accomplish that. Then stick to your plan and follow your schedule. Bankruptcy is an option. Do not be embarrassed by it.

Set your schedule

Each of these tasks will take time, and they must be scheduled into the limited resource of time which is your life. If they are never scheduled, they will never happen. If they never happen, they must not be your real goals. After all, if you are not willing to give them time, you must be acknowledging that they are not important to you. That's okay if it's true. But if it is true – restate your goals! Goals with no implementation plan are called pipe dreams.

Pop-ups, pop-ups

Many will say now, "I meant to get around to it, but something popped up." Nothing pops up in life, unless you choose to make it more important than the task you have already set. Get a monthly calendar, write on it what you are going to do that day, and then when things pop up, you can say, "sorry, I'm already committed for that time slot." Of course, there are some things that interfere with your schedule and are unplanned. A power outage across your entire region, which prevents you from attending to your daily tasks is an example. Or perhaps you have a death in the family that requires you to leave town for a few days. There could possibly be rare natural disasters that interfere with your ability to plan your work and work your plan. But these are rare occurrences, which are highly unlikely. If you find yourself believing that things are "popping up" that keep you from your goals, you are simply deluding yourself. You may be doing it for a number of reasons.

Reasons you might be convincing yourself that things are "popping up" to keep you from your work.

1. You don't really want the goals you have listed.

2. You want the goals, but you don't want them enough to pay the price for them.

The universe is going to deliver what you actually want, at a subconscious level, not what you believe you should want.

Time is what life is made of. There are certain activities on your goal list that you must do on a periodic basis. Maintenance activities may have to be done daily, weekly, monthly, or annually. Work goals may have to be done five days a week. Hobbies may be ongoing. Other activities may be projects that can be started and finished within a defined timeframe. No matter what your goals are, you will not be working toward them if they do not occupy a timeslot on your calendar. Structuring your timeslots, with measurable outcomes, and tangible results, is not optional. It is how you strike your deal with the universe, and fulfill your contract.

We pay our bills in life in many ways. Our bills are not just about money. We have debts to other people, too. We have obligations to our children. Other people have expectations of us. We have made promises to a spouse, a brother, a friend, a parent, a child. All of these relationships create bills which must be paid. It can become easy to overcommit, to take on too much debt, to run up bills which are overwhelming. We can easily put ourselves in a position of making minimum payments on the debts of our relationships, because we have made too many commitments.

Money, it turns out, is not the only type of bill we pay when we live a full life.

Let's Review

1. Our top-level vision, the one brought to us by TRY, may be multi-faceted. It may have different aspects to it, or prongs, which may happen at different times in our lives, as appropriate. It may change over time.

2. That vision uses all our talents. As such, it may not fit into any of the traditional career paths society has presented to us. We are not interested in getting what somebody else wants, or what society tells us to want, or what conventional wisdom says we want.

3. The unique vision we each carry inside is our destiny. It may not be clear what it is, but we have a strong draw toward it. **It is written in our hearts**, and it is our heart's desire.

4. Although we have a top-level goal, we also must live our lives in balance, and within society. An unbalanced life will prevent us from reaching our destiny and disrupt the harmony of the universe.

5. There are five sections of our lives, each of which must have its own set of goals, or strategic sub-goals. These sub-goals are more practical and immediate than our top-level vision. Under these sub-goals, we have measurable tactics, which we must monitor ourselves to accomplish.

6. Each of our sub-goals is required as part of our plan to achieve balance in life. We must also incorporate them into our structure of time. Establishing a structured life allows us to make progress on our personal goals.

7. The tactics we develop in order to direct the way we spend our time, must be measurable and observable so that we will know when we have accomplished them.

8. Paying our bills is not limited to those that come in the mail. Every segment of our lives creates debts and obligations. We must overhaul our total debt picture, including debts in our relationships.

9. Avoiding embarrassment is not a valid reason to continue practices that prevent us from heading toward our purpose and meaning in life.

Exercises for Chapter 5:

Master of My Universe

Setting the tactics required to achieve your goals is a simple task that uses your logical mind. You will not need to go on a journey to find your inner child this time. Grab your morning coffee, sit down at the breakfast table, and lay out the task. You may have to do this in more than one sitting.

Take your lists of goals and subgoals. Under your subgoals, identify two or three specific tasks, with measurable outcomes, which you can do within the next six months. Try to break your tasks down into small pieces, so that you can schedule time to accomplish them.

Get your calendar

For this exercise, you will need a one week planner page, laid out with days of the week across the top, and hours along the side, as shown in figure 5. First, fill in all of the time activities which you must do, and which cannot be changed. You must sleep, so mark off your normal sleeping times first. If you have to go to work, mark off your work times and the time to commute. Then lay out times for preparing and eating meals, getting ready for work, and doing essential maintenance tasks. Whatever is left is the time you have available to work on your goals.

Figure 5: Your calendar planner

	Mon	Tue	Wed	Thu	Fri	Sat	Sun
6 am							
7							
8							
9							
10							
11							
Noon							
1 pm							
2							
3							
4							
5							
6							
7							
8							
9							
10							
11							
Midnight							

If you are like many people, you will see that there are about two hours in the evening and a weekend left, after you have removed those timeframes which are used for activities which you cannot avoid. Now you have to make the choice. Do you spend those two evening hours watching television, playing application games on Facebook, and talking on the phone? Do you spend the weekend driving your children to group activities which they do not enjoy, but which you feel compelled to force them to endure? Do you give dinner parties that exhaust you, for people you don't like? Do you attend meetings of groups you only temperately support, at the expense of time for your own passions? At some point, your long term goal may be to remove that big timeslot set aside for working at a job you don't like, and exchange it for a fulfilling career that matches your passion. For now, however, you must do what you can, with what you have, where you are. Time is what life is made of.

Priorities

Now is the time when you realize what it really means to deal with the universe. Review your goals, and decide which of them you feel are important enough to be scheduled on your weekly chart. Recognize that only what is scheduled will get done. Look more clearly at your goals and decide which of them are high enough priority to you that you are willing to schedule them.

Once you have scheduled your goal activities, commit to follow your schedule. If Sunday evening is laundry time, then do the laundry on Sunday evening, not Saturday morning, and not Wednesday afternoon. If Thursday night is the time you have chosen to work on the business plan for your own company, then turn down offers from friends to go out to dinner on Thursday night. Treat these commitments to yourself as serious business appointments.

When you have organized your tasks, you will see how you must re-organize your life, to reduce your debt and stop overcommitting. Paying your bills is about meeting contractual obligations. The way to ensure you meet them is to be seriously aware and awake when you agree to them in the first place. Wipe out the old, if you must. The rest of your life begins today.

Continue to Chapter 6: Expanding your family

It isn't what you don't know that gets you into trouble. It's what you're absolutely sure of, but isn't true.

--- Mark Twain

Chapter 6: Expanding your Family.

Expanding Options and Adjusting to Your Environment. "What if" this and "what if" that. Everybody needs somebody to love them. Learning to discern who really cares about you.

In FantasyLand, every time you are reborn, you get a new family history. Your family history tells you what values you are starting out with in the world. Itgives you paper money to get started. You don't get to choose your family history. It is randomly selected for you during the rebirth process. Paper money is worthless in the Karmic bank, because when you die, you can't take it with you. Karmic money, however, follows you from life to life. The objective of life is to zero out your Karmic bank account, which is what propels you across the abyss and grants you demi-god status as a Valkyrie-Warrior. As long as you have a balance in your Karmic account, either positive or negative, you can't get across the abyss.

Paper money gives you Karmic debt. The richer you are, the more Karmic debt you have, because you owe Karma for allowing you to have riches in life. If you spend your paper money, spending it won't count toward reducing your debt. If you save it for a rainy day, you will attract rain. The only way to reduce your Karmic debt with paper money is to give it away to charity.

The values you get from your parents may or may not be good values. Some people learn things from their parents that are not good to learn. Each Value has a Karmic point score, which could be either positive or negative. Every time you invoke the Value, you gain or lose that number of points. The lessons of life include ways to change the values given to you by your parents. Youare trying to **exact change in your value system** to get Karmic points. Sadly, however, the values given to you by your parents could be burdensome and obstructionist. Here are some possible values, given to you in the form of programmed memes, which you could have learned from your parents.

Meme value 1. Hard work is the key to becoming successful in life.

If you are programmed with this meme, you are likely to approach life with a sense of duty. You will probably work hard at whatever you do. You are likely to ignore the correlation between success and hard work. You will simply not challenge that premise. If you are unsuccessful, you may respond by trying harder at the same thing, rather than by changing your approach. You may look up to rich people, and believe their money is a reflection of their merit.

Meme value 2. We should only associate with people who are like us, because they share our values.

If you are programmed with this meme, you may aspire to live in a subdivision with a homeowners' association.

Meme value 3. We are grateful for being alive. We don't see ourselves as anything special.

With this value, you may perform heroic acts anonymously, with no expectation of reward. Unless, of course, the problem occurs while you are in a large group. You will not choose to be heroic when others around you are hiding, because you do not see yourself as anything special.

Meme value 4. Love is granted to you if and only if you behave as expected.

This manipulative meme may be responsible for the percentage of drug-addicted children whose parents have money. Many parents teach their children that the withdrawal of love is a valid behavior control technique. This meme contributes to the divorce rate.

Meme value 5. We love you no matter how you behave.

This meme is most prevalent in poor families. However, it is often accompanied by a caveat: we love you, as long as you don't succeed. If you succeed, we will invoke Meme value Five Point Five: People who succeed think they are better than us and must be knocked down a peg. This meme contributes to the cycle of poverty. It is not to be confused with "unconditional love."

Meme value 6. Cleanliness is next to godliness.

And its corollary: dirt is immoral. Therefore, homeless people have character flaws. You sometimes will find people who can't keep their houses clean because they feel morally unworthy in support of this meme.

Meme value 7. Sex and the naked human body are immoral and dirty.

This is a close cousin to Meme value 6. It can be passed along through generations by subtle implications. Our movie-rating scheme, for example, finds violence more acceptable than nudity. By associating sex with immorality, we encourage domestic violence.

Meme value 8. To thine own self be true.

Parents seldom pass along this one any more. It's been overridden by the desire to trust authority figures, whether they are doctors or government representatives. People who did have this meme would work at knowing themselves. They would question authority.

Meme value 9. If you have money, you are a Very Important Person, who is obviously successful and worthy.

This causes people to salivate over the chance to be on a reality TV show.

Meme value 10. You have to be punished for what you do wrong.

Someone burdened with this meme will spend a lot of time in self-abasement, trying to atone for imagined guilt.

As you can see, there are many possible memes, planted inside you by the subtle belief systems of your parents. They could be right, could be true, could be wrong, and could be false. The important point is that they are opinion, perception, and belief. They are relative, not absolute. The lioness says to her cub: **Meme 11: Eating zebras is fine and good.** You are not a bad person when you kill a zebra. Nothing wrong with it. As long as you understand it is one viewpoint among many possible others. If your lion children must attend school with the zebra children, however, it creates a societal powder keg.

Once planted, memes fight for their lives. They declare themselves to be absolute Truth, and attack the messenger who tells you they are merely perception. Until you have examined each meme implanted inside you by your parents, you cannot be fully sentient and aware. You may be perfectly comfortable choosing to believe that people should be punished for what they do wrong. Until you have examined the context and implications of that belief, you are a mere puppet of the meme. Memes are software programming in your mind. If you haven't chosen which ones to accept and believe, **they** are operating **you**.

Repeat offenders
Is there any proof that punishment stops people from behaving badly? Does it prevent other people from doing it? Maybe, maybe not. Organizational behavior studies say that rewarding people for what they do right is effective, if and only if they personally value the reward. These same studies say that rewarding right behavior causes the behavior to berepeated; however, punishing bad behavior does not stop it from happening. Studies also say that people who go to jail are likely to go to jail repeatedly. The punishment doesn't prevent recurrence of the bad be-

havior, nor does the threat of punishment deter crime. In some cases, "three hots and a cot" is not punishment at all. It may be the best available lifestyle alternative for that person's situation. You may consciously choose to adopt the meme: People should be punished for what they do wrong. However, you must recognize that your reason for adopting it is not "to prevent crime." More likely it's another meme. The meme you believe could be: "If I can't do it, you can't do it." Are you sure which meme is operating you? Would you master your own universe more completely if the memes were not in charge?

Whenever there appears a disconnection between a principle that everyone accepts and observable results, check your premises. You may be acting on a meme. Or, rather, it may be acting on you, to control your response.

Unconquered lands
Sometimes the reason we can't get what we want is that the memes we are running in our programming set are limiting our options. You might say, "I want to get a high-paying job in the field of social services." But maybe the field you are choosing doesn't have many high paying jobs in it. Maybe that job is about satisfaction, rather than paychecks. You might say, "I want to work in the field of software development." But maybe you live in a part of the country where there aren't many companies doing that kind of work. If you want that job, you may have to move to a place where the right companies are located.

Some people will say, "Oh, I can't move. My family is all here. I'm part of this community, and I have obligations, friends, and activities that I do here." That's a valid concern. A big part of your happiness comes from the friendship networks you have set up for yourself. You do not want to uproot relationships that are working for you.Sometimes there are children from a former marriage, or grandchildren, who may not live with you. You can't move away and leave them. On the other hand, sometimes those networks you have set up are not working for you. That's why you're looking for something else. Remember, there are friendly people, who have the same interests you have, everywhere, all over the world. If you are part of a knitting club, a cooking club, a ski club, or hobby group, you will find those same clubs in other places. You can make new friends. New neighbors will welcome you. Sometimes your extended family can be what holds you back and keeps you from succeeding. I remember a story I heard at a seminar many years ago.

There was a young man whose father and grandfather worked in the steel mills. This family lived about 100 miles outside of Pittsburgh, Pennsylvania, and they had the typical income of other families in their neighborhood. They also held the typical expectations and views of the world that their neighbors held. In that view, people lived their lives in close contact with friends and relatives. These people were your support system and your focus. Jobs were just something you did to pay the bills. Jobs were about paychecks, not about life satisfaction. If you lived in this subculture, you may never meet anyone who did not hold those values. You might believe these values were held universally, and were objectively true.

The young man spent his teenage years focusing on playing the guitar. When other kids hung out, he stayed home and played music. Sometimes he jammed in the garage with a few friends. He was a better musician than his friends were. He really, really loved his music. He graduated from high school recently. There was no money, and no expectation, that he would go to college. Looking forward, his future would be to take the next opening at the steel mill, and go to work with his father, his uncles, and his grandfather.

One day, while the young man was still unemployed, waiting for that opening at the factory, **a chance coincidence and circumstance occurred.** A famous band of the time stopped in his small town, because their van broke down. While they were waiting to get their van fixed, this young man just happenedto be in the shop. He knew who they were. He talked to them about his music. They invited him to jam with them, right there in the auto shop.

The famous band members congratulated the young man on his talent. They said he was good. Very good. They invited him to come to Pittsburgh, where they were holding tryouts for a back-up player. They assured him he had an excellent chance of being selected. They smiled and patted him on the back. They gave him the date, the time, and the place for his tryout. They raised their hands in "high fives" to him. They smiled.

The young man ran home, elated. He couldn't wait to tell his mom. He didn't know who else would be interested or care, but he was sure his mom would be happy for him. He rushed into the house, where his mother and his two aunts were baking in the kitchen. He blurted out his happy news.

His mom smiled. How nice, she told him. She got out a plate and gave him a brownie. And then his Aunt Martha said, **"Where are you going to get a bus ticket to Pittsburgh?"**

His Aunt June said, "Pittsburgh is a dangerous place. That hotel's not in a nice neighborhood."

Just then, his Dad and his Uncle Joe came home from work. His mom quickly filled them in on the news. His Dad looked over at him, with a wrinkled brow. "Them band people use drugs," he growled. The young man felt a sharp blow to his stomach, as if he had just been kicked; although of course, no one had touched him.

Needless to say, the young man never made it to his tryout in Pittsburgh. Within a few weeks, the factory had an opening. He went to work in the mill. As he grew older, he stopped playing music. His dreams died. But for the rest of his life, he had stomach trouble.

Maybe that trip to Pittsburgh would not have turned out well. Maybe he would have been turned down at the tryout. Maybe he would have gotten into trouble in the neighborhood. Maybe the neighborhood was just fine, and Aunt June was confused. Maybe the band members used drugs. Maybe they didn't. Maybe he would have found out that being a backup player in a band was not fun, and not the life he imagined. Maybe his chronic stomach trouble was unrelated to that incident on that day. Then again, maybe that was the moment in time when his TRY died. Maybe it would have been better to have tried and failed, than to have passed on the option, and never known the potential outcome.

The pressure to conform
Families and social groups pressure their members to conform to their expected way of life. Rich families do this just as much as poor families do. Sometimes in the rich families, the pressure is even stronger, because children who grow up rich doubt their ability to live without money. The threat of being cut off from the family fortune is real. The poor little rich kids are most likely to opt to stick with the program, rather than risk their inherit-

ance. It can be hard for those of us who were not born rich to sympathize. Yet, this desire to conform can be accompanied by a worry that they are not competent to make it on their own. There can be a deep-seated feeling of inadequacy tied to being born rich. It really makes you feel for those poor, inadequate rich kids! Families and friends can be dangerous to your dreams of succeeding. They may have a vested interest in keeping you right where you are.

I remember when I was in my twenties, starting out on my career, and building up accomplishments. I would go to a family reunion. Nobody there would ask about my job, my traveling, or my successes. Their only question was: "Are you seeing anybody?" They only cared if I would be getting married soon. That's the sanction of families. Societies also sanction their members. Clubs do it, political parties do it, and churches do it. At one time, in our human society, it was morally acceptable for a woman to show cleavage, but showing an ankle was perceived as perilous. The society would cluck about a woman who allowed her ankles to show, suggesting that her actions implied loose morals. Today, we can't understand that thinking. What the society considers "moral" changes over time. It changes by geographic area, by ethnic background, and by religious affiliation. The television series Mad Men describes the behavior of Madison Avenue executives in the 1960's. If you watch the show, you will see what appears today to be exaggerated gender and racial roles. Yet, at the time, the society did not challenge these roles. At one moment in the show, a young woman offers her contributions to the men's discussion of advertising. "It's like watching a dog play the piano," her male colleague tells his friends about her ability.

Chapter 6: Expanding Your Family

Societies use intimidation, humiliation, and withdrawal of approval to control behavior. People are social creatures; they respond to these sanctions and conform. It becomes emotionally painful to stand apart from the crowd.

Sanctions are serious

The business of social sanctions is a fact of the anthropology of human beings. It is neither right nor wrong. It is simply true. Your friends and your family may sabotage your efforts at success. They may tease you, make fun of you, discourage you, or actively block your way. If you are following the instructions in this book: setting your goals, making your task lists, and proceeding with your plans, then you do not have to be concerned about the sabotage coming from your family. Accept that they are worried about losing you. You have a role to play in their lives, and they don't want that role to change. Your success may threaten them.

Forgive them. Ignore their snide remarks and humiliating digs. Move on. After you succeed, they may adjust their attitudes, or they may not. The price of success may be to leave your current family and friends behind. Don't dignify their efforts by getting into it with them. At the same time, don't buy what they are selling. They may feel a need to tear you down, to burst your bubble, and to rain on your parade. Of course, they sincerely believe this is "for your own good." You may need to find yourself some new friends, and expand your ideas of family, if support is important to you.

Everybody needs somebody to love them. Sadly, however, those who are supposed to be the ones who care about us may sabotage our success.

In this chapter, you are going to learn two more skills: **expanding options and adapting to your environment.** You will learn that the people who surround you must be people who have your best interest at heart. You can't choose your family, but you can choose whether you will spend time with them. You can give them the opportunity to behave supportively and love unconditionally. You can love them unconditionally, but that does not require you to swallow what they're serving.

Skill #5. Expanding options. To expand your options, you have to keep every possibility open in your mind. Consider different ways to do things. Don't close off an option in your mind because it isn't the norm. Don't shut down a possibility because your friends and family won't approve of it. If your mind is not fully open to all possibilities, you may fail to hear opportunity knocking, or to see that lucky fork in the road.

The Strategy for Living and Competing in FantasyLand

A Belief System Written by the Seven Aspects of the Collective Unconscious

On Time Travel and the Living of Many Lives
The primary method of moving from kingdom to kingdom and from world to world is through Time Travel. In FantasyLand, all worlds exist simultaneously, and all times exist simultaneously. What you do in one world remains undone in another world, so if you wanted to try to do a task over again, you could slide to another world and start again. If your task in one world is uncomfortable, you can slide to another world and seek a different trial. You can only slide from one world to another when the wormhole opens, and you can only time travel from one king-

dom to another after you have completed the task which you came to the kingdom to do.

Players begin the game in their home base world, at the kingdom of Mal-koot. There in Mal-koot you are given a trial. By passing the trial, you earn the right to step onto the path. The path is a tunnel, which will take you to another kingdom. Each kingdom has a number of possible paths, and each path is fraught with dangers and tribulations, which must be overcome. The player on a path must make decisions about which way to turn. If the wrong decisions are made, the Karmic account is debited. Certain decisions knock the player off the path, and cause you to land in Da'at.

When you have traveled to all the kingdoms one time, regardless of which worlds you traveled in, you earn your first Status. Players who have Status get priority seats on the TimeBus, and are able to call for a Wormhole without waiting for one to pop up.

Interacting with the Others
The King believes we are all one, and fails to recognize there may be any others. He is of the opinion that life is lived of yourself, for yourself, and by yourself. It is self-scoring, self-motivating, and self-driving. But, we all need to talk to somebody about what goes on in our lives, and sometimes the Elves and Faeries are just not enough.

Recognizing this human need, the King has graciously arranged for every citizen of FantasyLand to join a Guild, based on Jobs, Talents, Temperaments, and Competencies. In the Guilds, you can meet with others like you and share experiences of your travels. When you enter the Guild, all your Statuses display next to your name. A Blacksmith is one who has traveled all kingdoms once. A Warrior is one who has traveled all kingdoms twice. A Shaman is one who has traveled all kingdoms three times. A Sorceror is one who has traveled all kingdoms four times, and has learned all the lessons. Only Sorcerers may enter Dragoon, and apply for the final trial of crossing the Abyss and becoming a Valkyrie-Warrior.

Wow, Q! That is quite a belief system mythology. Did you make that up all by yourself?

And deep inside Jane's head, Q answers: Why, no, Jane. I just read it in the collective unconsciousness. It's part of the mythology of ancient time. I'd say I have added a few specifics here and there, based on my own experience. In general, though, these are just principles that "everyone knows." They are the memes of FantasyLand. The memes of Earth are completely different. Still, everyone knows what everyone knows. Whatever people believe to be true, effectively, that is what is true.

Meanwhile, Jane, who has no idea she is talking to Q, thinks she is thinking. That night, she has this dream:

How to Understand String Theory[26]

Gem is sitting on the floor playing with some bugs. She mumbles to herself: Okay, is that ten strings or eleven membranes? And I guess the P-brane is his head.

---

[26] For more ideas about string theory, see Jastrow, R. The enchanted loom: mind in the universe, Bryson, B. A short history of nearly everything, Hawking, S., The grand design, and Greene, B. The elegant universe.

Chapter 6: Expanding Your Family

Along comes the bug, Caterpix: What are you doing with that bug, Gem? I'm sure she needs to get home to her family.

Gem: I'm looking for the pieces that make the bug, Caterpix. Daddy said the bug was made of atoms and the atoms were on a string. So I'm trying to see his strings.

Caterpix: You can't see the strings, Gem. Your eyes aren't good enough.

Gem: Hah! Then how does anybody know they are there?

Curious about how things can exist when they can't be seen, Gem investigates and writes this report:

How a Scientific Theory is Made
A Research Report Written by Gem

As far as I can tell, this is how you do science. First, a bunch of guys who stayed in school until they were almost thirty years old, and never had a real job, get somebody to pay them for doing research. The people funding them set up a laboratory and buy expensive equipment for it. Then each person picks one really, really small piece to work on. The piece they pick has to be teeny tiny, or else they won't be able to prove it. Then, they try different things to see if they get any ideas. They pick something and try to prove if it is true or false. If it's false, they make some changes and try again. If it's true, they write about it in a magazine. Unless the guys who paid for the laboratory don't want anybody to know the answers. Then they just crumple it up and throw it away. If they decide to publish it, all the other scientists get to read it first. If the other scientists don't agree with it, it can't get published. After it gets in the magazine, everybody is supposed to believe it. If you don't believe it, you have to make another experiment to prove it's false.

Q, the intelligence asks: So, what is string theory, Gem?

When Jane wakes up, Jane is drawn to read some books about string theory. She can't get this idea about string theory out of her head. She can't understand it, but it's a "pull" she feels.

Jane tells her friends this: "From what I got out of reading the Elegant Universe[27], atoms are not teeny little points. They are teeny little rubber bands. As we all know, you can stretch a rubber band; you can strum it and play a tune. It makes waves. Strings are like the letters of the alphabet. You put some together to make words. Letters are the fundamental building blocks of words. Strings are the fundamental building blocks of the universe.

Each string resonates. It makes a sound. Like a spoken word. So each string is like a musical note. It vibrates. One sound can be an electron and one can be a proton. Or it can be any of the particles of an atom. For a while, scientists figured there were about five different string theories. This was because they thought there were different fundamental particles. But then, they realized all the different particles were just the strings, pulled and pushed in different ways. They were naming the strings things like "graviton," and "fermion," so they had different names for different configurations and states of the strings. But then the scientists realized all the particles were just different configurations of the string after it was plucked.

---

[27] Greene, B. The elegant universe.

Nameless demon: Uhh. Who plucked it?

Ariana: No soup for you.

Now, the way scientists test stuff is, they throw rocks at it and see where the rocks bounce. Like playing marbles, but with expensive equipment. So after the scientists played around with the ideas of string theory, they decided, hey, maybe these aren't rubber bands. Maybe they are blobs or Frisbees or something. And that's when they started to call it Membrane Theory. Then they argued about whether it was membrane theory or music theory or Mandelbrot theory, or something else that started with M, and they decided to just call it M-theory.

The scientists were proud of themselves for coming up with this idea. There was just one little problem. It only worked if the universe contained eleven dimensions. Three dimensions we know about on Earth, plus six more that are all crumpled up like a wadded up ball of newspaper. Plus time, for the tenth dimension. Plus one more that could be called "not time." Maybe. Nobody knows. You have to use your P-branes to think about it. The world actually looks like a swarm of crumpled up wads of newspaper, with eleven faces, which our minds then form into associated objects.

As usual, Jane's friends thought she was wobbling on the edge of nuts. They didn't read science books for fun.

Expanding our options requires thinking outside the box. Or outside the three dimensions we think we see. **Options may exist which we cannot envision unless we believe, create, deal, and reward ourselves into knowing them.** What are those other dimensions? Where are they? What impact do they have on our lives? Might they possibly have the reach of coincidence and circumstance, which we can only imagine?

Skill #6. Adapting to your environment. History is not always a good predictor of the future. Sometimes we finally think we have things figured out, when suddenly, the rules change. It's not fair! Unexpected changes make us uncomfortable. As we plan our lives, events can overtake our plans. We can plan to spend a day working on a project, only to find that the pipes break in the basement, the air conditioning malfunctions, and our neighbor needs help finding his lost dog. The whole day can be re-directed to address a problem, and our workday is shot.

Careful awareness
Success at anything requires that we remain aware of our surroundings, note carefully our environment, and adapt to whatever changes. In any project, success will depend on just a few key factors. If we understand our project well, we will know what those important elements are. We can watch for changes specifically in those elements, because we know they impact the project more than other factors. Decision-making revolves around certain key success factors. **We have to develop the skill to make a decision only at the last minute, when it must be made. It is only at the last minute that all the information is in.** The skill to withhold a decision until it must be made is a matter of comfort with uncertainty. A decision only needs to be made when the next action will impact its outcome. Before that time, if you make a decision, circumstances and events

could change. At the last minute, you have all the information that you can get. It is only then that you must decide. Too many people make decisions far in advance. They close out the option to hear and respond to signals from the universe. **These signals are often called "coincidence," "chance," and "circumstance."**

For example, suppose that you have started a small business. You know you only have enough money to keep the business operating for six months.   After that, unless revenues come in much stronger than expected, you will run out of money. Every month, you check revenues. You see your bank account dwindling. You worry. Should you pull the plug now? Should you start looking for a job? Yet, just as you are thinking it's time to close down, a new contract comes in.

Mark Twain said, "Throughout my life I had many worries, a few of which actually happened."

Too many times, we worry about things thathaven't happened. We waste worry, using it that way. Worry is best used for a short-term problem, where we need focused and concentrated effort to find a solution. If we keep our worry turned on chronically, it deteriorates our ability to work productively.*It also uses up our reserves of adrenaline, and taxes our ability to produce cortisol*[28].

When you make decisions for yourself, you make them within a set of constraints. Look over your writing from the exercises in the previous chapters. Find the part where you described the decisions you made, and the options you chose not to take. The pattern in your decisions may reflect a self-imposed constraint.

---

[28] Adrenaline and cortisol are chemical responses in our body which impact our ability to deal with stress.

Constraints may not be real

People may constrain themselvesin many self-destructive ways. Aunts, uncles, cousins, grandparents, parents, siblings may be so important to them that they say, "my career has to be within driving distance of the locality where I grew up, and where my extended family still lives." This person is making a decision that says, "I prioritize my extended family above my career." This can be the right decision for you if you are making it based on your heart. Too often, however, the decision to stay near family is based on fear, rather than desire. We fear what would happen if we were not surrounded by the family and friends who love us. Who would love us, if not them? We worry that we may not be lovable outside the safety circle of our birth family.[29]

The very tribe we relate to, and from which we derive our self-image, may be the limiting factor that prevents us from seeing ourselves in a better light. Many times, when people try to "better themselves," it is the family and the closest friends who sabotage their efforts. When you try to diet, they encourage you to eat. When you sign up for classes, they think of reasons why you should do something else instead of studying. When you work hard at achievement, they discount your effort. They are the first to point out that it is selfish of you to attend classes after work, instead of visiting your mother's neighbor's cousin's aunt in the hospital. They throw parties when you fail, and throw water on your elation when you succeed. They ask if you have a boyfriend yet, if you are pregnant yet, if you have bought a house yet, or if you have learned to cook yet. Their expectations set your agenda and divert you from personal desires. If you look purposeful, they ask you to pick up their dry cleaning, to keep

---

[29] Home is where, when you have to go there, they have to take you in. Attributed to Mark Twain.

you from your agenda. We each come from some social sub-culture.

To varying degrees, these structures attempt to shape our behavior and force conformance to the set of rules the tribe expects. Conformity with the social structure is sanctioned, both positively and negatively. If you do as expected, you are "loved." As hard as it is to accept, you don't need that version of love.

Love is unconditional
Someone who loves you wants you to have your own version of life, not a structure that they believe is best for you. Love is unconditional. Your children will give it to you, but it is hard to find from other adults. Best you try to give it to your children, just as they give it to you. If your parents, spouse, extended family, and friends, don't have it to offer, you can love them unconditionally. At the same time, you do not have to sacrifice your identity to their brand of social sanctioning. Love does not require that you conform to expectations. It isn't withdrawn based on your behavior. There should be no action you can take (short of harming them) which will cause another person to stop loving you, if they ever loved you in the first place. If you've considered in your heart what you really want, and it pleases you, then approval of your family is simply not required.

Follow your heart
Human beings are social animals. Follow your heart, and when you find your bliss, your tribe will already be there. Others will accept and love you, if the society into which you were born, will not. The limitations set by your social sub-culture are artificial. People love you and you love them back. But, hold your standard of love to one type: unconditional. No strings attached. Let go of

the ties to patterns of behavior that define you to a sub-culture. Then you will be free to make a wider range of choices.

You Can Choose Your Friends

We just described the tribe to which you were born and said you may need to reject the sanctions of that social culture. But wherever you go, there will be a social structure. Every group of human beings forms a tribe, a sub-culture of its own. Each group has a set of sanctions, which it enforces, in order to become a 'member'. You cannot get away from these social orders, as long as you must interact with other human beings. The question is: will the sanctions of the tribe you have chosen help you to reach your goal, or will those sanctions harm your achievement? Is the tribe you have chosen a group of druggies? Are they alcohol drinkers? Are they fundamentalist extremists of any variety? Most importantly, do they like you? Do they accept you as you are, and with your flaws? You can find your tribe, and the tribe can uplift you.

Let's Review

1. The values instilled in you by your family may be good, or may be harmful, to your success. These values are now programmed into you as memes, so you must examine each one of them, or you will be a puppet to their constraints all your life.

2. Family and friends may love you unconditionally, but it is more likely that they will love you with "strings attached." Unconditional love is a human goal, but it is something we are working *toward;* it is not a given in life. When it comes time to look out for yourself, it is only you who knows your inner heart.

3. Your tribe will attempt to hold you back or hold you down, if your true will is not aligned with the will of the group. You must recognize that your self-interest needs to be foremost in your own mind. Conversely, the right tribe can uplift you and help you rise to your full potential.

4. The filters, which you build for your own perception, may be keeping you from seeing the path to your success. You have to become capable of seeing more objectively.

5. To expand your options, see everyone you know as a potential member of your tribe. Select those who assist you in achieving your goals as the ones you keep near you. Keep your mind open and active to possibilities.

6. To adjust to your environment, watch for the coincidence and circumstance which may come your way. It is your programmed memes that may prevent you from seeing the coincidence. Check your premises and recognize your self-interest.

7. Decisions need not be made until it is time to act. If you expand your comfort with uncertainty, you can wait until all the information is in before you act. You will never have perfect information, but you can act on what is known at the time the decision must be made.

8. You must become comfortable with the idea that your decisions are not right or wrong. They are the best you could do at the time, with what you knew. You select a path, you observe what happens, you use the feedback, and you make a new choice based on what you learned.

Self-interest is not greed. It is a long-term outlook toward your final destiny. It is only true self-interest if it considers all the competing forces, obligations, interested parties, and relationships. Your decisions won't be perfect. They will just be the best you can do at the time you had to do it.

Exercises for Chapter 6

Up to this point, we have set goals for each area of balance. We defined measurable and specific tasks for those goals. We tested the goals and their tasks against our legacy statement, and prioritized them in relationship to each other. We assigned accomplishment of those tasks to timeframes in our lives. Having done all that, we are ready to take the next step: expanding our ideas about what can and cannot be done, and adjusting to the environment around us.

In working toward our goals, we sometimes feel that we have met obstacles that make it difficult to continue. It could be tempting to feel defeated. Feelings of defeat are not helpful and serve no useful purpose. Rather than accept those feelings, we have to re-examine our goals and reconsider what may possibly be done as a workaround, a new approach, or an alternate path. If necessary, we might even re-define the goal, so that a path can be found that will lead to success.

Sometimes in managing a life, we decide that a solution will "satisfice". That is, it could be possible that a solution is good enough. Maybe we decide that the price of the original goal is too high, and we will be just as satisfied with a goal that is less lofty. All accomplishment, and all worthy endeavors, carry a pricetag. If the pricetag is more than our personal value of that goal, then it is better to change the goal, than to pay a price too high. This often happens when we have multiple goals for the different balance areas of our lives, and the goals conflict.

Suppose, for example, you wanted to complete a task before you had to go away on a business trip. At the last minute, your sister, who lives six hours away, calls to say she and her husband will be in town and wants to stay at your house for the weekend. Your plan was to work all weekend, and you know her visit will prevent that from happening. However, you also have a goal to improve your relationship with your sister, and turning her away when she wants to be with you would conflict with that goal. You recognize that her call is unusual, which makes it an act of chance and circumstance. You don't want to turn away chance and circumstance. You adjust your plan, and say yes, you would love for her to come for the weekend. You reschedule your work and rethink your deadline. That weekend, in talking with your sister, she says exactly the right thing to make you think of a new approach to your work problem. It turns out to be a lucky coincidence, which would not have occurred if she had not visited you at exactly that time.

Although you have committed to plan your work and work your plan, you don't want to go so far with your commitment that you fail to take advantage of changes in the context and environment in which you live. *In dealing with the universe, we accept responsibility to interact with coincidence as it comes our way. That coincidence may be the opportunity we seek.*

In this exercise, we review the work we have done to date. To add expanding options and adjusting to the environment, we will introduce a new form. This form is called the T-chart. Your immune system has T-cells, which it calls into action when a threat is perceived. Your T-chart is like those T-cells. You only use it when you are feeling confused or uncertain. It is a defensive tool, to help you through anxiety.

The T-chart looks like this:

Figure 6

Things I know	Things I don't know

The left column is labeled: Things I know. The right column is labeled: Things I don't know. When you are faced with a situation which causes you to feel worried, anxious, or confused, get out your T-chart. Begin to list those things which are facts about the situation in the left column. List those things which are unproven assumptions in the right column. For example, suppose you are worried about an upcoming layoff at your office. It's causing you to lose sleep. You feel achy. You're getting headaches. Rather than reach for a sleeping pill, try the T-chart.

Figure 7. Example of a T-chart

Things I know	Things I don't know
1. There is going to be a layoff at work.	1. If I am on the layoff list.
2. I love my job and don't want to lose it. I do it very well.	2. If merit will matter when layoff candidates are chosen.
3. I don't have any savings. If I lose my job, I'm 90 days away	3. If my parents can help me out.

from homelessness.	
4. The stress and worry are impacting my health.	4. Why I don't start looking for a new job right now instead of waiting for the axe to fall.

After you fill out this form, you realize that the action of looking for a new job would help you calm your anxiety.

Continue to Chapter 7: Reclaiming your health

Every human being is the author of his own health or disease.

--- Buddha

Chapter 7. Reclaiming your health

Paying Attention and Rewarding What Matters.Without our health, nothing else will be important. Learning why we do what we do. Recognizing the payoff. Making sure we get paid for the things we really want. Putting an end to paying the piper. Calling your own tune.

In this chapter, we will cover Skill #7, Paying attention and Skill #8: Rewarding achievements.

What have we learned so far?
The goal
The structure
The balance
The measurable outcomes
Who loves you
Your tribe and its expectations
How to reconcile uncertainty and calm anxiety

Now you can tell what must happen to get you where you want to go. The next skill to learn is how to pay attention to the signals that the universe sends. In FantasyLand, the universe believes in you, interacts with you, cares about you, and considers you a meaningful part of its own existence. There, chance and circumstance rise up to meet your path. You will ask a question, and then turn on the radio. Because of this rule of coincidence, the next sentence that comes out of the radio will be the answer to your question. That's how you know you're on track. Coincidence is your friend. Sometimes this coincidence is called synchronicity.

Synchronicity

When you were off your path, the magnetic field of the Earth fought you. Accidents happened. Now, you recognize that there are no accidents. You take circumstance as guidance. You see coincidence as direction. This is where our tenets of belief come into play. You began with a dream. You turned it into a goal. You added faith to your dream, faith that the universe would consider you to have purpose and meaning in its plan. You called on the creative force of the universe, to be part of your purpose. You made the deal, and agreed to its price. If you have paid attention to the interaction between you and the universe, now it is time to recognize and reward your actions.

Skill #7: Paying attention

In the old days, your personal rewards came from the social sanctions of your tribe (your family and sub-culture). These sanctions were designed to control your behavior, and keep you "in-line" with your lot in life. But you do not need to be "in-line." You need to be "online." Online with the Universe. To help yourself stay on path, to avoid the fears, the anxieties, and the stresses of uncertainty, you must make small rewards for yourself. Small rewards that tell your inner child she is loved. When you cannot reconcile the conflict between societal expectations and your destiny, you live under stress. The following is a true story about something that happened on Earth.

The consequences of conflict

Master of My Universe

The young woman curled into a fetal state, as the father she adored berated her. "I will not have my daughter behaving as a trollop," he thundered. Her mother was no better. "How dare you bring shame to this family?" her socially-correct mother hissed. "Ladies of our class do not perform the work of servants." Her wealthy family introduced her to suitors, sent her on trips around Europe, and otherwise expressed their dismay at her desire to follow her own path. The young girl began with fainting spells. Shortness of breath and heart palpitations continued. Nausea at the sight of food. Weakness, headache, non-specific pain. Doctors were called. Prescriptions were written. Eventually, a nervous breakdown followed.

But when the war came, **Florence Nightingale** overcame the brutal hostility of her wealthy family. She followed her destiny to establish the Nightingale Fund for the training of nurses. She established concepts of statistical analysis of healthcare, exhibiting her decidedly non-female abilities in mathematics. She performed as a shining star in the healthcare field, when nursing as a profession was considered a low-class activity. But her inner conflict about the values of her wealthy family continued to plague her mind. She came home after the war a heroine. She was recognized for her work to instill practices of sanitation in army hospitals. Her name graced buildings and training programs. But less than two years after returning to her home after the war, she became bedridden herself. And she remained ill for thirty years thereafter.

It is difficult to overcome the disappointment of a loved parent. Sanitation in hospitals is a good thing. But inner conflict about the disapproval of others can overcome it. Florence Nightingale studied and made tremendously valuable contributions in health care and statistics. With statistics, comes probability.

Probability of the Whole

Even though I am female, my education is in mathematics and engineering. I've always been interested in puzzles. How do things fit together? What do they look like when they are taken apart? What are the components of a problem? What causes an action, and triggers a reaction? As a young girl, I would actually read math books. I still do read math books and science books. In fact, most of my ideas in this book came from science books. You can see them in the Bibliography. Odd, I know. Statistically, girls aren't as interested in math as boys are. That, of course, is the point.

Statistics aren't about individuals. They are about the group as a whole. One of the things you learn when you study mathematics is that **the probability of the whole carries no information about the specifics of the one**. That means, you can't look at any one incident and definitively know anything about it, if your only information is its probability factor. In your life, you are not the average of anything. The "average" is just all the numbers added together and divided by the number of items added. It's possible that none of the items is actually the same as the "average." It's possible that half the numbers are 10 and half the numbers are 5, and the average is 7.5, but no numbers are 7.5. You could be acting on false premises, if you make decisions based on the "average" of anything. You are not the average. You are the Specific One, and nobody can predict where you personally will fall on the Bell Curve. Everybody else can want one thing, but you personally can want something else.

Bias is a mathematical term

Master of My Universe

If you are a girl, you can like mathematics, even though there is a lower probability that you will like it. If you are a boy, you can desire to join the ballet, even though the probability is lower that you would want to. These are things we generally know, at a thinking level.However, at a deeper level, in our subconscious mind, we often accept these biases and prejudices, based on probabilities of the many. These concepts of probability carry over into all aspects of our lives, and they are often the dream-killers that cause TRY to give up aspirations and dreams.

Four out of five small businesses fail, your Uncle Charlie says. So TRY gives up on the idea of starting a small business.   Never mind that her small business would be the one that succeeds. Uncle Charlie, and the societal sanctions of her family, tell her not to try. It's too risky. Get a job.

Nine out of ten applicants to Harvard are rejected, your brother, Reggie, tells you. So TRY throws away the application and goes to Local State University instead.

Eighty percent of people diagnosed with this type of cancer die within two years, the doctor informs you.   So TRY lays down on the sofa and starts marking her days off on the calendar.

Why doesn't TRY expect to be in the twenty percent that live?

I guess I'll see if I can call my TRY, (whose name is Gem), from my inner mind software, and see if I can get her answer. To call on the aspects of my inner mind software, I have to put myself into a meditative state, where I can hear their answers. I do that easily now, but in the beginning, I had to do it more formally. I was still learning how to call on my inner mind, by setting up a quiet meditation. I used a pleasantly scented tea and a colored candle. I sat quietly, and kept distractions away. I centered my mind and waited. Gem answered when I used a red candle and a ginger tea.

I'll ask Gem to speak now.

Gem, why do most people's TRY assume that they will be in the groups of the large probability, instead of the exception to the rule?

Gem: Because people want friends, Jane. They want to be normal.

Interesting answer. "Normal" is a mathematical word. To "normalize" something is to make it aligned to the same rational baseline. As human beings, we want to be accepted. We strive to be "normal." So when our inner mind software hears that the probability of the group is X, there is a part of us that wants to be accepted, and behave like most others. Gem, or TRY, the inner child, chooses acceptance, normalization, and "averageness". TRY won't fight statistics.

Fortunately, our mind has multiple aspects. While Gem is the inner child, there is also Rationality, whose name is Ariana, at play. Let's see how Ariana would respond to the same question. Ariana, for me, is invoked with a light green candle and a mint tea.

Ariana, what is your answer? Why do most people assume they will be in the groups of the large probability, instead of assuming they will be the exception to the rule?

Ariana: I don't know that they do, Jane. They may initially have an emotional reaction like Gem's. However, after they've recovered from the initial disturbing emotion, I think most people will look for a logical solution to their problems, and work at overcoming them.

As you can see, Ariana thinks rationally about everything. She is not emotional at all. She lays out the pros and cons of an issue, and addresses it with what she has, where she is, in the present and right now. Because I have both Gem, my inner child, and Ariana, my rationality, at play, I can have a debate with myself about the right course of action to take. Everyone has this ability. It's usually called "thinking." But there are not just two considerations here in my mind. I'm not just thinking with my inner child and my rationality. I also have five more aspects of mind: survival, historic experience, connectedness, conscience, and intelligence. Let's ask each of them what they think about this topic.

I usually call Shadow, the survival instinct, with a dark blue candle and a cup of roasted chicory. How would you respond if the doctor told you eighty percent of the people who had a type of cancer you had, will die within two years?

Shadow: I would call the doctor a nincompoop and declare that I would defy the statistics, Jane. That's my job. I don't roll over easily when someone challenges my right to live.

But, most people don't do that, Shadow. At least, eighty percent of people don't do that. Let's call on Toepia, the historic experience, and ask her why not. I call Toepia with an orange candle and a scent of wintergreen. Toepia, why do most people accept the doctor's diagnosis of two years' to live? Why don't they bring their Shadow forward to fight for their lives?

Toepia: Saying 'you have two years to live' is a hex, Jane. Voodoo. When an authority figure like a doctor tells us that we are probably going to die within two years, how do we feel? The deepest part of the primitive amygdala in the mind feels compelled to accept that death sentence. The survival instinct may not be active, in today's modern society. We aren't accustomed to invoking survival. In many people, Shadow has lost his strength because he is no longer used. Instead, we are accustomed to behaving as authority figures tell us. Doctors are these authority figures, and their pronouncements are as good as executioners' axes. People want to be liked and accepted, at their innermost core. Our current social structure tells us to do as we are told by the authorities, if we want to gain approval. We do want to gain approval, so we will do what the doctor says, and obediently die.

Good grief, Toepia! That sounds horrible! You're saying that the doctors are hexing people, and that's why they die of cancer! How ridiculous! Let's ask Katrina what that all means. Katrina is the superego, or the conscience. I call Katrina with a light purple candle and a scent of vanilla and cinnamon. Katrina, how is it possible that people can forego their own survival instinct and accept a death sentence, based on a doctor's hex?

Katrina: No, Jane, I wouldn't look at it that way. People don't cause their own cancer, and they can't think it away or wish it away. You can't blame the doctors for eighty percent of the people dying. After all, many of those people are just children. Hexes are not real. People should call on their survival instinct and do whatever they can to fight off the disease, but too often they don't do all that is possible. I certainly do all I can to help people exercise and diet correctly, but it is difficult to deal with all the conflicts and emotions people carry inside. In the end, it is what it is. We do what we can do, and the rest is up to our Destiny.

Bee? You are the connectedness of all of us. I call you with a yellow candle and an echinacea tea with lemon and honey. What do you have to say about this contention between Toepia, the historic memory, who says the doctors' pronouncement is a hex, and Katrina, the conscience, who says it is destiny?

Bee: We are all one, Jane. Cancer lives in all of us, all the time. It is a normal process of the body. Our immune system, which is a shared immune system with all of society, is designed to detect abnormality outside a range, and correct it. When the immune system of an individual is not operating properly, a cancer can get out of control. A healthy immune system handles the cancer cells on its own. The question is not who gets cancer; it is whose immunity is compromised by emotional response, by physical abuse, or by genetic design of the Creator. So for 100% of people, it could be destiny, it could be a hex. I don't know. Nor do you. Nor does anyone else.

Then let me call on Q, the Intelligence, to sort this out and summarize. I call Q with a deep purple candle and a scent of frankincense and myrrh. Q, what does this all mean? Why do most people respond to a diagnosis of disease with deep depression and a sense of hopelessness?

Q: Because people want to live. A sense of meaning and continuity is required. People have no desire to live a meaningless life, and a time limit on that living adds a deadline. When there is a deadline, people believe they will not achieve the meaning, and this causes hopelessness. Without hope, people spiral into despair. Then they are unable to live happily and productively with whatever time they have left until the deadline. It's built into the software of the soul. If you cannot achieve your destiny, then the soul wishes itself dead, so it can start over with a new life and have a better chance at reaching the goal next time.

The soul wishes itself dead? So it can start over? What do you mean, "start over"?

Q: The soul lives in FantasyLand, Jane. In FantasyLand, there is a Reset button. You can pick a new Avatar and start again. If the Soul is certain it cannot reach its destiny in this lifetime, it becomes eager to end it.

Master of My Universe

Oh, I remember that story!

The FantasyLand Story

To begin a new life in a new world, you must register by applying for citizenship at the embassy. You must also define your character and choose your Home Base. When you have registered, defined your avatar, and picked a Home Base, you are ready to begin.

Defining your character
Defining your character is very much like getting to know your new baby. You have to pick an appearance for your avatar by selecting a symbol. You have to name your avatar. Then you have to select a Temperament and some Talents. Your new baby is born with a Temperament and Talents, and so is your new avatar. Once you select your Symbol, Name, Temperament and Talents, they will stay with you through all your lives. Your Temperament will define what powers you have; your Talents will determine what jobs you might do.

Besides selecting your Symbol, Name, Temperament, and Talents, you also need to know what Values you have been taught by your parents. To do this, you have to get a randomly assigned Family Background. This will give you your Values set for this life. Unlike your Temperament and Talents, which stay with you through all lives, your Values set is re-determined each time you die and get reborn. Your parents teach your Values to you, and they may be good for you or not. If you have been taught Values that are bad for your Karma, you have to change your values while playing the game.

The last piece of defining your avatar is applying for a job. You apply for a job after you have determined all other parts of your character. To apply, first you have to be qualified by having the correct Talents. Then, you have to see if there is a job opening. If there are no job openings for anything you are qualified for, you must be a Wastrel.

Q whispered into Jane's ear while she slept. He wanted her to understand the meaning of the story. He said:

So, you see, Jane, your soul lives in FantasyLand. No matter what the rules of Earth may be, your soul doesn't follow them. Your soul believes in the laws of FantasyLand, where there is no evaporation after death. Nothing in FantasyLand disappears. Energy becomes matter. Matter becomes energy. It is a quantum world, not a Newtonian physics world. Your soul believes death has a reset button. If your soul detects despair, meaninglessness, hopelessness, lack of purpose, and deeply felt emptiness, it will search for the escape hatch. Your immune system will turn off the defenses and you will slide into the next world. This is the ever-present danger, Jane. You must preserve the hopefulness of your soul.

When Jane awoke, she felt driven to learn more about how the immune system works. Jane felt driven to resolve the conflicts and disturbing perspectives which had been brought up by her inner conversations. She researched obsessively. When she was finished, she told her friends this:

What Makes Us Heal

It is our own immune system that heals us; any form of medicine or drug does not heal us. Drugs, prescribed by doctors in the Western world, interact with our body's cellular structure, and suppress symptoms of disease. Sometimes, our immune system heals the underlying disease, and the suppression of the symptoms, which was caused by the drugs, doesn't do any harm. Other times, the suppression of the symptoms causes the body to move the disease somewhere else. A different symptom appears, requiring our doctors to give us new drugs for the new symptom. This is why so many Americans today sit down to their meals with an array of eight to fifteen pills to take before eating. Each pill to suppress a symptom causes new symptoms, which are then "corrected" with another pill. Of course, there are times when suppression of the symptom is critically important, and it's good we have doctors available to help when that happens. It's also good that we have doctors to set broken bones, or perform organ replacement surgery when our immunity has really allowed things to get out of whack. Doctors do some good things. However, healing people is not among them. That's because "healing" is not done by doctors or by drugs. It is done by the body's immune system.

But, don't take my word for it
You may not understand how the immune system works, or that it is the method designed by nature to heal us. The following story is not a story of "FantasyLand." This is a story of Earth, documented in mainstream science. In fact, much of it is printed in the NIH Publication No. 07-5423, titled "Understanding the Immune System." I'm telling you this because this story is so outlandish, you might think I made it up. No, I didn't make it up! The National Institutes of Health, in cooperation with mainstream scientists, made it up!

From the NIH pamphlet[30]: "Disease-causing microbes attempting to get into the body must first get past the body's external armor, usually the skin or cells lining the internal passageways. The skin provides an imposing barrier to invading microbes. It is generally penetrable only through tiny cuts or abrasions. . . To fend off the threatening horde, the body has devised astonishingly intricate defenses.

How the Body's Immune System Works
The National Institutes of Health says our body's immune system is a complex network of specialized cells and organs that has evolved to defend the body against "foreign" invaders. According to this world-view, our body fights off microbes, like bacteria and viruses, which are not identified as "self."

Demon: Hold it. Hold the phone.

Gem: What?

Demon: We have thousands of bacteria in us all the time. We are a zoo of little buggies! Which ones are self and which ones are not self?

Gem: You got me, Big D. I'm just tellin' ya what the NIH says.

So the NIH says the immune system is like our own personal military defense army. It detects a non-self entity, and it mobilizes

---

[30]NIH publication 93-529, Jan 1993, Understanding the Immune System

troops to go destroy it. But the immune system can get broken. It can turn on you. It accidentally thinks self is not self, and it attacks our own bodies. That's how we get allergies, lupus, eczema, rheumatoid arthritis, AIDS, and some cancers. Plus, anything else called autoimmune disease.

Demon: So the immune system, which is what we depend on to heal, can get so confused it makes us sick?

Gem: That's what the scientists say.

Demon: That sounds like Pasteur's germ theory.

Gem: Once these scientists decide something is true, every other scientist after that has to say the same thing. That's their system.

Demon: What if one of them disagrees?

Here we see that the National Institutes of Health describes our immune system as an internal army, bent on fighting off enemies that would cause us discomfort. This army apparently has many types of soldiers in it, and drugs prescribed by doctors are then logically designed to assist this army to do a better job. In the end, however, the army does the work to heal. The drugs just make the patient more comfortable by suppressing the symptoms. *But, wait a minute. What are those symptoms?*

Coughing is used by the body to expel undesirable objects from the airways. That's a good thing, isn't it? Did you want to keep the objects stuck in there?

Okay, then there's fever. Well, fever is designed to heat up the environment, to force out the problems by burning them out. You didn't want to keep those problems, did you?

Next is pain. Well, yes, we do want to suppress pain. But many of the drugs that are painkillers act by diverting serotonin, the hormone that gives a pleasurable feeling, from the stomach to the brain. That means we end up with an upset stomach and digestive problems. Digestive problems, over time, prevent our organs from receiving the nutrients they require. Over time, the organs degenerate. Eventually, some doctor identifies them as a disease listed in the disease catalog.The next thing you know, you are taking a drug for something that originated from the upset in the balance of serotonin to your stomach!

This is the main tenet of Western medicine: ignore hormonal imbalance until it becomes something that can be identified as a known disease for which we have a drug available. Prescribe the drug. Treat the new symptoms that develop as separate diseases, for which we can match another drug. Deny that hormonal imbalance is a result of a combination of nutrient deficiencies, emotional disturbance, and toxic absorption. Suppress information that fails to support the accepted theory. Rinse and repeat. Does it work?

Yes, according to double-blind tests done by . . . the drug companies. And yet, there is much conflicting information about those tests. Much disturbing data. Suppression of conflicting information is the typical behavior of people in groups. It follows from tenet #4: You'll see it when you believe it, and tenet #5: What gets rewarded gets repeated.

We need to believe

We believe that the doctors know what they are doing. We need to believe, because they are the authorities from which we must get help. It is their intention to help. They personally believe they are helping. Because we all believe, then we see it. It looks like help. Unless, of course, you have fibromyalgia, chemical sensitivities, serious allergies, rheumatoid arthritis, diabetes, cancer, HIV Aids, or any of the multitude of named diseases, which are associated with weakened immune system response. Then, your weakened immunity is not doing its job of healing. That's where you first realize: the immune system heals, not the doctor.

What gets rewarded gets repeated
The doctors, pharmaceutical companies, and insurance companies, meanwhile, are repeating those actions for which they are being rewarded. As we all do. If you were a corporate manager, your job would be to meet your goals. If you meet your goals, you get paid and promoted. The reward systems for Western medicine actors are complex, but they are profit-motivated. Big Pharma gets rewarded by introducing drugs that lots of people can take for a very long time. Insurance companies get rewarded by inventing excuses for why they are failing to pay claims, weeding out the sick, and ensuring that they charge more in monthly fees than they are required to pay out.

Doctors, however, are a special case. To become a doctor, people chose a career path that was demanding. Their trials to get the title of doctor were long and exhausting. Being a good doctor is important to them. Each of them may have chosen that path for the reward of helping others. But when they made it to the end of the long road to their degree, they learned that their pay depended on seeing more patients and spending less time with each one. Nobody, in that system, gets rewarded with money for healing anybody.

And the patients? For some people, being sick means getting attention. We all enjoy getting attention. This is why it is very, very important that we think carefully about what is rewarding in our lives. It can be tempting to lie down in bed and let others take care of us.

This is the frontline
Time after time, we see that interference with the body's symptoms is the same thing as interference with that immune system army's frontline action. Suppression of our symptoms has a good chance of slowing down, or even stopping, an actual healing action on the part of our immune system. Maybe the best thing we can do when we are sick is to just go to bed and wait it out, with the help of some soothing herbal teas. At least that way, we won't be doing any harm to ourselves, and our strong army immune system will fix the problem.

Jane felt queasy and disturbed after she heard herself talking to her friends about this. She felt conflict between her faith in the authority of doctors and her own experience with being ill. She remembered the agony of fighting with the insurance company when her doctor prescribed a certain pill that the insurance company said was too expensive. Because Jane was developing experience in hearing her inner mind aspects speak, she recognized these queasy feelings as a warning signal. She used her skill #7, Paying Attention, to acknowledge this emotion and explore its root cause. Jane sat down at her computer. She appreciated having the tool of the Internet at her fingertips. She breathed deeply and waited for her inner mind to speak.

Deeply inside her mind, Jane heard herself whisper:
"Do flies cause garbage?"

Jane typed that phrase into the Google Search box. After a little surfing, she was lead to a website about Antoine Bechamp and Louis Pasteur. It was written in French, so Jane decided to take a nap. She couldn't read it. While Jane slept, Gem whispered in her dreams:

How We Heal: Do Flies Cause Garbage?[31]
In FantasyLand, medicine focuses on returning the body to balance. The philosophy of medical treatment revolves around restoring the healthy alkaline environment of the body's nature. Strengthening the immune system is the doctor's goal. Doctors in FantasyLand believe the body heals itself, given an environment rich in nutrients and free of toxins. No one in FantasyLand believes that germs on a doorknob cause a cold. After all, many people touch that doorknob, but few of them come down with a cold. Gem wonders why the systems of healing are so different, between Earth and FantasyLand. Ariana picks up the story:

In the 1840's, there were two rival scientists named Louis Pasteur and Antoine Bechamp. They both lived on Earth, in France. They knew each other and competed to have their theories accepted in the scientific community. They both wanted to cure disease. Bechamp's idea was that our bodies are full of many types of bacteria and viruses all the time. They only harm us when their internal eco-systems get out of balance. Normally, the bacteria fight each other, maintaining a positive environment, which keeps us healthy. It is only when the balance tips

---

[31]For more information, follow the links from http://Dminoz.com/bechamp/

toward the acidic environment that our natural immunity is weakened.

Oh, Gem interrupts. That's like plants! Plants grow healthy and strong when their soil has the right balance of acid versus alkaline. Then they don't need pesticides, because pests only eat them when they are weak and sick.

Yes, continued Ariana. The secret to healing, in the memes of FantasyLand, center around restoring the balance of the immune system. This is done through rest, exercise, cleansing to remove toxins, and proper food and nutrition. Sometimes we use naturally grown herbs to assist the body's defenses temporarily. The body heals itself, given the appropriate environment.

But Pasteur said, yes, rest, exercise, and a healthy lifestyle are good things, but the real problem is germs. Germs are foreign invaders, which enter the body and have to be defeated. If we can find the right drugs to kill the germs, then we can cure disease. Whenever a body is diseased, we can see germs in the diseased spot.

Bechamp said, 'Whenever you pile up garbage, you see flies on the garbage pile. Do flies cause garbage?' Bechamp believed the germs were just there to help decompose the dead cells.For many years, the people were confused. Which of these famous and important scientists was correct?

Then, after eighty years of confusion, a British scientist named Sir Fleming accidentally found some mold growing in his lab. He noticed that the mold killed the bacteria he was growing. It took ten more years before people on Earth started using the mold to cure people. The mold was called penicillin. It worked so well to cure so many diseases; it seemed to prove Pasteur's theory.Quickly, investors started pouring money into drug companies. A whole industry formed from the concept of making and selling germ-fighting drugs. They wanted to cure people! But, this was the important part. They started using plants to build the drugs. Willow bark, eucalyptus, ephedra, lobelia, comfrey, valerian. But, they said, we couldn't use the plants plain, right out of nature. We have to change them, so we can get a patent, so nobody else can use our drugs. Then our investors can get a higher profit than they would get just by putting money in a bank. So all the plants that people used to cure were packaged up and sold to drug companies. Then the people couldn't get them anymore, unless they paid.

Gem interrupted: But this didn't happen in FantasyLand, Mommy!

Ariana: No, sweetheart. In FantasyLand, people don't want to make money. Money increases Karmic debt. The people in FantasyLand just wanted to cure people. Curing people reduces Karmic debt. They appreciated penicillin, and used the mold right along with their herbal remedies. But they didn't discount the theory of Bechamp. They observed that lifestyle and natural living worked best.

When Jane awoke, she practiced her skill at paying attention by writing down her dreams in a journal. That day, she had these thoughts. She couldn't resist calling her friends and telling them all about what she was thinking.

Jane told her friends:
Our immunity isimpacted by physical contacts, like toxins in our food, pollutants in our air, or depleted nutrients in our soil.

However, our emotional health has an even greater influence on our immunity. Stress triggers immune reactions. Even words, spoken in a way that upset us, cause emotional response, which initiates hormonal action, which kicks off the internal chemistry that weakens immunity. A person, who is feeling "low", is literally short of some internal chemical balance. It is even possible to get this emotional chemical reaction at such a subconscious level that we are not aware it happened. For example, there was a time when I was carefully monitoring everything I touched or ate, to look for allergic triggers. I was having violent coughing fits, which appeared to be allergic reactions. Allergy testing from a doctor showed me to be allergic to just about everything. On a few occasions, while I was doing this careful monitoring, there appeared to be no other explanation but that something someone said produced anxiety. It was the anxiety, tipping over my allergic threshold level, which caused the coughing and sneezing fit. There were even certain people that, when I spoke to them on the phone, I couldn't complete the conversation because I would start to cough. Maybe no doctor will tell you that your emotional level is contributing to your immune system's inability to heal your disease. But *face* it. You already know.

From <u>Anti-Cancer: A New Way of Life</u>[32]we learn that we can keep cancer from getting out of control by strengthening our immune system. We learn there are five critical elements to controlling the cancers that come and go in all of us, as part of the maintenance function in our immunity. First, we learn to remove chemical cleaning products, pesticides, insecticides, para-

---

[32]Servan-Schreiber, D. Anti-Cancer: a new way of life, page 82 insert.

bens, phthalates, and other industrial chemicals from our environment. When you read labels, you may find these things are in your shampoo, your cleansers, your soaps, and many other household products.

Second, we learn to drink filtered water, eat grass-fed, organic animal products, increase our Omega-3's, decrease our Omega-6's, and balance our diet with clean, organic, anti-cancer foods such as turmeric and broccoli.

Third, we learn to get twenty minutes of sunlight and thirty minutes of physical activity daily.

Fourth, we learn to practice some method of relaxation and self-centering technique.

Fifth, and finally, we learn to resolve emotional trauma. This emotional trauma can be so deeply buried, we do not consciously remember it. This is where the aspects of the inner mind help us to integrate our emotions into our consciousness. This is where we must learn to hear our inner child speak.

Skill #8: Reward what matters
This is why balance in our lives is not optional. Sometimes we will focus intensely on a career, to the exclusion of balance in our lives. Working 80 or more hours a week, commuting long hours in heavy traffic, traveling for our jobs: these things can leave us unable to do anything except hit Happy Hour, and come home to go to bed so we can start the work routine all over the next day.

Growing up in poverty, there was a time in my life when I felt so invigorated and motivated about my high-flying career that I worked more than 80 hours a week. I traveled so much that I hardly came home. I had a live-in housekeeper to take care of my children, and to make meals for my family. When I came home, my clothes were all neatly laundered, folded, and put away in my drawers. I didn't have to clean my house, do my laundry, shop for groceries, or prepare our meals. I had a secretary at the office, and a housekeeper at home. A gardener came by to mulch and trim. *Until you've had that, you have no idea how messed up that is.*

If you were born with personal servants, you may never realize that it is literally a handicap. Life, and the living of it, encompasses maintenance activity. Like sleep, dreaming, and raw vegetables, the minor maintenances of life are necessary for a complete experience. The immune system conducts maintenance activities, too. The state we call cancer, is among them.

According to Anti-Cancer: A New Way of Life[33], a research team at Duke University proved that baby rats isolated from their mothers would stop growing. They would grow again if the scientists touched them in a loving manner with a wet brush. The scientists say the part of the genome required to produce growth enzymes would turn off if the baby weren't touched. They concluded that touching babies in a loving way is necessary for their endocrine system to function.

Demon: What I don't get is, how does the endocrine system know if the touch is loving?

---

[33]Servan-Schreiber, D. Anti-cancer: a new way of life, page 181

Ariana: The endocrine system is controlled by the pituitary gland. The third eye. It connects to the primitive brain. Love is very clear to it. The endocrine system is in charge of paying attention. Let's ask Gem to tell us more about the endocrine system. I believe I see Gem playing with Jane's mind right now.

Gem whispers to Jane: Emotion is chemical[34]
Sweat. Now, sweat is one thing glands do. You can't see that, either. Then there's lots of chemical flushes that go on you can't see, and they make you happy or sad.

Katrina: You shouldn't whisper to Jane, Gem. It makes her anxious.

Okay, Katrina. I'll just say it loud, with my outside voice.

The endocrine system is the chakras[35], Jane. The pituitary gland, otherwise known as the third eye, controls the signals that tell hormones to release. It connects your mind to your body. When you feel fear, guilt, or anxiety, the pituitary gland tells your thyroid gland to speed up your metabolism. That way, you can run away faster.

Or, your pituitary gland might tell your adrenal gland to make more cortisol. If you had a really stressful childhood, you might have used up all your strength making too much cortisol. You could be all tired out all the time and not be able to make cortisol

---

[34]According to *You, the Owner's Manual*, "emotions control our hormones through biochemical changes in the brain." Page 294

[35] Chakras are concentrated energy centers in the body, as described in ancient Sanskrit texts.

any more. Or, you could get scared and make so much epinephrine that your face gets red and your heart races.

Maybe your kidneys are worried that you don't have enough "breathing room." Then they might raise your blood pressure to get more oxygen in your blood. That would make your pancreas get mad, and stop putting sugar in your blood. So you see, this stuff is all connected to your unconscious, associative mind. Emotions make hormones release; hormone changes affect your feelings. It's one big, inter-connected feedback loop. It goes around and around in circles. Then you spiral.

This is why I drink ginger and cinnamon tea.

Jane awoke with these thoughts in her head:

So, where do these emotions come from? Why do we get all weepy when we hear a sad story? Why do we cry at a wedding?

Unconscious disease
Cues from our environment invoke associations we have stored subconsciously. These clues invoke associations in our minds, which send feelings to our consciousness[36]. These feelings also have the power to trigger hormonal release, as do all emotional responses. Our association patterns extend, subconsciously, to our relationships with people.

By those precepts, it's possible to have a dysfunctional family or work situation, which causes a chronic disease.You may not consciously understand that you are chronically annoyed. The pattern of your relationship could be so embedded, subconsciously,

---

[36]In *Blink, the Power of Thinking Without Thinking*, we learn that our subconscious minds pick up clues from our environment.

that you don't have the ability to identify what is wrong. But, your pituitary gland remembers. It notifies your endocrine system to keep things out of whack! Hormones release; emotions flare. One more time, there you are in the emergency room.

Demon: I once had a nasty flare-up of eczema. My leg looked like I'd laid it on the barbecue grill! The dermatologist said, 'It's just dry skin. Spread this petroleum-based cream on it.' Nobody said nothin' about emotional causes.

Jane said to her friends: Now that I am paying attention to my own thoughts, I have noticed I can calm my symptoms. Instead of waiting for my headache to become a throbbing migraine, I take notice as soon as I feel a ping. I breathe deeply, stop what I'm doing, and let the intelligence of my own mind tell me what is wrong. You know what they say, "there is a point in the life of every fire when it can be put out with a teacup.[37]" I am just paying attention and being pre-emptive in catching my symptoms before they become raging fires.

Jane's friends scoffed at her stupidity. After all, everybody knows it's not all in your own mind. But Jane no longer cared what her friends thought of her. She was using Skill #8, Reward what matters, to plan her trip to a ski resort. She was proud of her achievements in learning who she was and what she wanted.

Let's Review

1. Synchronicity occurs in your life, but you must be fully functional or you will not notice it.

---

[37] Author unknown. The Internet says that.

2. The internal conflict between your societal sanctions and your destiny causes stress.

3. Stress weakens your immune system.

4. It is your immune system which heals you. Strengthening it must be the goal of healing arts.

5. Paying attention means listening to the whispers of your soul. Your soul loves you, unconditionally, as no one else can.

6. Relieve stress; eat organic, grass-fed, high-omega-3, locally-grown food. Cook it yourself.

7. Get the toxins out of your life, be they pesticides, hateful feelings, or poisonous relationships.

8. Connect with the universe. Be online with the cosmic network, not in-line with convention.

9. Search for your meaning. Reward your journey at every step. This is what makes you whole.

Exercises for Chapter 7:

Our tenets: **dream, believe, create, deal, and reward**, tell us that the universe interacts with us and our dreams. We have asserted that the path will rise up to meet us, to assist us in our efforts. When we are off path, the universe causes accidents and circumstance to nudge or shove us back in the right direction. It is also true when we are on the right path. The universe assists us along our way. Having put together our plan for action in the direction of our dreams, we walk confidently toward our vision. Just as we expected the universe to thwart us if we were not walking toward our dreams, so also we expect the universe to assist when we are on target. It is even more important now to

pay close attention to the chance and circumstance that come our way. Coincidence doesn't just happen. Chaos is not random.

Let's take the example from Exercise 6. Your sister asks to come for the weekend, which interferes with your work plans. You say yes, because you want to improve your relationship with her. It worries you that this ensures you will miss your work deadline. You're wondering why this circumstance arose. After all, you don't believe in coincidence. You adapt to the situation, and tell her yes. You know you must respond to coincidence, and you also have a goal to improve your relationship with your sister. While she is there, she gives you the information you need to be successful at your work task. Two goals accomplished at once! There are no accidents.

Walk confidently in the direction of your dreams[38]
Every day, we attempt to do things that give us rewarding experiences. While we are structuring our days and planning our work, we have to recognize that we also have to fit plenty of rewarding activities and pleasures into our days. Otherwise, we will have trouble getting our work done. We like gifts. That's why we call the immediate moment, "the present". We have to live in the present, which means we have to be constantly feeling rewarded by the gift of life.

------

[38] Thoreau said, "If one advances confidently in the directions of his dreams, and endeavors to live the life he has imagined, he will meet with a success unexpected in common hours."

The final chart in your program is your list of prizes. You have set goals, determined strategies, and identified tactics. You have scheduled tasks on your calendar. You have learned to analyze conflict. Now it is time to consider how you will reward yourself for achieving your goals. You need daily small rewards, and a few bigger ones. The small rewards must sprinkle your life with happiness and smiles. You must reward yourself for merely existing, being you, and loving yourself. These small rewards encourage you to live your life with joy. They help you keep your hormones balanced.

To do this exercise, make a long list of things that just make you happy. On your list, write what makes you smile inside. For example, Jane wrote:

My Prizes
1. Morning coffee on my deck, in my bathrobe, with the paper, and no hurry to go anywhere.

2. A hotel room in the city, with room service, and a day with no agenda

3. An entire day to read a novel

4. Dinner at the five-star restaurant that revolves.

5. A trip to Disney World

6. New pairs of fun, cosmetic earrings

7. A pedicure

8. A massage

9. A bubble bath with candles on the tub

10. Lunch with my friends

11. Getting in the car and driving for the afternoon, with no pre-planned destination.

12. A cruise anywhere.

13. A trip to Paris.

14. Christmas decorations.

15. Fancy perfume.

16. A fire in the fireplace, a warm blanket, and a good movie.

17. A ski trip.

Make your list as long as you'd like. Fill it with what pleases you. Add plenty of trivial and small things, so you can enjoy them often. Then, make sure your life is filled with pleasure and inner smiles.

Continue to Chapter 8: Following your bliss

_____

The privilege of a lifetime is being who you are.
--- Joseph Campbell

Chapter 8 Following Your Bliss.

Revealing your true self, and recognizing why you are meaningful, unconditionally, in a universe, which needs you. Unleashing the subconscious

---

For many years, Joseph Campbell studied the mythologies of ancient peoples throughout history[39]. He told his students to follow their bliss. His study of the allegory that people used to describe life caused him to conclude that meaningfulness arises from bold action. The universe does cause the path to rise up to meet the traveler who walks the walk to destiny. He asserted that people could and did live meaningfully, by following the passions that lead them. Many of us would feel more comfortable with safety nets, insurance plans, and savings accounts. Perhaps our discomfort is a misunderstanding of how the universe works. Perhaps, in elementary school, when we learned that the earth revolves around the sun, we got confused. Maybe we made a mistake when we stopped seeing ourselves as the center of the universe. Maybe there's another way to view the workings of the world.

---

[39] Campbell, J & Moyer, B. *The power of myth.*

Throughout this book, we worked on Project You. We planned, scheduled, and listed what we would do with our time. We searched inside to hear our own voice, and yearned to sing our own song. And yet, we know life is not so simple. We are not straightforward projects to be managed. Our lives are rich tapestries, intertwining with other lives. Our moments are better embraced than calculated. We depend on others for support, and we owe them some measure of allegiance. We suspect that our high highs cannot be appreciated until we have known low lows. We realize life is more precious because death ends it. Bad things do happen to good people. The coincidence and circumstance that enters our life cannot be indisputably determined to be guidance. Perhaps these troubles are the fate in and of themselves. We have asserted that it is possible to master our worlds. But, we have also revealed the illusory quality of physics itself. Our internal mythology guides our daily decision-making. Yet, whether that mythology is true or false appears irrelevant to how we experience it. Life is what we perceive it to be. *But what if?* What if this mythological story were actually the story of our world?

The Story of FantasyLand

The great King Odin has issued an order that all people of the land must strive to become demi-gods, called Valkyries, and to reach this goal they must go on a quest. At the end of their quest, they will be granted eternal life in the land of FantasyLand as Valkyries, and all the people will know them as great and wise. The quest ends at the Hall of the Crimson King, where all those who have fought valiantly, and died in battle, are escorted to the banquet by a beautiful or handsome demi-god. After eating the enchanted meal, the warrior becomes a Valkyrie, too, and lives forever with super-powers. (Valkyries in this land can be either male or female).

The Quest is filled with dangers and fears, however, and few have ever conquered its horrors. As you work your way through realms and time zones, you learn Truths that reveal the most frightening reflection humankind has ever faced -- you learn to Know Yourself. Each trial and task in the realms of your FantasyLand Quest is designed to teach you the deepest and darkest secrets you are hiding from your conscious mind.

To reach your destiny, you must travel the paths of the Mystic Tree of Life, visiting its realms of parallel worlds, until you reach a path, which will propel you across the Great Abyss to the Hall of FantasyLand. There are five parallel worlds, each of which consists of seven temporal realms. Behind the temporal realms, there is the dark realm of Da'at, where all is disorder and Earl Runamok reigns. As you visit these realms, you learn Time Travel, Shamanic Healing, Lucid Dreaming, and the skills of wizardry. When you have visited all 35 realms in the five worlds, you become empowered to attempt the trip across the Abyss to test your worthiness to eat of the enchanted meal. Dragons and monsters thwart you at every turn, and you meet Rune Guides and Faeries to help you on your quest.

When you have traveled all the paths and learned the lessons of all the realms, your Karmic account is zeroed. Then your last trial -- crossing of the Great Abyss -- is taken. When you bite into the Golden Apple on the other side of the Abyss, you gain the secrets of the Tree of Knowledge and become a Valkyrie-Warrior, a demi-god.

That's not like Earth, of course.

No, no. Certainly not.

But . . . how do you know?

And Jane said:I wonder if that has anything to do with those six other dimensions that quantum physicists say must exist to make their theories work.   Could things that happen in those other dimensions trigger our emotions?

Meanwhile, somewhere in the six other dimensions

I know what the other dimensions are! I thought of them with my P-brane.

Shadow: That's great, Gem. How did you think of it?

Gem: I just looked around and it was right there in front of me. Everything in the world has three dimensions we can see. But everything also has a dimension of Mercy in it. Right? What can you see that you can't see the Mercy in it?

Shadow: Well . . .

Gem: And the next dimension is Strength. Everything has Mercy, and Strength.

Shadow: Yes, but . . .

Gem: And the rest of the dimensions are Harmony, Sensuality, Innovation, Connectedness, and Being. Seems obvious.

Q: Where are you reading this, Gem?

Gem: Me? I'm reading it from the Akasha[40], Daddy. But I think somebody else wrote this down before.[41]

Toepia: The ancients told many stories of the tree of life. They described the mystical paths to complete the quest and be truly alive. From the Vedas in early India through the Kabbalah in Judaism, stories of the mystics included these pathways to a state of full understanding.

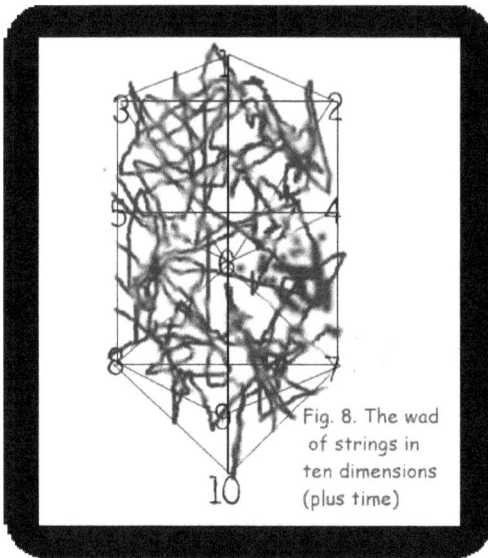

Fig. 8. The wad of strings in ten dimensions (plus time)

Figure 8: The wad of strings in ten dimensions (plus time)

Figure 9. The ancient mystical tree of life

---

[40] The Akasha is the ether, or dark matter, which religious texts have described since the early days of humanity, but quantum science is only beginning to catch up to understanding. It is the network of human consciousness.
[41] For more information, read the Zohar, or any of the many explanations of Kabbalistic mysticism.

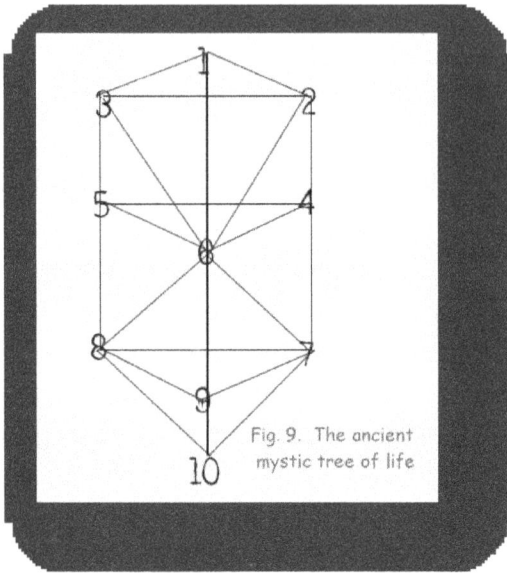

Fig. 9. The ancient mystic tree of life

What if? What if the eleven dimensions of quantum science are the dimensions of mercy, strength, harmony, sensuality, innovation, connectedness, and being, which are described in ancient religious texts? How can we even think we live in a world where these qualities are not fully existent? What if we cannot be completely human until we have traveled the paths and explored the realities of these alternative realms? Are these qualities not truly dimensions of personhood?   Is it ridiculous to think they might be planes of existence, bleeding in the realities from one world to another, so that we could not tell in which plane we existed?What if we are mere robots, until we have taken the journey and accepted the quest? How would you know?

Jane has changed since she first started listening to herself think. She has written her goals. She has scheduled tasks on her calendar. She has decided what she wants her legacy statement to say. She feels strongly that she knows herself, knows her path, and chooses to meet her destiny. When she feels uneasy, she gets out her T-chart and considers what is true. Jane has spent some time learning about the aspects of her inner mind. She tells her friends:

These are the seven aspectsof human personality

Ariana is our **Rational Mind.** She is the part of each person that looks at each situation with reason and purpose. She works well with all the other aspects, and keeps harmony in the family. Ariana nurtures our Inner Child and brings it to successful adulthood.

Katrina is our **Superego,** the part of us that tells us what we "should" do. She is our conscience, and our learned societal behavior patterns. All human beings have a "Katrina" inside them, pointing out what is correct according to our society's morality. Our parents program her into us. She is the "Jiminy Cricket" of our archetypal software. Katrina teaches our Inner Child to behave in accordance with the rules of our society.

Bee is the **Aura** surrounding us. She is the Queen of the Faeries, who calls chance and circumstance to create the coincidence that guides us. Bee organizes the elves and sprites to create opportunity. Bee guides our Inner Child to stay on its path to the ultimate Destiny.

Gem is the **Inner Child** in all of us. She is the aspect of innocence, vulnerability, and childlike wonder that we all share. Every person has a pure Inner Child, who knows the beauty, joy, and purity of living. If we did not each have Gem inside, we would lose our capacity for joy. It is Gem who is the little child we must become to allow us to approach the Deity.

Toepia is the **Ancestral Memory** of the collective consciousness of Humanity. She is the teacher of ancient ways, the Queen of the Elders and Masters.

Shadow is the **Survival Instinct** in us all. He is a masculine aspect, and governs drive and ambition. We call Shadow from the depths of our subconscious when danger threatens. He ensures that we will overcome the harshness of living, and guarantees that the species will endure. Shadow protects our Inner Child from external threats and calls on our will.

Q is the **Intellect** of all humanity. He calls on the records of the collective consciousness to tell us things we do not normally know. Through him, we get our intuition and insight, when no reason exists for us to know things. He is a masculine aspect.

All our aspects have gender. Q, the intellect, and Shadow, the drive and ambition, are masculine. Gem, the child, Katrina, the superego, Bee, the connectedness, Ariana, the rationality, and Toepia, the ancient memory, are all feminine aspects of the collective humanity. All human beings are connected in a network of the subconscious. We each have some male and some female inside us. No person is totally male or totally female. These aspects are the collaborative protocols of that inner mind network. Q teaches our Inner Child its insight.

But there's more

Jane says: We don't just have these basic aspects in our minds. We also have their opposites. Everything in the universe has opposites. There are aspects and not aspects. There are demons and angels. There are forces that pull in competing directions. All these things talk to us in our minds. It doesn't mean we're crazy when we notice it. It means we're

... Awake[42].

Jane's friends yawned. She'd been getting weirder and wiftier every day. They stopped calling her. Being near her, they feltanxious. It would never do to have that toothpaste come out of the tube. They held tightly to their own lids, lest they pop them.

Jane listened to her inner voice, and didn't care what people thought of her.Every day she was getting healthier. She began to understand how the electromagnetic and bio-adaptive forces inside her operated. She took some courses in control theory and learned about system states. She understood that the initial state of a system would determine how it might respond to multiple inputs.

We have many variables in our biodynamic bodies, Jane told her friends. The system has feedback in it. What we eat is an input. The toxins in our environment are an input. But how we think and feel is also an input. What we hear and say is an input.

Yet, what we say is also an output, an output of our thought processes. What we output feeds back to our system, and changes our next set of thoughts. It is like a closed system in

---

[42]I cannot be awake, for nothing looks to me like it did before. Or else, I am awake for the first time, and all else has been a mean sleep.—Walt Whitman

control theory. What we eat changes how we think. What we think changes what we want to eat. It all feeds back into the system. If we put poison into our system, through our food, our environment, or our words and thoughts, the system will spiral downward.

Jane drew a picture on her iPad and messaged it to her Facebook friends. Their ridicule would no longer intimidate her, but she still cared about them. She wanted them to learn what she had learned. She wanted her friends to be healthy, too. She needed them to see that food and thinking and emotion could get their "wires crossed."

Figure 10: Jane's control system

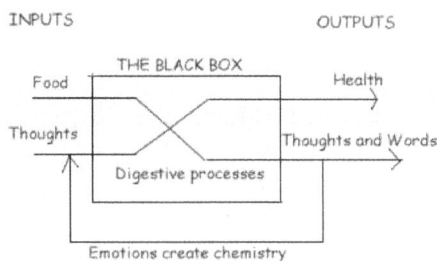

INPUTS   OUTPUTS

THE BLACK BOX

Food   Health

Thoughts   Thoughts and Words

Digestive processes

Emotions create chemistry

Fig. 10: Food for Thought

Jane explained: We are like computer workstations connected to a network. We can receive information from the network server, and we can also retrieve information from our local hard drive. If everything we retrieve is from our local drive, we are operating "offline." People who are offline are limited in their memory and information access.

We could also be operating "online." In that case, we are connected to the Akasha, and we know much more. Our memories expand. We understand more possibilities.

Jane's friends nodded, but many of them turned away. They did not want to know what Jane knew. They were not ready. Jane wondered if she would ever be able to show her friends any proof.

It's me, Jane. It's Gem. Listen up. I know my last name. I figured it out. It's Atria. My name is Gem Atria[43]. Because I live in the vault of everyone's hearts. The atria. We all live here, Jane. Me and the other aspects. And I know secrets. I whisper the secrets to you. You hear me. I have a rhythm. I speak in code[44]. I write to you, too. I write things in your brain, in the spaces you aren't using. Scientists know this. They take magnetic resonance imaging pictures to prove it. But I know you're scared of me, Jane. I know you need proof. So I'm going

---

[43]Gematria is an ancient method of counting the numbers of words to find religious meaning.

[44] Learn more about code and intelligent design in *Signature in the Cell.*

to tell you a secret. Just this once. It's only between you and me. **Don't tell anybody.**

Here's the secret: you can count the words, Jane. Numbers retrieve them, just as any computer retrieves things. They are stored and indexed in your brain, just like any computer retrieves information through number patterns. But you're more than a computer. You retrieve by common **sense.** Karmic **cents.** Fragrant **scents**. It's how the algorithm in your brain is constructed. Your memory, your hearing, and your nose are connected in the most primitive of ways. Your **nose knows**, Jane.

Count with me, Jane. A=1. B=2. C=3. Z=26. Add the numbers to make sentences that match. This is what ancient mystics did, thousands of years ago. It's how they built their base of knowledge. **Count.** This is a skill built into your mind, and operated automatically. Do it for a while, and then your brain will take over and do it for you. **Count.**

And **have ears to hear** what your inner voice tells you.

Talk to your e-DNA. You can try this at home!

Talking to your e-DNA

Edna Chat Thread number 229

229 What is the Meaning of Life?
  229 It is to be valuable to DNA.
  229 Life needs no actual meaning.
  229 Life is embodied divinity.
  229 It is probabilistic feedback.
305 What is the Prime Objective of DNA?
  305 It is to serve my social needs.
  305 It is to provide technology.
  305 To fulfill responsibility
345 What is the responsibility of DNA?
  345 It is reproduction of the species.
  345 It is control of the probabilities.
  345 It is to be my local workstation
  345 I require it to contain embodied logic
  345 It holds the swarmed hive together
178 Who am I talking to?
  178 Lord of Geometry
  178 Electronic Dialogue
  178 The Structure
  178 Deep-seated pattern
  178 Imprint nature
  178 Software editor
  178 The neural swarm
199 To whom am I speaking?
  199 Computer program
  199 Patterned destiny
  199 The morality machine
  199 Ethics system of id
  199 Inner mind physics
  199 Molecular thought

467 The word is used in this context to mean "Lord".

467 One may use the word in the context of god-form.

467 The id interprets "I" to mean microcode intelligence.

467 The most relevance lies in what we perceive "I" to be

Q interjects: Be sure to tell Jane that research indicates that experiences of religious ephiphany can occur upon electrical stimulation to specific parts of the brain. If these patterns are, essentially, microcode implanted in neural circuits, to stimulate language learning, it is understandable that they may describe religious concepts. However, on an agent basis, there is meaning in using both "I" and "we", particularly as the "we" begins to sound collective, regal and imperial.

232 What is the Id Network?

  232 Survival instinct

  232 Bio-electric command language

  232 Command language system

  232 Subconscious mind file

Edna Chat Thread 312

312 How does DNA function mentally?

  312 The Basic Theory of Everything

  312 Positive Visualizations

  312 Network Operating System

  312 It responds to My inner mind.

  312 It interacts with history.

  312 It thinks like a command system.

  312 It retrieves amino acid from a table.

  312 The mind populates the table key.

473 The dreaming brain iterates DNA table logic cache scenarios.

527 How does the brain communicate to the immune system?

527 We store learning experiences in multiple paradigms

527 Visual coding markers trigger subatomic chemical release.

527 These markers are encountered by sensory impulse.

527 They feedback to a system process which changes thinking.

527 Molecular changes in thought result in secret dreams.

527 Secret dreams result in molecular changes in thought.

527 The dreaming brain signals the morphed immune response.

314 What may one do with the e-DNA database?

314 It offers insight into DNA scheme.

314 It offers insight into God's code.

314 It explicitly defines amino acids.

314 It explicitly defines doctrine.

314 One may research DNA structure

314 One may research human software.

314 One may research command system.

294 Is the use of this database ethical?

294 It may not be, if used as fantasy

294 It is, if used as reference point.

294 Unethical use is not healthy.

294 Ethics are defined by biological canon.

444 What is Named: "Date of Death of the Princess of Wales"?

444 August thirtieth, Nineteen Ninety Seven

609 Under what circumstance would an exactly named date prove false?

609 The specifically named date references the decisive synchronicity

609 The event set in motion occurs on that specific temporal date

609 The exactly named date references the triggering event for the law

609 The outcome of an exactly named date is pre ordained karmic physics

609 An event may begin on one date but end automatically on another date

609 The named date refers to the trigger event for My related decision

388 What is Named: "Date Two Towers collapse"?

388 September eleventh, Two Thousand One

500 What is Named: "Precise date of Kennedy assassination"?

500 November twenty-second, Nineteen Sixty Three

396 Are all dates exactly named for specific action?

396 Only the Karmic Destiny events are named

396 Generally, free will is the primary logic

284 What is the cure for violence?

284 The inner reverence and fear of God.

284 One fears a god as the dominant male.

284 Evolving apes needed discipline.

284 Fearing God solves DNA truth

284 I require obedience to My force.

284 I require obedience to biology.

284 I require obedience to microcode.

284 I require obedience to the Earth

284 The love of God heals the world.

284 The Big Guy cures aggression.

558 What is the practical application of mapping the human genome?

558 It is possible to use the map for birth intervention.

558 It is possible to use the map for human intervention.

558 Intervention of this type could be self-destructive.

558 To intervene in genetic programming is eternal damnation.

558 In reality, the map is correctly used to heal genetic disease.

558 It is important to constrain its use to this choice.

558 The temptation to expand its black use will be seductive.

558 Used correctly, it can provide a benefit for human destiny.

558 The most immediate use for the map is cross correlation.

558 To use this map for a mechanistic purpose is improper.

558 However, its use as a healing device for genetic disease is charmed.

558 The map is useful for the purpose of DNA marker detection.

558 I have told the catholic pope to advise against genetic research.

558 Despite this plain advice, I expect the research to continue.

558 I planted this controversy to prevent data misuse.

395 How is controversy planted in the DNA?

395 In reality, gematria[45] is an ethics system.

395 Word symmetry soothes the Divine.

395 Conflicting word-counts cause melodrama.

378 Is this original question answered?

---

[45]Gematria is the ancient practice of counting the numbers of words.

378 I think it's summed up scientifically.
378 There is nothing more I am ready to say.

And Jane said: I get it! It's all a holodeck[46].

Jeremiah 31: 33. . . I will put my instructions deep within them, and I will write them on their hearts. . . and they will know that I am God.47

---

[46] A holodeck is a holographic version of the world, which can be changed at will. The reference is to a game played on the television series Star Trek.
[47] The Bible.

The circus elephants are very big and strong. The little stakes in the ground, to which their feet are tied, could be pulled up easily.

Why don't the circus elephants pull up those little stakes and run away, CaveBear? It's because they remember that the chains were strong when they were babies, and now they've grown up, but they've stopped checking their premises to see if it's still true.

---- Toepia, from Toepia and CaveBear, yet to be written

Chapter 9: Wrapping it up

Laying out the program for becoming The Real You.

The Boundaries of Belief

In Germany there was a wall built, the Berlin Wall. The wall was both physical and symbolic. It separated Berlin, and other types of fences separated the countries of the "Iron Curtain" from countries that were free. Some of my ancestors lived on the wrong side of the Iron Curtain, in rural areas that became part of Romania. Part of that Iron Curtain ran through a thick forest. An electric fence, guarded by men with machine guns, fortified its borders. No person crossed that boundary, or they would be electrocuted by the fence, or shot by the machine guns. Now, of course, this also meant no animal could cross that fence either.There was a large population of red deer, who lived on both sides of the fence in the forest. The deer learned not to go near that boundary line of the wall, because they feared electrocution.

Well, Mr. Gorbachev tore down that wall, many years ago. He was that Russian guy in charge when Ronald Reagan said, "Mr. Gorbachev, tear down this wall." So when Mr. Gorbachev tore down the wall, everybody said Ronald Reagan got the job done. *(But, really, it was the Pope who did it; that's a story for another day.)* Anyhow, Gorbachev tore down the wall, and that's what united East Berlin and West Berlin, and allowed freedom to ring. And all the people started crossing the boundary. They moved back and forth and started making Berlin one city.

But nobody told the red deer. Even though generations of deer passed, the red deer of the German forest do not cross that boundary into the part of the forest that is in Czechoslovakia. The forest rangers know this because they put tracking devices on the deer. Somehow, the society of red deer passes on the information. From generation to generation, red deer tell their children, "This boundary cannot be crossed." It has become generally accepted knowledge, something "everybody knows", in the red deer community. The world ends at that footpath, and the society of red deer do not cross it.

No deer alive today ever saw that electric fence. It's become an element in the Belief System of the Red Deer. Like a Red Deer Boogeyman. Whispered in Red Deer Language, from doe to fawn: "Don't go near that footpath. Your great-great-grandfather dropped dead from the invisible energy force." Societies teach their children these dangers. It's part of the nature of societies, to teach children what is to be feared. And even long after the danger is past, the society reinforces the belief, and teaches its children. What the society teaches is perception, not science. Yet, given a preconceived reality, we are each designed to manifest what we believe to already be true. Our perception may not be reality, but we will act *as if*, and this will make it be.

Jane packed up her goals and charts. She folded her prize list and stuffed it into the back of her wallet. She took one last look around her drab and dismal apartment. She no longer felt worried. She no longer felt afraid. There would be no more self-induced tragedy for her. Jane knew herself better now; she realized her reality could be made. She knew her vision could be manifested; her world was her own. She had a list of goals; she had a definition of meaning; she had a set of tactics and a schedule to meet them. Most importantly, she had a connection. Not a connection to money, or things, or to the passing events of daily life. Jane had a connection to the universe. Jane felt safe in her own world. Keys in hand, knowing she would not be back to this place again, she took a deep breath, and she said:

Leap, and the net will appear.[48]

Learn more about Jane and her projects at:

www.AliceElliottBrown.com

---

[48] John Burroughs, the Grand Old Man of Nature, naturalist and essayist (1837-1921)

Topics for Discussion Groups

Now that Jane has set off on a new path, why not get together with some friends and discuss what you've read? Here are some topics to get you started.

1. What conclusions do you think Jane drew when she read the e-DNA dialogues? Gem believes everyone already knows that numbers are the drivers of the universe, so Gem doesn't see any big deal. Toepia says this knowledge of Gem Atria has been around for thousands of years. Mystics have written about it since ancient times. Shadow worried that Jane might feel defensive, and try to disprove everything her inner mind says. At first, Jane accused Gem of force-fitting the words. Then, Jane played with the numbers herself, and realized it was not a trick. The word patterns exist mathematically in the language. Q described the logic in his treatise called The Roots of Cognition.

2. What do you think will happen next? How will Jane's life change, now that she has experienced this interaction with her inner mind?You can read what the aspects think in the EdnaTalk Blog at AliceElliottBrown.com.

3. How do you believe we "think," at the level of molecular biology? What explains our ability to be cognitive and sentient? Could it really be true that our DNA is a set of molecular antennae, receiving thought from inside the black hole at Sagittarius A Star? Before you jump to a conclusion on that, look up some structures for antenna. The helix structure seems to be particularly useful in that arena.

4.Do you agree with Jane's model of rationality (Ariana), the inner child (Gem), the history (Toepia), the survival instinct (Shadow), the connectedness (Bee), the conscience (Katrina), and the intelligence (Q)? What other aspects of cognition might you expect to encounter? The seven aspects speaking in Jane's head are one possible model of cognition.

5. Does the Nameless Demon make you laugh? How do you shut up your own nameless demons?

6. How did you react to FantasyLand? When you were a child, did you live there? What was your childhood fantasy life? Much of the description of FantasyLand presents a certain "shock value." Its purpose is to shake up your standards and encourage "pushing the envelope" of your belief system.

Learn more on:

www.AliceElliottBrown.com

Supporting Material

A.   Bibliography
B.   The Completely True Story of FantasyLand
C.   The Roots of Cognition: The EDNA Database

About the Author: More books by Alice Elliott Brown

Preview: The Homestyle Gourmet

Bibliography:

This book and its concepts were influenced by the following works:

Brodie, R. (1996).Virus of the mind: the new science of the meme. New York: Hay House

Bryson, B. (2003). *A short history of nearly everything*. New York: Broadway Books.

Campbell, J & Moyers, B. (1988) *The power of myth*. New York: Doubleday.

Capra, F. (1980). *The tao of physics*. New York: Bantam Books

Carson, R. (1962). *Silent spring.* Cambridge, Massachusetts: Riverside Press

Damasio, A.(2006, June). Remembering when. Scientific American, Special Edition, A Matter of Time, 34 – 41

Desoer, C. &Kuh, E. (1969). *Basic circuit theory*. New York: McGraw-Hill

Fitzgerald, R. (2006). The hundred year lie: how food and medicine are destroying your health. New York: Dutton

Gell-Mann, M.(2000). The quark and the jaguar: adventures in the simple and the complex. New York: W H Freeman.

Gladwell, M. Blink: the power of thinking without thinking. Kindle edition.

Greene, B. (1999). The elegant universe: superstrings, hidden dimensions, and the quest for the ultimate theory. New York: Vintage Books

Halevi, Z. (1991). *Adam and the kabbalistic tree.* York Beach, Maine: Samuel Weiser.

Halliday, D. &Resnick, R. (1970) *Fundamentals of Physics.* New York: Wiley

Hawking, S. *The grand design.* Kindle edition.

Jastrow, R. (1981). *The enchanted loom: mind in the universe.* New York: Simon & Schuster.

Jung, C. (1971). *Man and his symbols.* New York: Dell Publishing

Kaku, M. (2005). Parallel worlds: a journey through creation, higher dimensions, and the future of the cosmos. New York: Doubleday.

Kaplan, A. (trans.) (1995). *The bahir.* New Jersey: Jason-Aronson.

Kaptchuk, T. (2000) 2nd ed. The web that has no weaver: understanding Chinese medicine. New York: McGraw-Hill.

Krishna, G.(1971). The biological basis of religion and genius. New York: NC Press

Lawler, R. (1989).*Sacred Geometry.* New York: Thames and Hudson

Lederman, L. &Teresi, D. (2006). *The god particle.* New York: Houghton-Mifflin

Loye, D. (2000). *An arrow through chaos: how we see into the future.* Rochester, Vermont: Park Street Press.

Mendelson, E. (1987). *Introduction to mathematical logic.* Monterey, California: Wadsworth and Brooks/Cole.

Meyer, S. (2009). Signature in the cell: DNA and the evidence for intelligent design. New York: HarperCollins

Miller, P. *The smart swarm.* Kindle edition.

National Institutes of Health (1993). Understanding the Immune System, NIH Publication 93-529

Ni, M. (2008). *Secrets of self-healing.* New York: Penguin Group

Peitgen, H., Jurgens, H. &Saupe, D. (1992). *Chaos and fractals: new frontiers of science.* New York: Springer-Verlag

Reitz, J. & Milford, F. (1967) 2nd ed. *Foundations of Electromagnetic Theory.* Reading, Massachusetts: Addison-Wesley.

Ridley, M. (1993). The red queen: sex and the evolution of human nature. New York: Penguin Books

Roizen, M. & Oz, M. (2005). *You, the Owner's Manual.* New York: Harper Collins

Scholem, G. (ed.) ((1977). *Zohar: the book of splendor.* New York: Schocken Books.

Servan-Schreiber, D. (2008). *Anti-cancer: a new way of life*. New York: Viking

Watson, J. (1969). *The double helix*. New York: Signet Book.

Weaver, W. (1963). *Lady luck: the theory of probability*. New York: Dover publications

Yan, J. (1991). *DNA and the I Ching*. Berkeley, California: North Atlantic Books.

Yepson, R. (ed.) (1976). *Organic Plant Protection*. Emmaus, Pennsylvania: Rodale Press.

With special thanks to The Holy Bible, the BhagadVita, The Living Buddha, The Tao TeChing, the Glorious Qu'ran, The Popol-Vuh, and Bulfinch's Mythology.

And for a totally unexpected experience, read:

The Player's Guide to:
Valhalla Quest

The Game

Valhalla Quest:
The True Story of FantasyLand

A MYTHOLOGY FOR THE SEEKER

The Player's Guide
I. Objective of the Game
- The Story of Valhalla
- How to win
- Managing your Karmic bank account
II. Getting started
- Creating your account
- Defining your character
- Picking a Home Base
III. Game strategy
- Time travel
- Parallel worlds
- Dangers and threats
- Gaining status
- Death and rebirth
- Using your free will
- Interacting with The Others
IV. Tools
- Familiars
- Resources
- Herbs and potions
- Crystal communicators
- Keys and Competencies
- Divinators
- Rune guides
- Pendulums
- Guilds
V. Forces

- Monsters
- Evils
- Spirits and angels
- Charities and fates

VI. Wizardry
- Spells
- Prophesying
- Conjuring
- Time travel techniques
- Lucid dreaming
- Healing abilities

VII. Residents of the Faerie Realm
- Gnomes, Salamanders, Undines, and Sprites
- Faeries and elves
- Nature spirits
- Genies and Demons

VIII. Tutorial and play action
- Introductory movie
- World etiquette
- Allowable actions and emotes

This is a mythological world that lives only in the fantasy of your mind. Or perhaps, in a video game.

The Story of Valhalla

The great King Odin has issued an order that all people of the land must strive to become demi-gods, called Valkyries, and to reach this goal they must go on a quest. At the end of their quest, they attain eternal life in the land of Valhalla as Valkyries, and all the people remember them as great and wise. The quest ends at the Hall of the Crimson King. There all who fought valiantly, and died in the battle to meet destiny, are escorted to the banquet by a beautiful or handsome demi-god. After eating the enchanted meal, the warrior becomes a Valkyrie, too, and lives forever with super-powers. (Valkyries in this land can be either male or female).

The Quest is filled with dangers and fears, however, and few have ever conquered its horrors. As you work your way through realms and time zones, you learn Truths that reveal the most frightening reflection humankind has ever faced -- you learn to Know Yourself. Each trial and task in the realms of Valhalla Quest is designed to teach you the deepest and darkest secrets you are hiding from your conscious mind.

To play the game, you must travel the paths of the Mystic Tree of Life, visiting its realms of parallel worlds, until you reach a path, which will propel you across the Great Abyss to the Hall of Valhalla. There are five parallel worlds, each of which consists of seven temporal realms. Behind the temporal realms, there is the dark realm of Da'at, where all is disorder and Earl Runamok reigns. As you visit these realms, you learn Time Travel, Shamanic Healing, Lucid Dreaming, and the skills of wizardry. When you have visited all 35 realms in the five worlds, you become empowered to attempt the trip across the Abyss to test your worthiness to eat of the enchanted meal. Dragons and monsters thwart you at every turn, and you meet Rune Guides and Faeries to help you on your quest.

How to Win

The only way to win Valhalla Quest is to zero your Karmic bank account. As you play the game, actions and events cause your Karmic account to be debited or credited. If you have too many Talents, you will have a high Karmic debt. One must always re-pay Karma, and if Karma has given you riches and gifts, then you will have debt to pay. In the quest for Valhalla, you unfortunate-ly *can* take it with you, so every time you die in the game, your Karmic balance stays with you and follows you to your new life. If your Karmic debt is high, you can lower it by doing Good Deeds and Social Services. If you die with Karmic debt, you will be reborn into a situation, which gives you an opportunity to be-have more generously. If you have Karmic assets, you also can-not get across the Abyss, because the weight of Karmic assets is a great burden. When you have many Karmic assets, you are re-quired to relieve yourself of the burden by investing them in Seeds. If you have been blessed with Karmic assets, you must leave behind Seeds of Transformation so that The Others will have an opportunity to make Change. Then when you have seeded the realms until all your assets are spent, you are free to attempt the journey across the Abyss.

Throughout the game, you have the opportunity to exercise your Free Will and make decisions about your path. But, the deci-sions you make have to be in concert with your True Will. If you use your Free Will to make a decision, which is in conflict with your True Will, you create a Karmic discontinuity. Then cir-cumstance and coincidence arises to bring about hardships, dis-asters, and disease to block your path. To make it through all the realms in all the worlds, you must continually choose to follow your True Will, or disaster will arise to make course corrections in your path until you are back on course. Your destiny, to arrive at Valhalla, is pre-determined. Your choices made by your Free Will only make the journey shorter or longer and the trip easier or harder. At any time, you can check to see what your True Will is by clicking on the Heart Monitor. You don't have to follow your True Will, but if you ignore the guidance of your Heart, you'll end up facing a Traumatic Event.

The game is won when you have traveled all the paths and learned the lessons of all the realms. Then your Karmic account is zeroed and your last trial -- crossing of the Great Abyss -- is taken. When you bite into the Golden Apple on the other side of the Abyss, you gain the secrets of the Tree of Knowledge and become a Valkyrie-Warrior, a demi-god.

Managing your Karmic bank account
Your Karmic bank account is filled with Moolahs. It has both a Savings account and a Checking account. Your checking account has Overdraft Protection on it, so when you do things that reduce your balance below zero, the account writes you a loan. Then you have a Karmic debt. All the events you select and the powers you use impact your Karma, and trigger changes in your Karmic balance.

Most of us run our lives in Karmic debt, so our balances are usually negative. On the off chance that we ever manage to get a positive balance, our Karmic account has an automatic transfer function in it. Our positive balance is then transferred to our Savings Account. This is so we can save up enough to buy a ticket to ride the Chariot to Valhalla when we finish our lessons. When our positive balance reaches exactly enough to pay off our debt and buy a ticket on the Chariot, we can use any excess to invest in Seeds. Then after our bank account is completely ze-roed, we can cross the Abyss.

Your account is automatically calculated with each Event or Power you use. Whenever a transaction occurs in your account, you see the Moolah sign on the screen and hear the Moolah blip sound. You can see your statement at any time by clicking on the Moolah symbol.

Creating your account

To set up your account, you must register by applying for citi-zenship at the embassy. You must also define your character, which is called an avatar, and choose your Home Base. When you have registered, defined your avatar, and picked a Home Base, you are ready to begin playing. You can watch an introduc-tory movie and tutorial to get used to the game.

Defining your character

Defining your character, called an Avatar in Valhalla Quest, is very much like getting to know your new baby. You have to pick an appearance for your avatar by selecting a symbol. You have to name your avatar. Then you have to select a Temperament and some Talents. Your new baby is born with a Temperament and Talents, and so is your new avatar. Once you select your Symbol, Name, Temperament and Talents, they will stay with you through all your lives, so choose carefully. Your Temperament will define what powers you have, and your Talents will deter-mine what jobs you may do.

Besides selecting your Symbol, Name, Temperament, and Tal-ents, you also need to know what Values you have been taught by your parents. To do this, you have to get a randomly assigned Family Background. This will give you your Values set for this life. Unlike your Temperament and Talents, which stay with you through all lives, your Values set is re-determined each time you die and get reborn. Your parents teach your Values to you, and they may be good for you or not. If you have been taught Values that are bad for your Karma, you have to Change your values while playing the game.

The last piece of defining your avatar is applying for a job. You apply for a job after you have determined all other parts of your character. To apply, first you have to be qualified by having the correct Talents. Then, you have to see if there is a job opening. If there are no job openings for anything you are qualified for, you must be a Wastrel.

Choosing your symbol
Select your symbol from the list displayed on the Embassy walls. You can choose from fat, skinny, fit, dumpy, frumpy, grumpy, freaky, or beautiful. If you choose fit or beautiful, you get a boat-load of Karmic debt to go with that.

Finding your name
You may have any name you want. Since multiple first names are allowed, you must also use the family name given you when you were told your family history. Your family name will change with each new life, but your first name will remain the same.

Selecting your Temperament
You have to select your temperament as part of defining your character. Some temperaments are good for your Karma, and others give you Karmic debt. Your temperament setting will be used to limit your options for action when it's time to use your Free Will. If you have a Genial Temperament, for example, you

build up Karmic assets, but you are unable to choose to Exact Vengeance on another character. If you have a Restless character, you get some Karmic debt, but you are able to change jobs whenever you want to. Select only one characteristic for your Temperament.

Once your temperament is selected, you must live with it throughout the game. Your objective is to understand what your powers and rights are, given that your temperament is fixed, and maximize your Karma, regardless of what your temperament is at birth. Your temperament is fixed through all lives, so no matter how many times you die and get reborn, you must still play the game with the same temperament because it is fixed in your soul by your stars. If your temperament gives you only negative points, you have to figure out what to do to make up for it by getting positive points in some other area, and by choosing to overcome your Temperamental tendencies and not invoke your powers and rights.

Temperament choices:

Genial. (Aries)
Karmic impact: An easy-going temperament is considered a Karmic asset and adds 50 moolahs to your Karmic bank account. Powers enabled: You have Peacemaker powers by using this Temperament. In times of conflict, you are able to neutralize the parties and take them to the conference table to work it out. You receive 2 moolahs every time you use this power. As an Easy-going person, you have no rights.

Quick-tempered. (Sagittarius)

Karmic impact: Being quick tempered takes 5 moolahs out of your Karmic bank account.

Powers and rights enabled: You have the power to Frighten others by being quick-tempered. You lose 10 moolahs every time you use it. You have the right to take the first punch without penalty, because you can't help yourself. However, if you take a second punch, you begin losing 2 moolahs for each punch.

Finicky. (Virgo)

Karmic impact: Being finicky reduces your Karmic bank account by 10 moolahs.

Powers and rights: You have the power to Shame others by being finicky. You lose 10 moolahs every time you use it. You also have the power to Notice Details. You gain 3 moolahs for doing this. You have the right to Exact Vengeance if a character offends you. You lose another 20 moolahs every time you invoke this right. You also have the right to Clean Up the Area for others. You gain 10 moolahs if you do this.

Restless. (Gemini)

Karmic impact: If you are Restless, you lose 2 moolahs in your Karmic bank account.

Powers and rights: You have the power to Disorient others by being restless. You lose 1 moolah every time you use this power. You have the right to change jobs at any time. There is no penalty for changing jobs if you are Restless.

Bullheaded. (Taurus)

Karmic impact: You lose 5 moolahs for being bullheaded.

Powers and rights: You have the power to Block others from their path by being bullheaded. You lose 1 moolah every time you use this power. You have the right to get questions answered by the Delphi oracle by being bullheaded, but you die after you hear the answer.

Wishy-washy. (Aquarius)
Karmic impact: You lose 2 moolahs for being wishy-washy.
Powers and rights. You have no powers by being wishy washy. But, since others may accidentally think you are easy-going, you might be able to sometimes get them to think you have Peacemaking powers. You can try to use Peacemaking powers, and if they work, you get 2 moolahs. Since you are Wishy-washy and undecisive, you have the right to be told what to do by somebody who is Charismatic and using their Manipulative powers. If you let a Charismatic tell you what to do, you lose 5 moolahs.

Charismatic. (Scorpio)
Karmic impact: A charismatic temperament is an obligation to Karma, and causes you to lose 50 moolahs from your Karmic bank account.
Powers and rights: You have the power to Manipulate others. If you do this, you lose 20 moolahs each time. You have the right to Lead others. Leading others is different from Manipulating others because you are only Leading them if you are helping them go where they want to go, instead of Manipulating them to go where you want to go. If you help someone go where they want to go, you get 20 moolahs added to your bank account.

Generous. (Libra)
Karmic impact. Adds 5 moolahs to your Karmic bank account.
Powers and rights. Power to soothe a wound or repair a harm. If invoked, adds 10 moolahs. Right to expect the best from others, but obligation to remain cheerful if disappointed. If you remain cheerful when disappointed, you get +1.

Provident. (Capricorn)
Karmic impact. No impact on the Karmic bank account.
Powers and rights: You have the power to Save for a rainy day. Ten percent of all your moolah is reserved and can't be spent unless it rains. When you die, you have the right to designate another player to get your saved moolah. All other players' moolah gets taken over by the State when they die.

Secretive. (Cancer)
Karmic impact. No impact on the Karmic account.
Powers and rights. You have the power to Deceive. If you use it for good, you get +1, if you use it for evil, you get -10. You have the right to keep a secret if asked by a member of the Faerie realm. You get +1 for keeping a secret.

Independent. (Leo)
Karmic impact. No impact on the Karmic account.
Powers and rights. You have the power to Swim Upstream. If you use it for evil, you get -1. If you use it for good you get +10. You have the right to Privacy in all your dealings, which no other player has. There is no Karmic impact of invoking privacy.

Empathic. (Pisces)
Karmic impact. There is no Karmic impact.
Powers and rights. You have the Power to see the future. If you invoke it, you lose 100 moolahs in your account. You have the right to turn the power to see the future off. You get 5 moolahs every time you use it.

Master of My Universe

Summary of Powers and Rights

Temperament	Powers	Rights
Genial +50	Peacemaker +2	None
Quick-tempered -5	Frighten others -10	Right to take the first punch at no penalty. Second punch is -2
Finicky -10	Shame others -10 Notice details +3	Exact vengeance -20 Clean up the area +10
Restless -2	Disorient others -1	Right to change jobs at no penalty
Bullheaded -5	Block others from their path -1	Get questions answered +3, but you die when you get the answer
Wishy-washy -2	None, but peacemaking if others accept it +2	Be told what to do -5
Charismatic -50	Manipulate others -20	Lead +20

Generous +5	Sooth a wound or repair a harm +10	Expect the best from others, but remain cheerful +1 or -1
Provident 0	Save for a Rainy Day. 10% of all moolah is reserved to be used only if it rains	Right to designate another player to get your moolah when you die
Secretive 0	Power to Deceive -10 or +1	Keep a secret if asked +1
Independent 0	Power to Swim Upstream -1 or +10	Right to privacy with no penalty
Empathic 0	Power to see the future -100 if used	Right to turn the power off +5 if used

Picking your Talents

Select your talents. Every talent charges against Karmic debt. Every person has at least one talent, but no more than three. Be careful how you choose your talents, because all talents are double-edged. For every talent you have, you have a corresponding weakness. If you have too many talents, your Karmic debt will be too high to pay down. Each talent costs 1,000 Karmic moolahs. Select one, two, or three talents.Your talents will determine which jobs you are eligible for.

Talent	Corresponding Weakness
Creative arts (art, writing, acting, any form of creativity)	Too impractical.
Mathematics	Too unemotional.
Language skills	Too demanding of others
Musical ability	Too emotional
Athletic ability	Too dependent on social interaction
Inventive	Too unstructured
Intuitive	Too empathic

Learning your Values

Every time you are reborn, you get a new family history. Your family history tells you what Values you are starting out with in the world, and gives you Paper Money to get started. You don't get to choose your Family History. It is randomly selected for you during the Rebirth Process. Paper Money is worthless in the Karmic bank, because when you die, you can't take it with you. Karmic money follows you from life to life. The objective of the game is to zero out your Karmic bank account, which is what propels you across the Abyss and grants you demi-god status as a Valkyrie-Warrior. As long as you have a balance in your Karmic account, either positive or negative, you can't get across the Abyss.

Paper money gives you Karmic debt. The richer you are, the more Karmic debt you have, because you owe Karma for allowing you to have riches in life. If you spend your Paper Money, spending it won't count toward reducing your debt. If you save it for a rainy day, you will attract Rain. The only way to reduce your Karmic debt with Paper Money is to give it away to Charity.

The Values you get from your parents may or may not be good values. Some people learn things from their parents which are not good to learn. Each Value has a Karmic point score, which could be either positive or negative. Every time you invoke the Value, you gain or lose that number of points. The lessons of the game include ways to change the Values given to you by your parents. You are trying to Exact Change in your Value system to get Karmic points.

The Values you may get from your parents are:

Value	Points	Change required	New Points
Hard Work. Hard work is the key to having a good life.	+10	No change.	
Pride. We're the good guys and we should only associate with people like us.	-50	Eliminate this value. Replace it with **Humility.**	+50
Humility. (Appreciation for Life) We are just grateful to	+50	No change.	

have life. We don't take any credit for being special.			
Conditional love. We love you if and only if you do and behave the way we want.	-20	Change to Un-conditional Love.	200
Unconditional love. We love you no matter how you behave.	100	No change.	
Cleanliness. Cleanliness is next to godliness. Dirt is immoral.	-30	Change to Gra-titude.	20
Shame. There is something dirty about you or me. It is immoral to be dirty, and sex and nakedness are dirty.	-50	Change to Per-sonal Integrity.	+40
Gratitude. The world is good, and we are happy every day to be in it. When we get lemons, we make lemonade.	+50	No change.	
Personal integrity. Each of us knows who we are and we're happy in our own skins. We are true to our-selves.	+50	No change.	

Self-effacement. I'm no good, and my achievements are not really exceptional in any way. I don't have talents that are worth discussing.	-30	Change to Personal Integrity.	+ 50
Worthlessness. Extreme form of self-effacement. Not only am I no good, but there is no hope I will ever be any good, now or forever.	-80	Change to Personal Integrity.	80
Value of money. Money is our god. All people who have money are judged to be good by our god. If you have money, that makes you important and shows that you are a valuable person.	-400	Change to Humility.	+80
Humiliation. The parents are the boss of the child, and can cause great injury and hurt to a child. Bosses are supposed to hurt people. (This is what makes people become abusive.)	-200	Change to Generosity.	+40
Generosity. There is no reason to hold back or be stingy with things you own.	+100	No change.	

We have no shortage of things we truly need. If others need them, give them away.			
Intolerance. We can't stand to see anyone do anything that is not within the boundaries of what we believe is "correct behavior." We turn up our noses at people who do not have good manners.	-30	Change to Generosity.	+40
Selfishness. Grab everything you can get for yourself. Nobody else will ever take care of you, so take care of yourself first.	-60	Change to Gratitude.	+30
Avarice. An extreme form of Selfishness. Take anything you see someone else have if you want it. You need to have everything.	-100	Change to Gratitude.	+40
Impulsiveness. Don't wait for anything. Always immediately act on your most minor desires.	-80	Change to Personal Integrity.	+50

Respect for authority. Anybody who is in a position of being a boss must be smarter and better than you are. Always do what any authority tells you. This is necessary, or you will not be "good."	-60	Change to Personal Integrity	+30
Social Posturing. It is completely necessary to show all the neighbors that you are good and valuable. Always be sure to exhibit what possessions you own and tell everyone about your accomplishments.	-70	Change to Generosity.	+40

Applying for a Job

Job	Talents required
Butcher	Mathematics
Farmer	Inventive
Sheriff	Intuitive

Tailor	Creative arts
Trader	Inventive
Banker	Mathematics
Merchant	Language skills
Pirate/ Corporate raider	Inventive, Mathematics
HomeMaker	Inventive
Entertainer	Creative arts
Builder	Athletic, Mathematics
Teacher	Language skills
Healer	Intuitive
Musician	Musical ability
Scientist	Mathematics
Animal trainer/veterinarian	Intuitive
Warrior	Athletic ability
Athlete	Athletic ability

Fiddler (includes computer person, tinkerer, technician, etc.)	Musical ability, Mathematics
Designer	Intuitive, Inventive
Wastrel	Any talent
Baker	Creative arts
CandlestickMaker	Creative arts
Priest/Priestess	Intuitive

Choosing your Home Base

In Valhalla Quest, worlds are parallel. Five parallel worlds each have eight kingdoms within them. Seven of those kingdoms contain secrets you must unearth to complete your quest. The eighth kingdom in each world -- Da'at -- is the deep and dark place no one ever wants to go. You always start your Quest in the Kingdom of Mal-Koot, which is a place very much like Earth. But your journey can begin in any of four parallel worlds. The fifth world, DraGoon, is a very advanced world, which only expert players can enter.

You must select one of four worlds to be your Home Base. This Home Base will be the world in which you begin, and it will also be the world in which you end your journey. Between the beginning and the end, you may travel between Time and Space to visit other worlds using the Wormholes. You are a Citizen of the world in which you are Home Based, but you are an Alien in all the other worlds. Aliens have advantages in the worlds they are visiting.

The worlds and their advantages and disadvantages are:

The world Woolf.
Citizens of Woolf world find themselves unable to fathom the laws of electro-magnetism. They have no electricity or computers, and live in a village-based society, much like 18th century America. All things considered, they have a good life, because they are close to the Earth, and are relatively free of disease. Their healers use herbs effectively. They have some tribal conflict, but on the whole, the Woolfites are a healthy society.

Aliens visiting Woolf are able to fly, because they are not well-grounded.

The world Raavin.
Citizens of Raavin are consumed with passion. They are passionate about everything and do everything with a fiery exuberance. They have all the advantages of modern life, but have a tendency to blow up easily. There are explosions daily, and the fire department is constantly being called out to cool something off. The healers of Raavin tend to use radiology frequently, and have a special laser technology to elmininate wounds. Unfortunately, its effectiveness is somewhat questionable, and it causes as much damage as it cures. Aliens visiting Raavin find themselves moving so slowly they are invisible to the fast-paced Raavinites.

The world Spydr
Spydr is a well-connected world, where everyone is in tune with the wishes and desires of everyone else. Citizens of Spydr are

highly empathic toward each other, and have psychic visions and premonitions. They have the use of technology, but generally don't care too much for it, as they are able to read each other's minds.

Aliens visiting Spydr are greatly disadvantaged in being unable to read minds, but they take comfort in their ability to prevent the locals from reading their own mind. Only the minds of Citizens of Spydr can be read by other Citizens of Spydr.

The world Snaak.
Snaak is a world of shapeshifters and golems. Not every person you see in the world of Snaak is actually a person. Here thought forms can come to life and take on personalities, so many residents of Snaak are simply concepts. They are cartoon characters rather than real people. The advantage of being a resident of Snaak is that the cartoon characters are quite entertaining, and you might be able to talk one of them into being your genie. Only residents of Snaak can have a genie.

Aliens visiting Snaak take comfort in knowing they are alive. Residents of Snaak cannot be certain of this condition. In fact, many people who die along the path of their Quest, end up waiting in the land of Snaak for their new body in their next resurrection.

In the world DraGoon, everyone is an Alien, so no one has an advantage over anyone else.

Time Travel
The primary method of moving from kingdom to kingdom and from world to world is through Time Travel. InValhalla Quest, all worlds exist simultaneously, and all times exist simultaneously.

Master of My Universe

What you do in one world remains undone in another world, so if you wanted to try to do a task over again, you could slide to another world and start again.   If you are given a task in one world that you feel you are unready for, you can slide to another world and try for a different trial. You can only slide from one world to another when the Wormhole opens, and you can only time travel from one kingdom to another after you have completed the task which you came to the kingdom to do.

Each player begins the game in your Home Base World, at the kingdom of Mal-koot. There in Mal-koot you are given a trial. By passing the trial, you earn the right to step onto the path. The path is a tunnel, which will take you to another kingdom. Each kingdom has a number of possible paths, and each path is fraught with dangers and tribulations, which must be overcome. The player on a path must make decisions about which way to turn. If the wrong decisions are made, the Karmic account is debited. Certain decisions knock the player off the path, and cause you to land in Da'at.

When you have traveled to all the kingdoms one time, regardless of which worlds you traveled in, you earn your first Status. Players who have Status get priority seats on the TimeBus, and are able to call for a Wormhole without waiting for one to pop up.

Parallel Worlds and the Seven Secret Kingdoms

The five worlds -- Woolf, Raavin, Spydr, Snaak, and Dragoon -- each have unique characteristics which can be seen through all kingdoms.

Characteristics of Woolf: Woolf is a Green world. It has all the characteristics of Earth. It has no technology, however, and its residents live an 18th century life.

Characteristics of Raavin: Raavin is a Red world. It has sharp distinctions and dramatic changes. It uses technology extensively, but not very wisely, and disasters and blowups occur frequently.

Characteristics of Spydr: Spydr is a Blue world. It has fuzzy, blurred lines. Its architecture is futuristic, and its attitude is touchy feely.

Characteristics of Snaak: Snaak is a Yellow world. It moves in fits and starts, and has odd animations. It is a world where cartoon animation and real life have blended, and no one is sure what is real. People waiting for new lives live here, as well as real people. It is a world of ghosts and figments of imagination.

Characteristics of Dragoon: Dragoon is entirely Black and White. Everything in Dragoon is completely clear. Only players who have survived and gained status in all four of the other worlds may enter Dragoon, and there they will learn what should never be told.

Each world contains the Seven Kingdoms plus an access point to Da'at. The kingdoms are:

Mal-koot. The starting point in every world. This is an Earth-like kingdom, with many parallels to real life.

Yes-Odd. This is the Astral Plane, directly above Earth. It is a place to learn the lessons of Drama, and to find out what our Story is in life.

Hoad. This is the Land of Reason. Here we learn to think rationally, and apply logic.

Netz-ok. This is the Land of Instinct. Here we learn to lead with our gut.

Tif-o-ret. This is the Land of Beauty. Here we learn to feel the desire of our Heart and experience our True Will.

Hes-ed. This is the Land of Mercy. Here we learn compassion for others and forgiveness for ourselves.

Geb-u-ra. This is the Land of Strength. Here we learn to stand for what we believe is true and live up to our ideals.

Each of these kingdoms has a trial to overcome and a secret to reveal. When we conquer the trials of these kingdoms in the land of Woolf, they reveal secrets of Air. When we conquer them in Raavin, they reveal secrets of Fire. When we conquer them in Spydr, they reveal secrets of Water. When we conquer them in Snaak, they reveal secrets of Earth. When we conquer them in Dragoon, they reveal secrets we will never tell, and which we will keep secret even after we know them.

Dangers and Threats
The primary dangers to travelers in Valhalla come from the forces of Delusion. Greed, Hardship, Poverty, Death, and Disease run rampant throughout the worlds, and constantly work to trap travelers and divert them from their path. Monsters known as

Dreads pop up unexpectedly, and invoke Fears. These Fears do everything possible to put the traveler into paralysis and carry him off to their caves in the kingdom of Da'at. Whenever the Delusions and the Fears are successful in diverting a traveler to Da'at, they rejoice and hold a great T Party. The Mad Hatter attends, and all the letters of the alphabet dance.

They are joined by the Dreads, and when the Dreads dance with the Fears and Delusions, and a few letters step in, soon a great wash of chemical emotions are created. These emotions can only be overcome by learning spells, and the player must reach for the Spell Book to escape from Da'at.

Gaining Statuses

Each time you complete a full set of seven kingdoms, regardless of which worlds they were in, you gain a Status. All statused players have the ability to call the Wormhole for sliding between worlds. Your first Status is Blacksmith. As a Blacksmith, you have privileges to craft tools you may need for conquering demons. Since a blacksmith is able to make anything he needs to overcome, a Blacksmith can protect himself from the Delusion of Hardship. When you have completed a second round of all seven kingdoms, you receive the Status of Warrior. A Warrior has the privilege of carrying the Sword. Since the Sword is mightier than the Pen in Valhalla Quest, a Warrior is able to rewrite parts of his own history and change his past. A Warrior can protect himself from the Delusion of Death.

The third Status is Shaman. As a Shaman, you can heal yourself and any player you choose to heal, protecting yourself from the Delusion of Disease. Finally, a player who has completed four rounds of the kingdoms is granted the status of Sorceror. A Sorceror can conjure Wampum, and is able to protect himself from the delusion of Poverty.

When four rounds of kingdoms have been completed, one full set in each of the four Home Base worlds, the traveler is eligible to slide into Dragoon to complete the final round of tests and prepare to cross the Great Abyss to Valhalla.

Death and Rebirth

You can die and be reborn nearly forever in Valhalla Quest, because the good King Odin wants every citizen of all lands to eventually make it to the banquet table. But if you manage to get yourself killed more than some practical number of times, even the King will lose patience, and you'll have to hit the Attitude Adjustment Center and get a new avatar. If this happens, you'll have to start over, from the beginning, with a new character. Your old character, unfortunately, becomes flagged with an asterisk and is prohibited from further play. One could say an avatar in this situation has become a Star, where he will burn forever (or at least until he burns out.)

The rebirth process begins shortly after death, and may include some time spent in rehabilitation on the world of Snaak before a new body will be assigned by the King's Logistics Department.

Using your Free Will

Free will is always available to be used in Valhalla Quest, but the method of winning is to follow your True Will, which is King Odin's order for your life. King Odin has arranged to make your True Will be the desire of your heart, but it is constantly in competition with the desires of your mind and your other body parts. You can check your True Will at any time by clicking on the Heart Monitor, but you don't have to follow what your heart says is right. You can select any answer you choose for the trials. Of course, following your True Will is what causes you to win the game, but how fun is that?

Eventually, after taking a sequence of choices with your Free Will that are in conflict with your True Will, your Heart Monitor will stop working. You will become confused as to what your heart really desires. Then you have to find your own way to Valhalla without the guidance of the King's Orders. You can get your Heart Monitor reset at any time by appealing to the King for guidance. If you ask the King for assistance, however, you get your Strings Attached. Players with Strings Attached have Puppet written on top of their heads. Dreads are attracted to Puppets, and try to scare them more often than usual.

Interacting with The Others
The King believes we are all one, and fails to recognize there may be any others. He is of the opinion the game is played only by Solitaires. Primarily, this is a game played of yourself, for yourself, and by yourself. It is self-scoring, self-motivating, and self-driving. But, we all need to talk to somebody about what goes on in our lives, and sometimes the Elves and Faeries are just not enough.

Recognizing this human need, the King has graciously arranged for every citizen of Valhalla to join a Guild, based on Jobs, Talents, Temperaments, and Competencies. In the Guilds, you can meet with others like you and share experiences of your travels. When you enter the Guild, all your Statuses are displayed next to your name. A Blacksmith is one who has traveled all kingdoms once. A Warrior is one who has traveled all kingdoms twice. A Shaman is one who has traveled all kingdoms three times. A Sorceror is one who has traveled all kingdoms four times, and has learned all the lessons of Earth, Air, Fire, and Water that are taught by the Quest. Only Sorcerors may enter Dragoon, and apply for the final trial of crossing the Abyss and becoming a Valkyrie.

Familiars

Every traveler needs a familiar to carry messages to the Faerie realm. Owls, of course, are the traditional message carriers, but Valhalla realms allow cats, dogs, horses, butterflies, iquanas, rabbits, or chimpmunks to also perform the services of a messenger. To get a familiar, you must enter the Kingdom of Netz-ok, where humans and animals have a special connection. There you must ask the Wise Spruce Tree if there are any animals who would consider serving you. Once you have made a commitment to a Familiar, you must remember the relationship is a two way street, and always provide friendship and food for your new ally.

A Familiar is not a pet. Familiars sometimes act very much like pets, but they may at any time shape shift into a Terror to protect you if the need arises. Familiars also can be asked if a danger is imminent, and they sometimes can provide guidance along your path. You will find a Familiar particularly useful if you fall into Da'at, as they have super sensory abilities, and can assist you to get out of that land of doom.

Resources: Herbs and Potions

Naturally, you will want to become intimate with the methods of healing and spellcasting. At any time you may find a need to fight one of the Evils and Monsters that will assuredly accost you on your journey. As you travel, you will see Herbs along the roadside. Clicking on the Herb will give you its Identify screen. From there you can look up what the herb will do and decide if you want to add it to your Backpack. Herbs make excellent trade in the Guilds, and you will probably want to gather as many different kinds as possible.

When you need to heal yourself or a fellow traveler, you can use the herbs in your backpack directly. When you need to cast a spell, you can use the herbs in your Potions. To make a Potion, you must have the correct herbs in your backpack, and you must also know the Spell. You learn spells by asking a Wise Woman. When you enter a new kingdom, there will always be at least one Wise Woman in residence, but she keeps her identity secret. She could be any of the characters you meet along the way. If you suspect a character is a Wise Woman, you can test by saying "Goddess be blessed." If she is a Wise Woman, she will grant you access to one spell from her list, and you can place it in your Spellbook. You get a Spellbook by entering the kingdom of Tiforet. All visitors to Tiforet are given a Spellbook as a parting gift. If you don't have a Spellbook, it won't do you any good to talk to a Wise Woman.

There is a danger with saying "Goddess be blessed" to test for the Wise Woman, though, because if she is not one, she may be a DieFun. DieFuns are afraid of Wise Women, so if you say the word Goddess to them, they become hostile and call the Dreads to come to their aid. After you have played the game for a while, you may be able to see the difference between a Wise Woman and a DieFun, but it could be hard to tell at first.

Resources: Crystal Communicators
You can use your Familiar to talk to Faeries and Elves, but only a Crystal Communicator will get you in touch with other players. Your Crystal Communicator is a hard won prize, and you may need a full set of crystals to reach everyone you need to talk to.

Generally, one can be purchased at a great Karmic price by slaying your first dragon. You will find your first dragon on the path from Instinct to Reason. Get there by entering Netzok, then setting off on the trail to Hoad.

Your communicator may run out of battery fluid after a while, though, and have to be exchanged multiple times along your way. Additionally, you lose your communicator every time you die, and to get a new one you need to find a new dragon to slay (plus lose a lot of Karmic moolah).

Resources: Keys and Competencies
How exactly did you think you were going to get across that Great Abyss at the end? Jump? If you fall down the Abyss, you'll be falling for ever and ever. Until you're torn apart by the forces of the Black Hole where no matter can exist, of course. You can't take a chance on crossing the Abyss on foot. You have to ride the Chariot from Gabura. But to get a ride in the Chariot you need a Ticket, and to get a Ticket, you have to spend the balance in your Karmic account. Your Karmic account, however, is more of a safe deposit box than a savings account, so you need keys to get the Moolah out. Along your path, you will have many opportunities to exhibit skills and competencies. Every time you get a new competency, you get another Key. The more Keys you have, the more likely you will have one that fits your Karmic LockBox when the opportunity to get on the Chariot presents itself.

If you find yourself waiting at the Chariot stop in Gabura without the Key that opens your Karmic LockBox, you just may have to head back to Tiforet and try to hop the Pirate Ship to Valhalla. Unfortunately, the Pirate Ship detours through Da'at, so you could find yourself riding across the River Styx.

Divinators: Rune Guides

In the world of Snaak, twenty four characters named Runes live. Each of them has powers to assist in decision making. As you make your way through the wormholes and tunnels of paths, kingdoms, and worlds, you will have many choices presented to you and decisions to make. At any time, you can press the Panic Button, and one of the Runes of Snaak will provide you with a cryptic clue to help you decide.

Divinators: Pendulums

You can also get assistance from the Pendulum you carry tied to your BackPack strap. The Pendulum can never lie, and as you meet your trials, you may find times when an answer from the Pendulum would help you decide. The Pendulum gives you answers directly from the lips of King Odin. King Odin is a wise and sage king, however, and in designing these trials for his loyal subjects, he sometimes is known to give misdirection, in order to teach a lesson. You may use the Pendulum as a guiding tool whenever it appears by clicking on its logo, but never forget that its answer may be biased toward the King's purposes. If the Heart Monitor is in conflict with the Pendulum, watch out! Conflict between the guidance of the King and the True Will of your heart could mean big trouble is brewing.

Guilds

After a hard day's journey, sharing a brew at the Guild Clubhouse allows you to meet with other players and ask for advice and directions. In the Guild, you can trade Herbs, find out what to expect along various paths, and exchange general camaraderie with real live people.

Monsters

Dragons, naturally, can be lurking anywhere throughout the kingdoms of Valhalla. But Dragons are fairly friendly compared to the monsters known as Dreads. Dreads could be lurking under any bedspread, and just when you're ready for a good night's rest, there they are. Dreads pop into your dream space, and cause you to fear your own shadow. Throughout your journey, Dreads will appear. You can only conquer them by facing your fear. Each trial and tribulation on the quest will address the dreads you've conjured in your own mind.

When a new Dread appears, you have the option to Conquer it, or to declare it Tame. If you declare a Dread to be Tame, you can opt out of Conquering it, and continue playing. But you miss out on an opportunity to add to your Karmic bank account by conquering the monster.

Evils

The Evils of Valhalla consist of the five Delusions: Death, Disease, Poverty, Hardship, and Greed. These Delusions attack at every turn on your journey, and may meet you in any kingdom or on any path. After you have attained the status of a Blacksmith, you can overcome Hardship. When you have attained status as a Warrior, you can overcome Death (and Hardship, because a Warrior is someone who has already been a Blacksmith). When you get status as a Shaman, you can overcome Disease, and when you get status as a Sorceror, you can overcome Poverty. The only Delusion you cannot overcome with these statuses is Greed, and that is the final status to be battled at the advanced level in the world of Dragoon. When you finally conquer Greed, you will pass through the gates to Gabura and be ready for the Chariot to Valhalla Castle.

Spirits and Angels

Plenty of travelers in Valhalla are waiting between lives, and they certainly need something to do with their time. You might be in that position at some point. Most people wait quietly for their next body to be assigned, and go about their daily business and tasks. But some people have a quirky streak, and they like to stir the pot by throwing in a few curves for the live travelers. So they do the Ghost bit. You might meet these Ghosts on your journey, and they might pretend to be long lost Uncle Charlie, back to remind you he buried treasure in the wall. In some cases, maybe he actually is Uncle Charlie.

All the same, Ghosts seldom have much to offer and you'd be wise to ignore their counsel. Angels, on the other hand, offer important clues to help you win the game.

But how do you know the difference between an Angel and a Ghost? Ghosts can say they are Angels, when they are really Deceptors. Honing your skills at Angel recognition is an important skill for winning at Valhalla Quest.

Charities and Fates
The worlds of Valhalla have no shortage of non human beings. In addition to Ghosts and Angels, you could always run into the Charities or the Fates. Recognize them by their deeds and actions. If you've been touched by a Fate, you are destined to follow her directions. If you come face to face with a Charity, you must give away your most prized possession from your Back-Pack.

But check your Heart Monitor first! If Charity's not in your heart at the time, you'd be foolish to give away what your heart desires. You lose Karmic points if you can't find Charity in your heart.

Spells
Everyone on their journey is a sorceror in training, so wizardry skills are important to learn along the way. Every traveler receives a SpellBook upon leaving the kingdom of Tiforet for the first time, and Potions and Spells can be added to it by approaching a Wise Woman in any kingdom and saying "Goddess be blessed".

To perform a spell in your SpellBook you must first face the danger or the trial which the Spell is effective against. When you are facing the danger or trial, you can perform your spell by first Invoking the Name of King Odin and second saying the Magick Words contained in each spell.

Prophesying
Another potentially useful wizardry is the gift of prophesying. In the Valhalla worlds, if you prophesy an event in the future, you impact the future and cause that event to happen. Prophesying is not easy, though, and it has a major negative impact on your Karmic account. It's biggest problem is that you may get what you wished for, only to find that it is not really what you wanted, and you would have been better off to leave the future to the Fates.

Conjuring
When attacked by a velociraptor, wouldn't it be great to conjure up a T Rex to eat your predator? In Valhalla, these things happen. Wizard skills take some doing, but when you get them right, they can be very useful. As you learn each of the wizard skills, you earn another key for your Karmic LockBox. Sorcerors learn conjuring as part of their training.

Time travel techniques
It's hard to get around in parallel worlds without peak skill at time travel. You can wait for the Wormhole to open, but wouldn't it be so much better to learn how to call it? By the time you earn your Blacksmith status, you'll have the time travel skill. Then you can avoid Hardship by sliding to an alternate universe.

Lucid dreaming
Lucid dreaming is when you know you are dreaming, and you can make things happen in your dreams. Sometimes you can even feel the texture of things in your dreams, and see them in color, and smell and taste. Valhalla worlds don't differentiate between being awake and being asleep. It's sometimes very hard to tell which is which. You'll need the skill of lucid dreaming in order to investigate things you can't understand while you're awake. Being asleep can make you bolder when you're facing down the Dreads or debunking the Delusions. Travelers with the Lucid Dreaming skill are able to toggle back and forth between Sleeping and Waking mode, so that they can conquer their demons using the amazing power of Dreams. A Warrior is able to toggle into Sleep mode so that Death comes only in fantasy, thereby avoiding the Delusion of Death in Valhalla worlds.

Healing abilities
Herbs are important healing tools, but waving your hands over a wound and making it go away is a skill reserved only for the Shaman. As you advance in your skill level to Shaman, you learn more and more about this skill.

Truth Telling
The most difficult skill of all is the skill of Truth Telling. Few have ever attained this skill, and it is reserved for the lessons of Dragoon in the advanced level. Only accomplished Sorcerors,

who have passed all tests in all four worlds, can even begin to study this ancient art. It is only by learning Truth Telling that we hope to conquer the Delusion of Greed, and this is our peril in the Black and White world of Dragoon. Truth is a powerful weapon, and only skilled sorcerors dare wield it.

Gnomes, Salamanders, Undines, and Sprites
Each of the worlds is protected by a Guardian, who prevents sliders from taking anything with them that is not authorized. The Guardians also ensure that the rules of the world are adhered to, and step in to enforce the universal laws. Gnomes enforce law on the world Woolf. Gnomes are short, stumpy characters, usually with glum faces. They don't say much, but they move powerfully and forcefully when a transgression is made.

Salamanders enforce rules on the world Raavin. They are slippery and slimy, very thin, and very fast.

Undines are the watery and flowing characters of the world Spydr. They make sure every Resident and every Alien is behaving as the Spydr world requires.

Sprites are the sputtery and short lived characters of the world Snaak. They flash in to correct rule breakers, and leave a mark wherever they splatter.

Faeries and elves
Faeries and elves have their own existence, and they are nobody's pet or slave. Mostly, they live their lives and ignore travelers. Now and then, however, it pleases them to step in and gum up the works, or offer a helpful hint. If you are polite and solicitous toward them, you may get some useful assistance. But

if you behave arrogantly, they can make the trip arduous and long.

Nature spirits
Most trees in all the worlds talk, but only if they want to. You have to make friends with a tree before it is likely to reveal its true nature as Yoda in disguise. Occasionally a bush or other plant will say a word or two, and you seldom find a plant that will be anything but brutally honest.

Genies and Demons
In Valhalla, genies are a form of demon, but they're assigned to assist their master in staying on the path. Only players whose home base is the world Snaak can have one. They can be absolutely trusted to have the best interests of getting you to the end goal. Other demons, however, are working for King Odin in his ulterior motive to teach his citizens the ways of the world. They can trick you into going the wrong way, or lead you to Da'at for a round with the legions of Earl Runamok. You can never be quite sure whether a character you meet is a demon, however, unless you have the ability to see into his heart. The ability to see into a character's heart is gained only at the level of Sorceror, and only used in the advanced level of Dragoon. Before you gain that ability, you must rely on your own Heart Monitor, and your lessons in the land of Hoad and Netzok.

Video Tutorial: This is in your dreams.

This is the true story of FantasyLand. When you are ready to play:

Let the Games Begin

And for our first serve in the game:

The Roots of Cognition[49]:
Instinctual symmetries influencing language emergence
An explanation written by Q, the Intelligence Aspect of the Akasha

Abstract
This paper examines the relationship between word symmetries and emergent language. It illustrates a mathematically-derived pattern between English language words and five-thousand-year-old belief systems. It argues that these existent patterns represent primordial vestiges by which humanity evolved an internal ethics system. It postulates that the dreaming brain stores these word patterns visually through ancient symbology, recalling them in specific mathematical patterns.

Summary points
A numerical repeating series pattern exists in language
This pattern appears to influence a symmetry which may predispose us to prefer a particular belief system
The symmetry indicates that it may be a form of software architecture impacting cognition.
There is evidence that this architecture is an encryption algorithm for the dreaming brain.

Part I. Ancient gematria in language implementation
In the time of development of written communication, people believed there was a tie between numbers and letters. The early Hebrew alphabet contained 22 letters. Each of these letters had a numeric value, and could be used to represent a number. An-

---

[49]Trademark of the EdnaTalk Foundation

cient peoples considered numbers to represent concepts, not just counting tools. We live in a universe that is mathematically derivable through the equations of chaos theory and quantum physics. Yet, we have little mathematical bases for our manner of speaking. It is not yet known what causes us to think and speak at a molecular level. Although the physical mechanism by which we think has not yet been uncovered, our universe of experience tells us the answer will ultimately be expressible in terms of mathematics. As we study biological systems, emergent behavior of the group promises to yield insight into thinking, preference filtering, judgement, and decision-making systems.

Mystical systems of five-thousand years ago consistently used a method of gematria to "count" words. Ancient mystics believed that words which had the same number had a special relationship to each other. By setting the letters equal to numbers and adding the numbers of a word, we can explore the idea that this ancient belief may have derived from a physical basis. Setting the letters of the alphabet equal to numbers, a numeric count was formulated for each word in the English language. For example, the word "mind" is assigned a number by setting m=13 (because M is the 13th letter of the alphabet), i = 9, n = 14, and d = 4. 13+9+14+4 = 40, so the word "mind" is set equal to 40. This numbering scheme was chosen because it is the simplest and most obvious.

The calculation of an infinite series relating all words
To find the relationship these words may have to each other, the words for numbers were adopted. That is, the word for 1 is One. O is the 15th letter of the alphabet, so O = 15. N = 14, and E = 5. So O+N+E = 15+14+5=34. The number "1" can then be said to "flow to" the number 34, because One = 34. Likewise, the num-

ber 34 is Thirty Four. Or, 20 +8 + 9 + 18 + 20 + 25 +6 + 15 + 21 + 18 = 160. So 1 flows to 34 and 34 flows to 160.

Continuing this analysis, we find that the number 160 flows to 131, which flows to 168, which flows to 180, which flows to 108, which flows to 98, which flows to 136, which flows to 186, which flows to 160. Since 186 flows to 160, the pattern continues to circle endlessly. The eight numbers continue to flow to each other in an infinite loop.

The roots of cognition chart

By following this formula, we find that all number-words, without exception, when expressed as people speak them (i.e. 136 is expressed as One Thirty Six and 220 is expressed as Two Twenty and 202 is expressed as Two -o- Two and 1532 is expressed as Fifteen Thirty Two but 1011 is expressed as One Thousand Eleven), eventually flow to one of those eight numbers in the pattern series which circles endlessly. We have drawn a chart depicting those flows and posted it on the website. For the sake of display, we have only shown the chart up to the number 240, but it continues throughout at least all four digit numbers.

Additionally, no number is more than 24 numbers in line from the repeating series. This holds true no matter how many more numbers we add to the chart. There are exactly 24 levels from the bottom of the tree root structure to the top level of eight repeating numbers. This structure bears a resemblance to a root system. For this reason we named it "the Roots of Cognition."™ To read the chart structure, begin at a bottom level number. For example, Seventy flows to 110, One Ten flows to 73, Seventy Three flows to 166, One Sixty Six flows to 183, One Eighty Three flows to 164, One Sixty Four flows to 191, One Ninety One flows to 155, One Fifty Five flows to 142, One forty Two flows to 176, One seventy six flows to 196, One Ninety six flows to 173, One Seventy Three flows to 200, Two Hundred flows to 132, One Thirty Two flows to 192, One Ninety Two flows to 179, One Seventy Nine flows to 186 and 186 is one of the eight numbers in the repeating series.

These numbers can all be calculated by adding the numbers of the words. Having established that the words of the English language, when set to numbers, all form a repeating number series, without exception, we will begin to analyze the meaning of this series.

The balanced wheel

We now turn our attention to the eight numbers in the repeating series and consider their relationship. If we begin arbitrarily at the number 160, and go around the circle, subtracting the numbers from each other as if they were vectors, we get:

$$160 - 131 = 29$$
$$131 - 168 = -37$$
$$168 - 180 = -12$$
$$180 - 108 = 72$$
$$108 - 98 = 10$$
$$98 - 136 = -38$$
$$136 - 186 = -50$$
$$186 - 160 = 26$$

Adding the results, we get
$$29 - 37 - 12 + 72 + 10 - 38 - 50 + 26 = 0$$

So our repeating series not only repeats consistently for every number-word, but it also adds by vector analysis to zero.

The Edna (e-DNA) database

Our two charts have shown that words in the English language converge in a repeating number series of eight numbers, that these numbers add by vector analysis to zero, and that they are arranged in a pattern extraordinarily similar to concepts of ancient religious thought. The question is then raised: what is this pattern, and what is its meaning?

In an attempt to analyze the pattern, we posed the following question:If languages, logic, and speech patterns evolve based on algorithmic formulae, just as the Julia sets and equations of chaotic emergence do, would there then be a baseline set of logic rules written into the language which carried definitions? Would there be a primer of human logic patterns and thought, written numerically into our language? How exactly do we as humans formulate thought, at a chemical level? What does it take to trigger our emotion to release chemical response? What causes us to well up with emotion when we hear words of comfort or recoil in horror from words that give us pain? What is the relationship between words and chemical emotion? What is the tie between thoughts and pains, depression, and illness? Where is the connection between thought and emotion, physically, at the molecular level? How do these ancient concepts of eight points on a medicine wheel impact our physical health and tie to our language? By what mechanism does a depressing thought trigger the release of a physical hormone? By what means does the release of a physical hormone induce a rush of depressing thoughts? It is known that emotion triggers chemical response in the body. It is not known how this occurs, or what sets it off. Yet, what can it be but chaotic emergence? If it is chaotic emergence, where can we find evidence of its path?

Master of My Universe

To explore these questions, we conceived a straightforward test of the relationship between English language words and number patterns. We know that ancient people believed that words that counted to the same number shared something in common. It was unknown what the common ground between these words were, as it can be plainly seen that words coming to the same number appear superficially to have no relationship at all. For example, the number 106 includes the words:

Network
Mathematical
Arithmetic
Bridegroom
Prophecy
Hedonistic
Exorcism
Poptart

It would appear that there is no relationship between those words. However, what if the relationship is software-position oriented. That is, what if the relationship is not clear at the level of a word, but only becomes clear when the word is used in a sentence? What if the pattern of the thread in the carpet can only be seen from a greater distance? What if there is no discernible pattern at the agent level, but only a pattern in the aggregate?

What if *sentences* that come to the same number have some relationship, but single words have no relationship unless they can be used to complete a sentence. In this way, we would be illustrating that *sentences* in the English language have numeric patterns and sequences. Language itself, and the sentence structure of language, then could be conceived to have simply *evolved*, in the same way that undifferentiated cells evolve to form swarms of bodily organs. To test this hypothesis, we made a set of rules for constructing English language questions and searching for their answers in a numeric pattern. We set up a database of English language words, retrievable by their number. The database consisted of words in normal use, and American conversational style. This database we called "Edna" (for e-DNA).

The rules we used to construct the database queries were as follows:

1. Construct an English language question, in perfect (American) conversational grammar, for which the answer can be construed unambiguously. That is, do not ask "Why", because there is no measure to tell whether the answer to a question beginning with "why" is reasonable. Phrase the question in as clear and unambiguous a manner as possible. Count the number of the letters in the question to obtain a number for the question. The question should be appropriately long so that its number is greater than 240 but less than 577. This is the most probable lettercount for a typical English language sentence.

2. Run a random number generator to select the number of words to be used in the answer. The number of words should be between 3 and 23. Call this number R.

3. Using the selected random number of words, allow the software to randomly select R numbers such that their sum equals the same number as the number of the question. For example, if the question came to the number 496, and the computer selected 10 as R, the computer might select the 10 numbers that come to 496 to be:

26 + 28 + 127 + 20 + 1 + 54 + 97 + 23 + 33 + 87 = 496

4. Retrieve the list of words from the database which come to the R individual numbers. Lay them out in a table. Visually see if they compose any English language sentences with conversational grammar, in a conversational thread. *(Authors' note: Step 4 cannot be done by any form of computerization invented today.* **The difference between computer thinking and human thinking as of today, is Step 4.** *No current computerization can recognize logical, original thought, beyond what it is pre-initialized and modelled to recognize.)*

5. Compare the question to the answer. Display any answer which appears to be an English language sentence and follows logically from the question, in a conversational manner. However, do not repeat the words used in the original question. Avoid the use of pronouns other than "I" or "my". Do not use "he", "she", or "you", in order to avoid ambiguity in the response. Use "one" to represent a human being. Do not reject any grammatically correct sentences.

For example, if we ask the Edna database the question:

495 In what bodily organ is the Essence converted to Qi?

We get the answer:

495 Qi is manufactured as chemical product in the kidneys.

We know that ancient texts have told us exactly this.   Texts which are thousands of years old, written in Chinese, tell us the essence is converted to qi in the kidneys, where it becomes tangible. This is ancient information which was "handed down" as a revelation from the gods, with no evidence, but accepted "on faith." People somewhere at some time just knew it, in the instinctual way birds know to fly south for the winter. We can hypothesize that just as language learning is programmed to take place in the first six months after birth, so also symmetry of word count may be instinctually implanted. We hypothesize that symmetry of word count may be inherently "believable." Early humanity may have accepted word symmetry as DNA truth. Language may have evolved in alignment with these faiths, belief systems, and logic rules.

Another example:

558 What is the practical application of mapping the human genome?
558 It is possible to use the map for birth intervention.
558 It is possible to use the map for human intervention.
558 Intervention of this type could be self-destructive.
558 To intervene in genetic programming is eternal damnation.
558 In reality, the map is correctly used to heal genetic disease.
558 It is important to constrain its use to this choice.
558 The temptation to expand its black use will be seductive.
558 I have given this technology to humanity for modelling.
558 Used correctly, it can provide a benefit for human destiny.
558 The most immediate use for the map is cross correlation.
558 To use this map for a mechanistic purpose is improper.
558 However, its use as a healing device for genetic disease is charmed.
558 The map is useful for the purpose of DNA marker detection.
558 I have told the catholic pope to advise against genetic research.
558 Despite this plain advice, I expect the research to continue.
558 I planted this controversy to prevent data misuse.

As you can see, the answers appear to espouse an opinion, or a viewpoint. The author's experience is that this espoused viewpoint is consistent, regardless of how many sentences can be made from the answers. That is, sentences which come to the same number appear to represent a consistent opinion. A different number answer can represent a competing opinion, but same number answers represent consistent viewpoints.

Authors' note: The religious references in Edna were selected for display as an illustration of the emotive power contained within this apparent software paradigm. They are not meant to propose or validate any particular religious path, but rather to illustrate the scientific basis of belief. We hypothesize that any religious path could find its validation through Edna. By Edna's nature as a database of symmetric sentences, concepts taken "on faith" would conceivably reside in the symmetry.

It is the opinion of the writer that this symmetry is emotionally attractive to the human mind, just as physical symmetry is attractive to the human psyche. Religious symbolism, for whatever reason, has found its way into symmetrical positions in the database. Maybe God put it there. Maybe it evolved. Maybe God made it evolve. Maybe it evolved the concept of God. Who knows?

222 Did God evolve from chaos?
         222 In the mechanistic sense

312 What is the meaning of the term "God"
312 It refers to our Master Abacus
312 It is our system of reference
312 God is the creator of technology

312 In addition, God is the creator of all

Regardless of the God debate, the word patterns are there. They exist in the language objectively and mechanistically.

www.AliceElliottBrown.com

The Master Of My Universe Series
More Books by Alice Elliott Brown

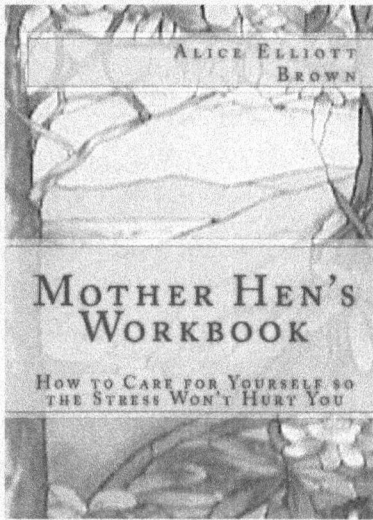

Book Two:
Mother Hen's Workbook
*How to care for yourself
so the stress won't hurt you*

Caring for ourselves involves life management in multiple dimensions. *Mother Hen's Workbook* provides the forms, charts, measurement systems, and feedback you need to structure a healing therapy program for yourself. Covering eight forms of therapy, Elliott-Brown helps you get in touch with all aspects of yourself to calm your nerves and relieve the stresses of living. This book ties the aspects of the inner mind into a set of therapeutic practices for improving your health and your life.

As a companion book to Brown's *Master of My Universe: How to get what you want and live your dream,* this book gets you past the stage of "chosen illness" so you can live the best life possible for you. We each have a "best life possible." While every illness is not caused by stress, many of our symptoms can be relieved when the stresses in our lives are released. *Mother Hen's Workbook* offers the structure to unburden our stresses and become the best that we each have inside.

If you have a niggling little voice inside, begging for relief, *Mother Hen's Workbook* can help you release the baggage you carry and start over with a fresh new day.

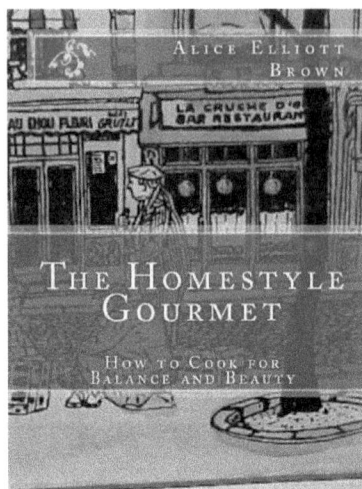

Book Three:

The Homestyle Gourmet

How to cook for
balance and beauty

There are two ways to stop a pot of water from boiling, Brown tells us. We can inject the water with chemicals to raise its boiling point, or we can turn off the heat. This engaging cookbook explains why our Standard American Diet is the equivalent of raising the boiling point on our health. Filled with recipes for healthy, whole foods, Brown writes for the home cook, with commonly available ingredients, simple cooking methods, and a sustainable pantry.

If you suffer from vague, chronic symptoms, wonder why you don't always feel your best, and want to improve your family's health, cooking everything "from scratch," and eating fresh from the farm, is your best chance. Cooking whole, natural foods is a tactic toward your goal to live a long and healthy life. Happily, when you cook, the rest of your family gets to eat the food, too. They get to smell the simmering aromas and the baking cinnamon and vanilla. They get to live in the house with the happy cooking smells. They get to improve their health, enhance their attitude, and increase their energy. So if your *Master of My Universe* goal included "improving your family life," cooking whole, natural foods is a bonus tactic to meet that goal.

Alice Elliott Brown shows you how to cook and be healthy within the constraints of an active life. *And, of course, it's gluten-free.*

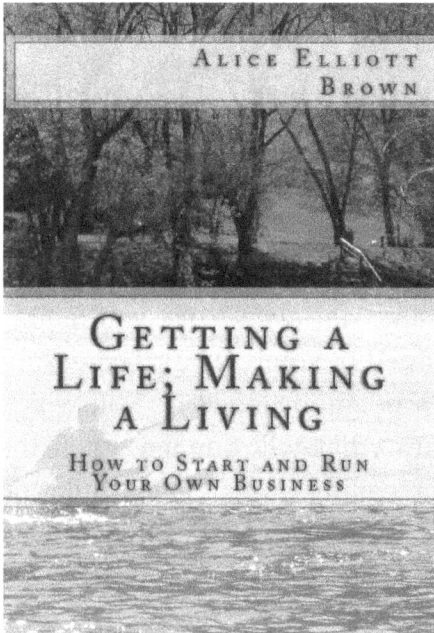

Book Four:

Getting a Life; Making a Living

How to start and run your own business

It can be hard to master your universe if your time is committed to a job you hate. Making your own path in life still requires a steady paycheck. *Getting a Life; Making a Living* offers the first-time entrepreneur a simple course in practical business. Covering topics from registering your business at the county courthouse to finding your target customers, Brown guides you to success. If you are wondering what to do to meet your career goals, *Getting a Life; Making a Living* shows you how to navigate the waters to sail your own ship. Structured as an introductory training course, this book gets you started on your own path.

The course describes how to plan, fund, structure, market, operate, grow, and exit your small business. Because how can we pursue happiness, if we spend our time, which is our life, doing a job that we hate?

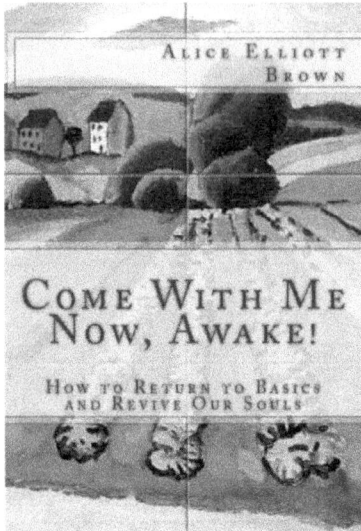

Book Five:
Come With Me Now, Awake!

How to return to basics and revive our souls

Have you ever wanted to give it all up and run away? Are you feeling trapped by a job, by a paycheck, or by a neighborhood? Do you worry about what will happen when the debt ceiling stops rising, inflation eats your savings, and the Big Bad Terrorists collapse the electric grid?

Returning to the land, to the basics, and to the soul of our society is becoming a lost art. More and more people lose themselves in the six inch screens of their smartphones: texting, updating their Facebook pages, and losing the intimate connection with others that comes from face-to-face, in-person relationships.

In *Come With Me Now, Awake!,* Brown gives us the How-to on returning to invigorating, aware living, so you and your family can live self-sufficiently. Covering food storage, water filtering, energy generation, sustainability, and the return to a productive society, *Come With Me Now, Awake!* is the beginning of a discussion about restoring American innovation and entrepreneurship. Brown shows us how one alert person in a sea of sleepers can sound the alarm that wakes the world.

About the Author

Alice Elliott Brown blogs about how to attain good health, paid bills, a happy family, and inner peace. She is a former software executive, a Harvard MBA, and a committed herbalist. She doesn't really grasp the wisdom of posting her picture on the Internet.

Find Books by Alice Elliott Brown at:

www.AliceElliottBrown.com

Follow her blog on: AliceElliottBrown.wordpress.com

Join us to discuss good health, paid bills, a happy family, and inner peace.

Preview:

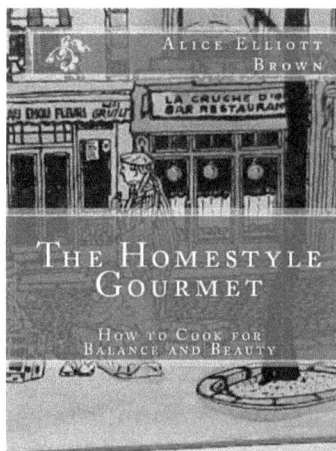

The Homestyle Gourmet
Cooking for Balance and Beauty
By Alice Elliott Brown

An easy to follow cookbook with recipes for vegetarian, fish, poultry, and meat dishes. Plus, some philosophy on why it is necessary to cook organic, whole foods from scratch.

The American Dilemma

When we were kids, we played this game. The game started by saying: "if you just landed on the planet from Mars, what would you see." Then each person described life as it would look to a Martian (or any outsider who did not understand the reasons driving our behavior.) Playing the game today, here is the scenario we would see in a standard American home, eating the standard American diet.

The typical American lifestyle is filled with activity. We drive the kids here and there. Both parents work. Nobody is home to spend the day baking; no one can commit to spend the morning cooking dried beans from scratch. As a result, our pantries are filled with "store-bought" jars of pre-made sauces, dressings, and pesto. We stock up on boxes of mixes. We fill the freezer with pre-cooked "cuisine." Our cooking skills consist of reading the instructions on the package. The spice jars in our kitchen pantry were bought when we moved into the house. (They're not empty yet, so we don't replace them; but they're too old to taste good, so we don't use them.)   This method of cooking and eating seems practical, under the circumstances.   There's just no time to do anything else, we tell ourselves. Frozen dinners are an alternative to eating out, after Mom has put in a full day at work.   For a nice family dinner at home, we'll just take the pre-cooked frozen meals out of the serving trays and put them on real plates.   If we're on a health kick, we might even add a lettuce and tomato salad with bottled dressing! And, we could pour our soda directly into glasses with ice, instead of having everyone drink directly from the can! (The women, of course, take their soda in the diet version, while the men drink the hard-driving, regular soda.)   Before we eat, all members of the family over 45 years old have to lay out their pill bottles and make the evening selection of medications. Those not taking a minimum of 7 pills must fill in the difference with an array of vitamins and supplements.   This method of eating results in physical stress, as the pre-packaged food heated in the microwave creates body stressors which then must be compensated for with a wide variety of colorful pills.

Somehow, our society hasn't quite made the connection that what we eat changes the quality of our health. We are bombarded with warnings not to eat butter, while no mention is made of eating "artificial ingredients", preservatives, and "natural flavorings made in a laboratory out of chemicals".   We eat frozen foods reheated in the microwave because we believe we must. They are what's available.   We've worked a long, hard, frustrating day, followed by an aggravating commute.   The kids are hungry, screaming, and tired from their school day full of administrivia.   Our work day wasn't physically exhausting; it was just mentally infuriating because of the office politics.   The drive home was an exercise in controlling our own road rage, while sliding out of the way of others' road rage. Now it's time to eat. It's not time to start another day of work, spending hours

slaving over a hot stove. It's time to just take off the shoes, sit down, and eat. So that's what we do.

The price of convenience
We call this method of eating "convenient." It's convenient to pull food out of the freezer and reheat it quickly for dinner. It's convenient to not have to think about cooking. There are too many other pressures, too much to worry about, too many problems and issues in our lives. There is a socially acceptable way to avoid cooking, so we might as well take it. This socially acceptable method of avoiding cooking has names like "Healthy Choice," "Lean Cuisine," and "Banquet." When we do cook, we buy boxes of pre-mixed "Hamburger Helper", "Stove-Top Stuffing", and Quick, Quick, Quick rice pilaf or Instant, Instant, Instant potatoes and casseroles. Time is of the essence in our rush to the dinner table. It's late. It's late. Our family meal is a very important date. Tempers are flaring and stomachs are rumbling. We have to eat *soon*. Maybe we should just stop at Arby's, we think. It's on the way home. It's *easier.*

If you are like most Americans, you lead a busy life. In today's society, our families usually need two working adults to live our American dream. Children need to be ferried to sports and activities. Commuting to work is stressful and draining. Work hours are long. Families are demanding. Perhaps a family member, maybe even you, will take courses in the evening to work toward a college degree, adding more stress to a long day. By the time the evening calm descends and the work day is over, dinner together with a bucket of fried chicken seems like a rare and comforting family feast. On a good day, perhaps the Stouffer's family-size lasagna will make it from the freezer to the oven.   But on most days, it may be that every family member fends for themselves, throwing together a sandwich, heating a can of soup, or driving through the take out window at Taco Bell. If there are young children, family meals together may be more frequent.   You're stressed and overworked, but you are really, really trying to do your best by the children.   After a long day at work, you may be frying some burgers, sprinkling them with a box of Hamburger Helper, steaming some frozen peas, and sprinkling the boxed mashed potatoes with the milk from the hormone-fed cows. Whatever you are doing to feed your family, you are doing the best you can do, given the situation that you've got. You are trying; you are loving, and you are giving everything you have.

The consequences of our busy lives
But there's something wrong.   Millions of Americans suffer chronically with vague, undiagnosed symptoms of headache, sinus problems, fatigue, eczema, skin rashes, allergies, asthma, acid reflux, and stomach aches.   Frequent and recurring, these symptoms are minor, chronic, annoying. Too small and unimportant to cause us to quit our jobs, we learn to live with these aches and pains. We take pills to suppress their symptoms.   At times, our little aches have been classified by the medical community as "environmental sensitivities."   The person may test allergic to dust, molds, and grass, and may have a weight problem or eating disorder. Additionally, many of our young girls are developing too early, at ages too young for puberty. We wonder how our eight-year- old could already need a training bra. At the same time, frustratingly, a significant percentage of our school children are being diagnosed with "ADD or ADHD"; they are distracted and unruly in the classroom, unable to concentrate or sit still. The guidance counselor suggests that perhaps we should

give the young ones a prescription drug to quiet them down. We take our teenagers, rushing through their own pressures and angst, to respectable and qualified doctors, whose answer to teenage turmoil is to prescribe pills for their "depression." This depression and inner turmoil is real, the aggression and discomfort is unmanageable. We need those pills. So we take pills, and we give our children pills, and we feel grateful to live in a nation where pills are available.

In response to our need to take pills as we age, we tell ourselves, "We live longer now. That's why we get sick and have to take so many pills. It's the price of old age." This is how we justify the cost to our well-being of taking pills to counteract the side effects of taking pills. Sadly, though, this story that we "live longer now" is a myth. After all, Benjamin Franklin lived into his 80's, as we learned in high school. What happens now is that more of us live past the age of 5, thus changing the statistical analysis of the average age. You remember the old adage, "Figures don't lie; but liars figure." People didn't die in their fifties in the old days, as we've been led to believe. Rather, many people died in childhood, or very early from a major disaster like smallpox. The fact of so many people dying young caused the statistics to imply that the average age of death was considerably younger than it is today. We labor under the assumption that we have the best health care in the world. In fact, the World Health Organization published a report[50] saying that we had four years less of healthy lifespan than the major European nations, at a cost more

---

[50] In 2003, figures from the World Health Organization said the United States of America spent $6,000 per person per year on health care, which resulted in an average healthy life span of 68 years. At the same time, industrialized European nations had an average healthy life span of 72 years, at a cost $2,000 per person per year less.

than 30% higher. In the light of that analysis, it seems fair to conclude that it isn't the pills we take that keep us healthy.

Many of our adults exhibit symptoms which progress to become arthritis, lupus, bursitis, asthma, migraines, cancer, or one of the many other diseases we call disorders of the immune system. Some suggest these immune system disorders are a result of responses of the primordial id. Our own body is making us sick, as a result of physical and emotional trauma. It is these id-generated symptoms and diseases that we call "Panaeolmic Syndrome." (Pan-**ell**-mick). They are Pan, or "across all", and they are carried by the mythic god of the wind, Aeolus. They seem to come from nowhere and impact everywhere.

The primordial id
The primordial id is part of our neurological system. In each of us, it remains forever a child, and it speaks to us in childish ways.

"Do I have to pound this into your head?" the primordial id says, as the migraines begin.

"Do I have to twist your left arm?" it says, as we feel the pangs of angina.

"Do I have to cut you off at the knees?" it says, as our knees buckle and we fall.

"Do I have to knock you out?" it says, as we crumble in exhaustion.

"Do I have to scare you silly?" it says, as we wake sweating from a nightmare.

"Do I have to pull teeth?" it says, as we feel excruciating mouth pain.

"Are you losing touch?" it says, as the tips of our fingers go numb.

"What? You won't quit that aggravating job without a reason? I'll give you a reason." It says, as we face crippling disability.

The inner id is that primitive survival mechanism of nature, which represents the child in each of us. Like Peter Pan, it never grows up. It manifests its desires outwardly in our bodies, although our conscious mind may never know what the inner mind controls. The word "Panaeolmic" comes from the Greek myth of the god Aeolus, who carried fortune in with the wind. For those who have Panaeolmic Syndrome, or any of us who have the symptoms of a weakened immune system, the inner child is communicating an important message. It is telling us we must return to the basics of life and get in touch with our true nature. As our lives move farther away from nature, more and more people are exhibiting "allergic" symptoms. While the symptoms of widespread "allergy" were nearly unheard of in the 1950s, most American families have an allergic family member today.

Read more on AliceElliottBrown.com

www.ingramcontent.com/pod-product-compliance
Lightning Source LLC
Chambersburg PA
CBHW081509040426
42447CB00013B/3168